CW01263789

2023

To dear Dad,
Happy Christmas
lots of love,
Joanie & Paul
xxx

FENDER
TELECASTER & STRATOCASTER

THE STORY OF THE WORLD'S MOST ICONIC GUITARS

by Dave Hunter

Introduction by Tony Bacon

VOYAGEUR
PRESS

Brimming with creative inspiration, how-to projects, and useful information to enrich your everyday life, Quarto Knows is a favorite destination for those pursuing their interests and passions. Visit our site and dig deeper with our books into your area of interest: Quarto Creates, Quarto Cooks, Quarto Homes, Quarto Lives, Quarto Drives, Quarto Explores, Quarto Gifts, or Quarto Kids.

First Published in 2020 by Voyageur Press, an imprint of The Quarto Group, 100 Cummings Center, Suite 265-D, Beverly, MA 01915, USA.
T (978) 282-9590 F (978) 283-2742 QuartoKnows.com

The content in this book previously appeared in *The Fender Telecaster* by Dave Hunter (Voyageur Press, 2012) and *The Fender Stratocaster* by Dave Hunter (Voyageur Press, 2013).

Voyageur Press titles are also available at discount for retail, wholesale, promotional, and bulk purchase. For details, contact the Special Sales Manager by email at specialsales@quarto.com or by mail at The Quarto Group, Attn: Special Sales Manager, 100 Cummings Center, Suite 265-D, Beverly, MA 01915, USA.

10 9 8 7 6 5 4 3 2

ISBN: 978-0-7603-7010-0
Digital edition published in 2020
eISBN: 978-0-7603-7011-7

Library of Congress Cataloging-in-Publication Data is available.

Design and page layout: Tango Media Publishing Services, LLC
All photographs are from the collection of Voyageur Press unless otherwise noted.

This publication has not been prepared, approved, or licensed by Fender Musical Instruments Corporation. Fender®, Stratocaster®, Esquire®, Telecaster®, Broadcaster®, Nocaster®, and the distinctive headstock designs commonly found on those guitars are registered trademarks of Fender Musical Instruments Corporation and used herein with express written permission. We recognize, further, that some words, model names, and designations mentioned herein are the property of the trademark holder. We use them for identification purposes only. This is not an official publication.

Printed in China

FRONT COVER: *(left)* 1950 Broadcaster. *Steve Catlin/Redferns/Getty Images; (right)* 1954 Stratocaster. *Chicago Music Exchange (www.chicagomusicexchange.com)*

FRONTIS: A well-traveled case with a jewel inside. *Chicago Music Exchange (www.chicagomusicexchange.com)*

TITLE PAGE: Muddy Waters holds his red Telecaster at a concert in Denmark in 1970. *Jan Persson/Redferns/Getty Images*

BACK COVER: *(left)* 1960 Custom Telecaster. *Fretted Americana; (middle)* 1965 Stratocasters in blue, red, gold, and charcoal. *Rumble Seat Music; (right)* Early white-guard 1954 Telecaster. *Guitar courtesy of Elderly Instruments/Photo Dave Matchette*

CONTENTS

Introduction by Tony Bacon • 9

**PART I:
LEO AND THE ORIGIN OF FENDER • 19**

**PART II:
THE TELECASTER • 35**

History of the Telecaster • 37
Telecaster Tone and Construction • 131

Artist Profiles

PART III:
THE STRATOCASTER • 181

History of the Stratocaster • 183
Stratocaster Tone and Construction • 281

Artist Profiles

INTRODUCTION

WHEN LEO FENDER WAS INDUCTED INTO the Rock and Roll Hall of Fame in 1992 alongside Jimi Hendrix and Johnny Cash, Keith Richards was there at the podium to speak on behalf of Leo, who had died less than a year earlier. "He gave us the weapons," Keith told a hushed gathering at the Hall of Fame. It was a thoughtful, concise tribute. Without the principal Fender weapons—known more prosaically as the Fender Telecaster and the Fender Stratocaster electric guitars—music would sound very different.

It all started way back in the forties, when Leo Fender moved on from an early collaboration with a guitarist, Doc Kauffman. The pair had started a modest company in Fullerton in Orange County, California, called K&F (Kauffman & Fender), and they made electric lap-steel guitars and small amplifiers in the back of Leo's radio store.

Doc soon decided he'd had enough, but the undaunted Leo pressed on, setting up a new firm in 1946, at first called Fender Manufacturing and renamed the Fender Electric Instrument Co. toward the end of 1947. Leo's revived operation continued to make lap-steels and amps, and gradually over the following years, into the early fifties, he gathered around him a capable and enterprising team: Don Randall as sales boss, Forrest White to organize the factory, and Freddie Tavares, who helped guide the development of new models.

In 1950, the new Fender company launched the world's first commercial solid-body electric guitar, at first named the Fender Esquire and then the Fender Broadcaster. It was renamed the Fender Telecaster in 1951—almost everyone calls it simply the Tele. Three years later, Fender completed its remarkable brace of original electrics with the introduction of the Fender Stratocaster guitar—better known as the Strat.

The new company ignored the contemporary conventions of guitar production and did not care for the way long-established guitar makers such as Gibson would hand-carve selected timbers. Instead, the fresh-faced Fender operation relied on factory methods to manufacture its radical solid-body electric guitars, stripping down the products to their essential elements, putting them together from easily assembled parts, and selling their guitars (and amps) at relatively affordable prices.

The firm's methods made for easier, consistent production—and in the process, gave its instruments a different sound. Not for Fender the woody Gibson-style jazz tone, but instead a clearer, spikier sound, something like a cross between a clean acoustic guitar and a cutting electric lap steel. It wasn't long before that sound would be heard ringing out around the world.

And it wasn't long before Fender introduced additional models to its lines, including the cheaper "student" Musicmaster and Duo-Sonic (1956) and Mustang (1964), the offset-waist Jazzmaster (1958), and the high-end Jaguar (1962). As the firm grew in confidence, the original Teles and Strats, and to a lesser extent, some of these newer models, began to attract more and more guitar players. And alongside all this, amplifiers remained a backbone of Fender's product lines and would prove as important to its success as the solid-body guitars and basses.

Since the company's beginnings, most major guitarists have played a Fender at some time during their life. Some have built entire careers playing Fenders. Muddy Waters regularly played a '57 Tele through most of his life and times, and an interviewer asked him later how he'd managed to rely more or less on a single instrument. "What would I look like with two or three guitars like these kids?" Muddy said to *Guitar Player*, probably with one of his twinkly smiles. "I don't need to be bothered with that. I got my one old guitar."

◆ ◆ ◆

The Telecaster in its original design has remained more or less unchanged in the Fender line since its launch at the start of the '50s. It's a classic that is about as simple as a solid-body guitar can be. And it occupies a unique position in history as the oldest solid-body electric guitar model still in regular production—which is hardly surprising, because it was the first.

Back at the time of the Telecaster's birth, before anyone had even thought about rock 'n' roll, Fender had come up with the first commercial solidbody electric. It was uncluttered and plain-speaking, and those qualities remain today at the heart of the Tele's appeal. It still has that dry bite and twangy, cutting punch that so many great and almost-great players have learned to love and continue to relish. The Telecaster is an unfussy, honest, playable guitar.

But the original-design Telecaster and Stratocaster have not been alone in the Fender lines. Over the years, Fender has offered many alternatives, exploiting these willing testbeds that seem to accept whatever their creator might throw at them, no matter how far the result might be from the basic template. Sometimes, modification has involved adding a humbucking pickup or two—even though that's enough to make some purists wince.

More pickup updates have appeared in recent years, and over time Fender has introduced colorful custom finishes, gold-plated metalwork options, control modifications, twelve-string versions, signature models, synthesizer hookups, and plenty more besides. Yet for some players, it's still the classic originals that deliver exactly what they're looking and listening and feeling for, many decades since the instruments were first designed.

The twenty-first century Fender is serious about recreating those originals. In the early eighties, when the firm's bosses first considered reissuing vintage-style guitars, the company had no collection of original instruments that they could study to help get the details right. So they paid a visit to a vintage guitar dealer, and there they carefully examined some old Fenders, taking measurements, making paint tests, snapping photographs. And at the end of a long day, they bought some vintage Fenders. That's correct—Fender had little choice but to buy back its own product. The result is that, today, players can get as close as they dare in a

2009 limited-edition 1958 Candy Apple Red Stratocaster with gold-anodized pickguard. *Fender Musical Instruments Corporation*

Dr. Feelgood guitarist Wilko Johnson's Stratocaster and 1962 Telecaster in his trademark black-and-red color scheme. *Kevin Nixon/Guitarist Magazine/Getty Images*

gun. "I could really hit a target with that old rifle," Leo told the *Washington Post*. "One time, I got a jack rabbit at better than 300 yards. You see, some pieces of machinery just suit people." Leo loved gadgets, and it's not too hard to imagine that if, somehow, he could come back for a tour of Fender's current American factory, he would adore it.

The company had started life at its home in Fullerton, moving in 1953 to a three-and-a-half acre plot where it put up three new buildings. Gradually Fender expanded, and by 1964 it employed more than six hundred people there, spread over twenty-nine buildings. At that time, the huge CBS corporation was on a mission to scoop up any broadly entertainment-based company that caught its acquisitive eye. In January 1965, CBS bought Fender in a deal worth $13 million. Under the new owner, Fender sales increased and profits went up, but Leo and most of the old guard soon left, and gradually it seemed to some players that the guitars and the amps were not like they used to be.

That trend continued into the seventies, and in 1985 CBS sold Fender to the company's existing management team. Fender Japan, set up a few years earlier, became the sole supplier of instruments for a while, because the Fullerton factories were not included in the deal. But a new US factory was soon established in Corona, about twenty miles east of the defunct Fullerton site, and a few years later a second factory was added just across the border in Ensenada, Mexico. Fender guitars continue to be made in Corona and Ensenada today, and through the years the company has also manufactured in China, India, Indonesia, Japan, and Korea.

✦ ✦ ✦

Back in the day, Leo and his team were always looking out for what tomorrow might bring. In fact, he thought

2013 Custom Shop 1956 Candy Tangerine Stratocaster. *Fender Musical Instruments Corporation*

new instrument to the curious voodoo that is a real live vintage Fender.

Someone asked Leo Fender in the seventies why he thought players had started seeking out old Fenders, which had come to be known as vintage guitars. He said he understood that people liked the early stuff—guitars that were gradually creeping up in value, too—and he compared the phenomenon to the way he felt about his trusty Remington

that when the Stratocaster was launched it would replace the Telecaster—because it was better and newer. We know better now, of course. And it's a constant source of delight and wonder to see Fender's dynamic duo turning up in all manner of new music. The Strat is as versatile as a player needs it to be, and you'll see it in almost as many settings as there are genres of music. The Tele, too, can go way beyond the chicken-pickin' and country-inflected beauty that for some players passes as the regular Tele fare.

On its launch in '54, the Strat was the first solidbody electric with three pickups, it had a new built-in vibrato bridge, and its radically sleek solid body was contoured for the player's comfort. It became the most popular, the most copied, the most desired, and very probably the most played solid electric guitar ever. As for the Tele, it can offer a welcome oasis of direct simplicity for guitarists who have braved the heat and sweat of the latest gimmicks and hip gadgetry. Relaxing instead with a fifties-style Tele, they might just wonder what all the fuss is about with this modern stacked humbucker, say, or that new-fangled modeling amp or stomp box.

Just take a look at one of those original Teles for a moment. Yes, it has a body and it has a neck. And yes, there are some pickups and some knobs. But there's not much more—and nothing less. Take a look at a couple more guitars: here, an old Stratocaster from the guitar's earliest years in the '50s; over there a brand new twenty-first-century Strat, maybe a starter guitar with Fender's budget Squier brand, or perhaps one of the lofty high-end wonder machines made in the firm's Custom Shop. You might be forgiven for thinking that nothing much has changed in the decades between their origins. And you'd be right and you'd be wrong, both at the same time.

♦ ♦ ♦

For the dyed-in-the-wool Fender fan or the newbie who's just discovered their first example, it can be comforting to discover they're in good company. Among the great players through the decades who have found themselves at ease with a Tele or a Strat, some names loom larger than others. We might mention Eric Clapton, Steve Cropper, Bob Dylan, George Harrison, Jimi Hendrix, Buddy Holly, Mark Knopfler, Bonnie Raitt, Bruce Springsteen, Andy Summers, and Stevie Ray Vaughan. We could go on. And on. It would probably be easier to list those who haven't played one.

Leo Fender's favorite music was said to be that made by old-fashioned Western singing groups like the Sons of the Pioneers. So it's unlikely he would have had much time for Jonathan Richman. But Jonathan is one of the few songwriters to have written a song about a specific guitar. The song is "Fender Stratocaster" on an album from 1989. Jonathan Richman was too smart to get bogged down in the origins of the Stratocaster name when he wrote that song. Don Randall, who headed up Fender's early sales efforts, named most of the early Fender models, and he told me that when it came to the Strat, his fifties' mind turned to the stratosphere and the dawning space age.

Don was a keen pilot, too, so he'd almost certainly noticed that Boeing was calling its B-47 jet bomber the Stratojet. He'd probably seen that Pontiac had a new car called the Strato-Streak, too. And he went to all the instrument trade shows of the era, so he must have sniffed around the Harmony booth and seen the Chicago brand's new Stratotone electric. Nothing comes from nowhere.

1952 Telecaster. *Steve Catlin/ Redferns/Getty Images*

David Gilmour's view is that the Fender Stratocaster is the most versatile guitar ever made. He reckons it has a funny way of making players sound like themselves. Assuming they are content with how they sound, this is another decisive advantage.

David was one of the performers at a show Fender staged in 2004 at London's Wembley Arena to celebrate the Strat's fiftieth birthday. It was quite a moment when he came on with one of his best-known Stratocasters, a first-year 1954 model that bore the serial number 0001. It wasn't actually the first one made, but that didn't stop it selling at auction in 2019 for a little short of $2,000,000. David had no trouble at all making his storied instrument sound wonderful at that Wembley celebration. There it was, clear as a bell—fifty years of the Stratocaster before everyone's eyes and ears.

Today, the Strat and the Tele are in their seventh decades, at a time when the Fender company is celebrating its seventy-fifth birthday. Both instruments and the company itself show little signs of old age. Another pair of sprightly old guys pushing well into their seventies are Jeff Beck and Jimmy Page.

Jeff Beck is prone to nostalgia when he thinks about the Strat, which he blames for his early conversion to the power of rock music. "The reason I left school was because of that guitar," he told me. "I mean, that is brain damage when you're a kid of fourteen and you see something like that. It's just a piece of equipment that you dream about touching, never mind owning.

"The first day I stood looking at one in one of those London shops, I just went into a trance—and I got the wrong bus home, just dreaming about it. You know? It just blew my brains apart, and it's never been any different since," Jeff concluded. "It's taken me all round the world and given me everything I've got—just that Strat, really. So it is a particular favorite of mine."

I once asked Jimmy Page about pulling out his old Telecaster to play the solo on "Stairway to Heaven" at a time when he was much more inclined to use his beloved Gibson Les Paul. "People say why did you do that, and . . . I don't know," Jimmy admitted, with a laugh. "There was no particular reason other than: that's what I did. It's funny, isn't it?" Well, it was a long time ago. But sometimes it just has to be a Tele—or a Strat—or both.

Back at that Rock and Roll Hall of Fame event in 1992, Leo Fender's second wife, Phyllis, was there for him. "When I accepted his award, I said that Leo truly believed that musicians were special angels, special envoys from the Lord," she recalled. "He believed he was put here to make the very best instruments in the world, because these special angels would help us get through this life, would ease our pain and ease our sadness, and help us celebrate."

—Tony Bacon
Bristol, England, March 2020

David Gilmour's 1954 Stratocaster guitar, serial number 0001.
Outline Press Ltd.

2007 George Fullerton 1957 Stratocaster with matching
Pro Junior amp. *Fender Musical Instruments Corporation*

B.B. King poses for a promotional portrait in Memphis, Tennessee, circa 1950, holding his black-guard Esquire. *Michael Ochs Archives/Getty Images*

PART I

LEO AND THE ORIGIN OF FENDER

WHAT A FEELING, to live in an age when simple old rock 'n' roll seemed at the forefront of a cultural revolution, and a curvaceous new solidbody electric guitar with unprecedented features seemed about as radical a work of design-art as could be imagined. We like to think that things move fast in our current age. Certainly iProgress, and the consumer products that go hand in hand with it, has ramped up to a heady pace. And yet, briefly consider how fast things were moving in an earlier age—a predigital, pre-"information" age, sure, but one in which an early–Cold War Western world was jogging swiftly toward a level of technical innovation in everyday life that was staggeringly advanced over what was known just a couple of decades before. Now apply that to the world that is of immediate concern to us—which is to say, guitarists and fans of guitar history—and the mid-twentieth century really does appear to have been the dawn of a brave new world, and one in which the advances in how we made music came on fast and furious.

Any in-depth look at the history of the Fender company is really an exploration of mid-century American history from several perspectives. It traces the birth of an industry that was truly in its infancy, which in itself is fascinating, with roots not only in the early years of the electric guitar market, but also in the dawn of amplification itself, and the front edge of a wave in consumer electronics that continues to curl to this day. Even beyond this, though, any such study inevitably plumbs a field that, more than any

other developing industry or technology, was one in which technological progress—the evolution of the product—directly influenced the art itself, and, therefore, the national and international culture. The early history of Fender and its most famous guitars is inextricably entwined with a major shift in the ways and means of popular music, and even if that music would seem to sound very different today than it did seventy years ago, it is still rolling forward in the same direction, set in motion by the same initial force.

LEO'S EARLY YEARS

Clarence Leonidas "Leo" Fender was born in 1909 on his parents' orange grove in what was then the bountiful farmland that stretched between Anaheim and Fullerton, California. He attended the local public schools throughout his childhood, and he began tinkering with radios and electronics in his early teens, as well as working with tools and mechanics in general while helping out on the family farm. It is widely reported that Fender was not a guitarist himself, although he showed an interest in music from a fairly early age, learned to play the piano and the saxophone, and even built an acoustic guitar at the age of sixteen. Fender graduated from Fullerton Union High School in 1928 (coincidentally the same year the first AC vacuum tubes were issued, making amplifier design and construction much easier), and went on to Fullerton Junior College later that year to

study accounting. Although he continued to improve his skills with radios and amplifiers throughout that two-year accounting course, he took no formal training in electronics.

While working as a bookkeeper in the early thirties, Fender was asked to build a PA system for a local band, and the fulfillment of that request proved the first step in a small side-line that found him building, then renting out and maintaining, as many as half a dozen PA systems that were used for musical performances, baseball games, and other events around Orange County and the environs surrounding Los Angeles. He married his first wife, Esther, in 1934, and the couple moved to San Luis Obispo, California, for another job in accounting. After he lost what would be the last of a series of accounting positions in 1938, Leo and Esther returned to Fullerton, and he borrowed six hundred dollars to open his own store, Fender's Radio Service. The shop sold records, radios, and record players—as well as servicing the latter two—but soon the musicians who frequented the place began to bring in instruments and amplifiers for repair, and were eventually asking him to build amps and PAs, too.

In the course of this work, Fender quickly showed a knack for discerning the flaws in the circuits and construction of many of the amps made by others, and, in addition to repairing them, avoiding these pitfalls in the amps he would produce himself. As he told *Guitar Player* magazine in 1971, "Originally my work was design, modification, repair, and custom building. This gave me a wide acquaintance with competitive products and users' needs. Since my work encompassed more than musical equipments, I knew of benefits I could apply to the musicians' gear. I guess you would say the objectives were durability, performance, and tone."

Clearly, Fender also enjoyed hanging out, chatting, and exchanging ideas with the musicians who frequented Fender's Radio Service, and in so doing, he developed another of his great skills: the ability to take on outside input and constructive criticism from players "in the trenches" and to use it in the upward evolution of his own designs. The effort became more difficult,

however, as the shortages of the war years forced him to work with scavenged parts and leftover scraps. The situation might have slowed his development in some ways, as it did that of established guitar and amplifier makers, who largely shut down production for the war effort, but being a small operator also allowed Fender to fulfill a demand that existed in the market, war or no war. Fender progressed his notion of the business through the early forties and into the middle of the decade and moved further toward the idea of manufacturing and away from radio sales and repairs. "I liked developing new items that people needed. Working with tools and equipment was more to my liking than retail sales," he said (*Guitar Player*, 1971). By this time, it seemed to make sense to take on a knowledgeable partner, and to formally establish a presence in the musical instrument industry.

THE BIRTH, AND SHORT LIFE, OF K&F

One of the musicians who wandered into Fender's Radio Service in the early forties was Clayton Orr "Doc" Kauffman, and, while discussing some instrument pickups that Fender had on display in his shop window, the pair revealed a mutual inclination for inventing and developing electronic gadgets. Although Kauffman's association with Fender would be relatively brief, the men's early work together sowed the seeds for the eventual bombshell that Leo could barely have foreseen at the time.

Still involved in the radio and phonograph business, the pair developed a precision 45-RPM record changer and sold the rights to the design for $5,000, a sum that would provide seed money for their own manufacturing efforts. Perhaps more foretelling of things to come, however, was the patent application filed in 1944 for a strings-through-coil pickup design that Fender and Kauffman had begun developing

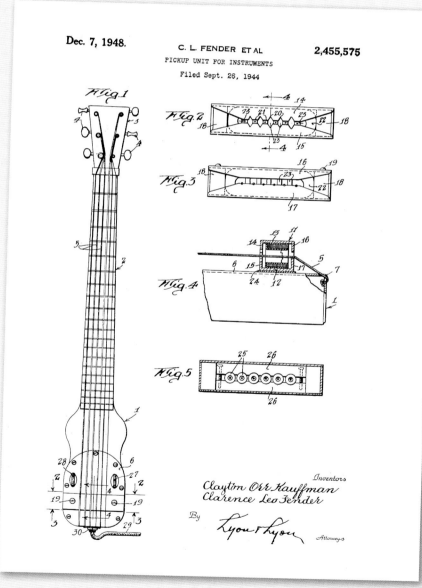

Above: The 1944 patent drawing for Leo Fender's early electric lap steel.

The construction of early Fender lap steel guitars in the 1940s led the way to building solid-body "Spanish" electric guitars. **Left:** 1955 Fender Champion model lap steel electric guitar; **right:** 1952 Fender Student model lap steel electric guitar. *Outline Press Ltd.*

in 1943. Eventually granted on December 7, 1948, the patent shows the pickup mounted to an instrument that appears much like an early lap-steel guitar, but which, in fact, carries a thinner, narrower neck intended to be played in the conventional upright (or "Spanish") style. It shows, in fact, the first non-Hawaiian solidbody electric guitar that Leo Fender built, along with Kauffman, an instrument now on display in Roy Acuff's museum at Opryland in Nashville, Tennessee.

Kauffman and Fender formed K&F Manufacturing Corporation and, during the course of 1945, produced six different models of lap steel (Hawaiian) electric guitars, and three amplifiers, which were paired in sets aimed at students, novices, and professional players. All was apparently rather promising, but any major success was still unforeseen beyond the horizon. Kauffman's fear of the risks involved in expanding the business led him to trade his share of the company to Fender late in 1945 in exchange for a punch press. Now active as sole proprietor, Leo established Fender Electric Instrument Company in 1946, and carried on in much the same manner as he and Kauffman had, building lap steel electrics and the amplifiers they were played through.

The latter were particularly successful—or relatively so, given the Fender company's modest means at the time—on a scene where that technology might have seemed to be lagging behind the musical times. Leo Fender's vast experience in repairing commercial radios and related products gave him great insight into both the virtues and flaws in many such designs, which he applied to his designs for musical instrument amplifiers. As a result, as young as his company was, Fender amps were generally sturdier and more roadworthy than almost anything else on the market by the late 1940s and yielded volume levels and a quality of tone that were equally elevated. His stated belief was that a product that would be easy to repair would also be easier to manufacture; the tone factor relied upon how you put those low-maintenance ingredients together.

If the amps arguably proved Leo's greatest early success, his formative years of building lap steel guitars and learning from the musicians who played them would be crucial in helping to distinguish Fender's eventual electric Spanish guitars from anything else that was already on the scene. Leo's goals of durability, ease of maintenance, and ease of manufacture would be transported from the amp line to the guitars, but the sonic goals of "performance and tone" would be more directly derived from the input of musicians who primarily played "hillbilly" and Western Swing. They wanted instruments that were bright, firm, punchy, and feedback-resistant, and Fender already knew how to deliver, even before the Broadcaster hit the scene. Essentially, Fender guitars were not designed to sound like amplified versions of traditional guitars, but to be very much an evolution of the existing Hawaiian lap steel guitars—which displayed these characteristics in abundance—that could be played fretted in the "upright" Spanish style, in standard tuning.

As a result, while more traditional makers such as Gibson, Epiphone, Gretsch, and a few others already had the template for the electric guitar in hand in the form of their existing archtop acoustic guitars, and approached the task mainly from the perspective of amplifying these, Leo went at it tone-first, abandoning all preconceptions of the form and designing his guitar from the ground up. He already knew the sound and how to get it; he just needed a playable and visually acceptable instrument to produce it.

FENDER'S—AND THE WORLD'S— FIRST PRODUCTION SOLIDBODY

Leo nailed the "playable" part of the equation in 1950 with the release of a guitar that was briefly called the Esquire, then Broadcaster, and eventually and forever after, Telecaster (the name that will be used here for ease of reference). From the start of the Telecaster's production, players lauded the fast, comfortable feel and easy playability of Fender's guitar necks, and this characteristic would form a significant component of their reputation going forward. As for the "visually acceptable" component, well, that wasn't quite there yet, in many people's view at least. (For a detailed history on the development of the Telecaster, see page 37.)

Today the Telecaster is considered an undeniable classic, an iconic piece of midcentury-modern guitar design, so elegant in its simplicity that it's hard to conceive of it causing any offense.

The first prototype of the Esquire was believed completed in 1949. The early production Esquires from 1950 did not have truss rods; they were added late that year. By 1952, when this Telecaster was made, the features of Fender's solidbody electric were set. *Fretted Americana*

THE
TELECASTER AND ESQUIRE
MODELS

An unknown country western band from the early 1950s poses for a publicity photo with their tripleneck Fender pedal steel and early Telecaster.

When they first set out to get the Telecaster into the guitar stores, though, Fender's salesmen encountered some resistance from players and merchants who derided it as a "plank," a "canoe paddle," and worse. In short, the Tele was far from traditional, but that was exactly the point. For forward-looking players in search of a much-needed new tool to play a sonically demanding new form of music, the Tele fit the bill exactly.

In 1984, Leo Fender told *Guitar Player* magazine of taking a guitar, early in the new solidbody's existence, to the Riverside Rancho Dance Hall in Riverside, California, for up-and-coming country virtuoso Jimmy Bryant to check out. Bryant took it up on stage with Little Jimmy Dickens and his band and started playing, and, as Leo told it, "Pretty soon the band stopped, everybody on the dance floor stopped, and they all gathered around Jimmy when he played." If the solid-body electric guitar is "old hat" now—a thing that we feel has always been with us—this window into one of the new creation's first public appearances in 1950 hints at just how revolutionary it must have appeared and sounded. Clear, bright, cutting, sustaining, and feedback-free at higher volumes, Fender's guitar was exactly what Bryant had been looking for and soon proved to be the sharpest tool in the box for plenty of other players besides. The simple fact was, plank or not, this thing boasted qualities that the hollow-body archtop electrics by Gibson, Epiphone, and so many others just couldn't claim for themselves, and it established that essence known as "the Fender sound," defined by a sonic personality that Leo would seek to repeat in all his guitars.

Despite early nay-sayers, the Fender brand was more and more in the sites of Spanish-style guitarists on the Western scene, and Leo was priming the rig to lure in even those who weren't entirely enamored of the first solidbody out of the gates.

ONGOING EXPANSION

Having started out in 1939 in the back of the original Fender's Radio Service premises, at 107 and then 112 South Spadra in Fullerton (a road that is now called Harbor Boulevard), Fender was setting up in two purpose-built corrugated metal buildings on Santa Fe Avenue by 1946, around the time of the establishment of the Fender Electric Instrument Company. A few years later, even before the Esquire/Broadcaster was ready for the market, Fender was feeling cramped, and had a third building—this time a sturdy brick construction with a flat roof—built on the adjacent lot at the corner of Santa Fe Avenue and South Pomona Street.

Just three years after, even these three buildings would prove insufficient to contain the steadily expanding company. In late 1953, Fender moved lock, stock, and barrel to a new premises at 500 South Raymond in Fullerton with four adjacent cinder-block buildings and plenty of vacant land around it, which would be used for the company's steady further expansion in the years that followed. Before the end of the decade, four more buildings would be constructed on that land, providing Fender with more than fifty thousand square feet to work with throughout the facility as a whole.

A few months before this move, in June of 1953, having outgrown the distribution services of the Radio and Television Equipment Company (RTEC), Fender Electric Instrument Company set up its own distribution and sales arm. This new independent company, Fender Sales, Inc., was initially owned in equal partnership by Leo Fender, Don Randall (general manager of RTEC), Charlie Hayes (RTEC salesman), and RTEC's owner Francis Hall, and for the most part, it simply brought key Fender-related RTEC personnel into the operation to affect a smooth transition. Hall, however, also purchased Electro String Instrument Corporation from Adolph Rickenbacker later in 1953, a move with obvious potential for conflict. After the death of Charlie Hayes in a car accident in 1955, Fender and Randall bought out Hall's share in Fender Sales, thus bringing the sales and distribution entirely into the fold.

By 1954, a significant layer of management personnel was established at Fender, and the manufacturer was more and more reflecting the structure of any traditional company. Don Randall was established as president of Fender Sales, George Fullerton had been promoted to production foreman the year before, and Forrest White was hired as plant manager. Freddie Tavares, a Hawaiian-born musician and experienced mechanical and electrical engineer, had also started working for Fender in early 1953. Tavares was himself a skilled and in-demand session musician both on steel and Spanish-style guitar, and his work has been heard by millions—if unbeknownst to most of them—in the famous steel-guitar slide crescendo that introduces the theme song to Warner Brothers' *Looney Tunes* cartoon series. Acting as Leo's chief assistant in R&D, Tavares would be seen more and more as Leo's "right-hand man" in that department through the course of the 1950s and into the '60s, and would have a major role in developing the Stratocaster in particular. By the end of the decade, there would be more than one hundred employees at Fender to fill the ever-expanding manufacturing premises.

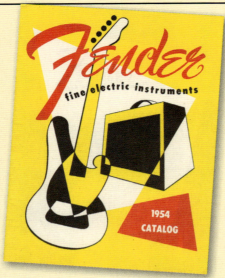

REACHING FOR THE STRATOSPHERE

Whether spurred on in the face of the competition from makers like Gibson and Gretsch or encouraged by the guitar world's increasingly warm reception of the solidbody with this proliferation from some better-established makers, Fender went from strength to strength through the mid-fifties and on toward the end of the decade. An uncontested Fender first, the Precision Bass, had been released in 1951 to wide acclaim, and thus helped to bolster the company's profile with musicians in general. Then in 1954, the unveiling of the revolutionary Fender Stratocaster—a guitar that would become the most widely emulated solid-body design over the next half a century—gave the Telecaster an exciting stablemate, and helped to ensure that Fender was here to stay. (For a detailed history on the development of the Stratocaster, see page 183.)

In fact, amid the genuine competition for the Telecaster, the Stratocaster was virtually on top of the heap. Several Tele players moved over to Fender's fancy new three-pickup electric with its efficient new vibrato bridge. One was Bill Carson, whom Leo had tapped for constructive input on the guitar's design, while others like Eldon Shamblin, who had never embraced the Telecaster, took enthusiastically to the Strat.

As radical and space-aged as the Stratocaster was, however, and as much excitement and seemingly easy acceptance as its release received, by the time the dust had settled, the Telecaster remained king of the heap for the majority of country players, and would prove a favorite with plenty of blues and rock 'n' roll artists, too.

CBS ACQUIRES FENDER ELECTRONIC INSTRUMENTS

Although the deal had been sought by Leo Fender and Don Randall as early as mid-1964 and negotiated throughout the latter part of that year, its finalization on January 5, 1965—and the departure of Leo Fender from Fender Electric Instruments—is probably best embodied by Forrest White:

"Monday evening, January 4, 1965, I went down to see Leo in his lab for the last time. We both found it difficult to act nonchalant. I helped him carry his personal belongings out to his car, pretended not to notice the tears in his eyes, hoped he hadn't noticed mine. He got into his car and I walked to the side gate. He stopped briefly on his way out, paused and said, 'I don't know what I would have done without you.' . . . He stepped on the gas and was out the gate before I could answer. That was the last time I would let him out the gate as I had done so many times before. I watched until his car was out of sight." (*Fender: The Inside Story*)

Having been unable to shake a strep infection contracted in the mid-'50s that continually aggravated his sinuses, Leo Fender had, by the mid-'60s, been feeling more and more run-down from his illness, and further exhausted by the effort of running the ever-expanding business. By 1964 Fender employed approximately five hundred workers in a premises that had expanded to twenty-seven buildings in Fullerton. Business was good—business was great, even—but Leo Fender himself just wasn't up to it.

Leo instructed Don Randall to quietly begin searching for a suitable buyer, and Randall's request to the investment firm Merrill Lynch for appropriate introductions eventually led to the Columbia Broadcasting System, Inc. (CBS). Looking to expand its portfolio, CBS was keen to acquire a leading electric guitar and amplifier manufacturer during a boom time in that industry. A deal to purchase both Fender Electronic Instruments and Fender Sales was hammered out, and the price, a staggering $13.5 million, was the highest paid to date for a musical instrument manufacturer.

Upon completion of the sale, the company name was changed to Fender Musical Instruments, now a division of Columbia Records Distribution Corporation under CBS. Don Randall was named vice president and general manager, the title Forrest White had held with Fender Electronic Instruments, while White was made plant manager again, the position he had held in the mid-'50s. Fender had hired guitarist Bill Carson in 1957 to work in quality control. Having been promoted to guitar production foreman in 1959, Carson also stayed with Fender through the sale to CBS, and would move over Fender Sales in 1967. Among other formative Fender employees that stuck it out with CBS, in the beginning at least, were George Fullerton and Freddie Tavares, although Dale Hyatt left around the time of the sale's completion.

As part of the sale agreement, Leo Fender was retained as a consultant in research and development for five years, with a "non-compete" clause of ten years that would prevent him from setting himself up in the musical instrument business independent of the now CBS-owned Fender company. The consultation role seems to have been largely a token gesture on CBS's part, and his input apparently carried relatively little weight.

Some reports, though unconfirmed, indicate that Leo Fender's doctors had him believing that he didn't have long to live, and that his sale of Fender was a clear move to get out from under the burden of the company and enjoy what time he had left. In any case, three years after selling the company that he had built from the ground up over the course of twenty years to become one of the world's most successful musical instrument manufacturers, Fender finally found relief from his affliction. "About 1968, I found a doctor who knew the appropriate treatment for the infection," he told *Guitar Player* in 1971, "and I haven't been bothered with it since."

1954 Stratocaster. *Chicago Music Exchange, www.chicagomusicexchange.com*

Fender's 1966-67 catalog.

Just a year after CBS's Fender acquisition, the factory had increased its guitar and amplifier production by approximately 30 percent, though with no noticeable decline in quality as of yet. In 1966, however, CBS completed construction on an enormous new facility at 1300 S. Valencia Drive, adjacent to the previous site at 500 South Raymond Avenue in Fullerton. Soon after the move into the new premises, production increased another 45 percent, and the first signs of what would be a steady decline in quality in general began to be apparent.

Several of the old guard that had transitioned to CBS from the former Fender Electronic Instruments expressed increasing displeasure with the large company's emphasis on production numbers over all else. As the new decade approached, it also became apparent that CBS was bleeding the profits from the continued business success of Fender Musical Instruments (now officially called CBS Musical Instruments Division other than in the brand line used on the instruments and amplifiers themselves) to offset losses from other divisions. Division head Don Randall, who was on the same five-year contract term as an executive that Leo Fender had as a consultant, was also dissatisfied with the way the business was going under CBS by this time. Randall departed in 1969, well before the official end of his tenure, and in 1971 he set up his own company, Randall Instruments.

FENDER AFTER FENDER

At the end of his consultation contract with CBS, Leo Fender established the Tri-Sonic company in 1971, along with Forrest White and former Fender Sales rep Tom Walker. Fender and White began developing ideas for a new line of amplifiers and guitars, with White patenting a design for a bass headstock with three keys on the bass side and one key on the treble that would soon be a familiar new sight on the market. In 1973 the three partners changed the company name to Musitek, then changed it again in 1974 to Music Man, and took old Fender colleague George Fullerton onboard soon after. In 1975, with his noncompete clause completed, Leo Fender stepped forward as president of Music Man, and the company soon hit the ground running with a line of products that had already been in development. Music Man's amps of the mid- to late-1970s, in what were clearly Fender-like configurations but with solid-state preamps and tube output stages, proved fairly successful and were used by major pros such as Eric Clapton and Mark Knopfler. The Stingray bass, with its unusual 3-and-1 headstock, also

A well-gigged 1968 Telecaster updated with a 1970s six-saddle bridge. *Doug Youland, Willie's American Guitars*

became a standard of many reputable studio and touring pros, although the six-string guitars were slower to achieve wide acceptance among working musicians. That Music Man guitars, under the latter-day ownership of Ernie Ball, were eventually endorsed by Albert Lee, Steve Morse, and for a time, Edward Van Halen, finally put those on the map, too.

In 1979 Leo Fender and George Fullerton started G&L—for "George and Leo"—in Fullerton, California, and the pair began to produce a range of guitars in competition with both Fender and Music Man. In 1985 G&L introduced its Broadcaster model, a guitar clearly patterned after the Fender Telecaster, with similar body and headstock shapes but powered by Leo Fender's newly developed Magnetic Field Design pickups. Fender Musical Instruments, rather ironically, objected to the use of the Broadcaster name—denied to them by Gretsch some thirty-five years before—and in 1986 G&L changed the name of its Tele-like model to ASAT (as in the anti-satellite missile). After George Fullerton's interest in G&L was bought out by Leo Fender in the mid-1980s, the company name was changed to "Guitars by Leo"; former Fender employee Dale Hyatt joined the fold, and Forrest White was soon taken on, too. G&L would be Leo's final home as a guitar maker.

Former Fender associates Doc Kauffman and Freddie Tavares died in June and July 1990, respectively. Less than a year later, Leo Fender passed away on March 21, 1991. Following Leo Fender's death, ownership of G&L eventually passed to BBE Sound, which still maintains Fender's final workshop on the premises as a memorial to the man who brought so much to the guitar world.

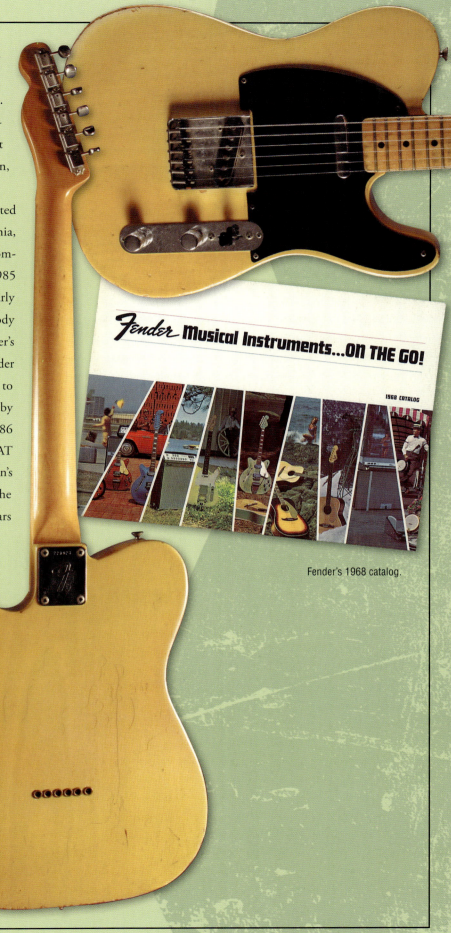

Fender's 1968 catalog.

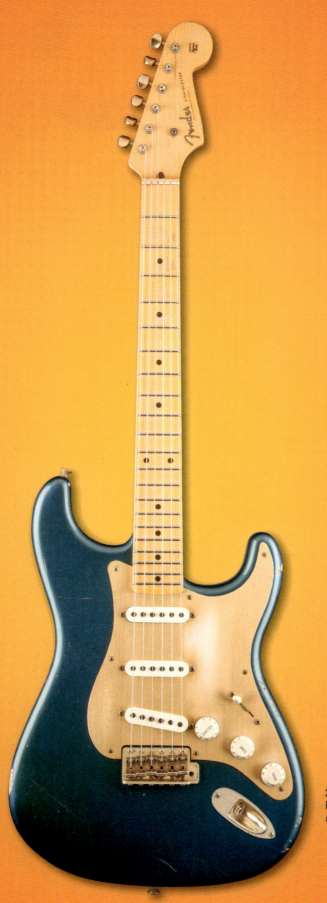

2012 Custom Shop 1956 Aged Lake Placid Blue Relic Stratocaster. *Fender Musical Instruments Corporation*

GAZING BACKWARD TO MOVE FORWARD

Following a decade of increasing struggle to maintain a foothold in the marketplace, which often found Fender's reputation slipping down between the expectations established by its former glories and the sketchy quality of its current production, a major shift toward the better was in the wind in the early 1980s. In an effort to revive the company's fortunes, CBS brought in John McLaren, Bill Schultz, and Dan Smith in 1981, all young executives from the American branch of Japanese instrument maker Yamaha. Rather ironically (or perhaps not), the new team started production of a Fender line in Japan in order to compete with the cut-price Fender copies that had been coming from that country for some time, and the Squier and Japanese-made Fender series were born.

At the same time, the Smith, Schultz, and McLaren team saw the virtue of returning to Fender's past strengths and launched the company's first-ever reissue-style Stratocasters (and Telecasters) in Japan and the United States in 1982 and 1983, respectively. It was a wise move. The growing success of the reissue lines arguably saved Fender's reputation when the very existence of the company was on the line, and decades later similar reissue guitars in their various guises have continued to prove the backbone of the lineup.

Shortly after these initiatives, however, twenty years after Leo Fender sold his company, CBS decided to divest itself of its holdings in the musical instrument industry and, following a search for a suitable buyer, sold to a group of investors headed by then-Fender president Bill Schultz. The deal, inked in March of 1985, gave the new owners the Fender brand and designs and some stock for $12.5 million, although the Fullerton factories were not included in the bargain (a point which makes it difficult to directly compare the price to the $13.5 million tag on Fender circa 1965, as purchased by CBS in the first place).

After struggling to maintain a place in the market while ramping up production in new premises in the United States and maintaining Japanese production, Schultz and company steered Fender onto a stronger and stronger footing, and did so largely by remembering—and recreating—what had made the guitars so popular in the company's glory days of 1950 to 1965.

2010 Custom Shop 1956 Stratocaster. *Fender Musical Instruments Corporation*

Custom Shop 1953 Telecaster. *Fender Musical Instruments Corporation*

Fender's Vintage '52 Telecaster Reissue has become famous and beloved since its introduction in 1982—and as many great licks and songs have probably been played on them as the original black-guard models! *Fender Musical Instruments Corporation*

PART II

THE TELECASTER

WORKING-CLASS HERO. The ultimate blue-collar guitar. That is the Fender Telecaster. It wasn't made to be elegant, or pretty, or sophisticated—although it can claim the first two qualities in spades. It was constructed as a tool for the working musician, an optimally functional guitar to get the job done. The Telecaster aimed, in short, to be the ultimate utilitarian musical instrument, and it far and away exceeded that goal.

In the hands of Luther Perkins, Buck Owens, Muddy Waters, Joe Strummer, and Bruce Springsteen, the Telecaster and its brethren have made the music of working people: country, blues, punk, and rock 'n' roll. Strap on its solid slab of swamp-grown southern hardwood, plug straight into an old tube combo, and let it rip. The Telecaster offers no adornment, and needs none: no abalone inlays, no scrollwork, no marquetry or purfling. It's a pure music-maker, raw and in your face, ready to take on what you throw at it. In short, it is the simple, naked form of the solid-body electric six-string. It gives you nothing more than is needed to attack the job at hand, and certainly delivers nothing less.

This is the complete tale of an electric guitar that came to work, and that continues to work hard seventy years after its birth, still resonating with the purity of the first slab of swamp ash that was carved to that iconic single-cutaway design.

1950 Broadcaster. *Steve Catlin/Redferns/Getty Images*

Clarence "Gatemouth" Brown totes his early Telecaster in a 1950s Peacock Records publicity photo.
Gilles Petard/Redferns/Getty Images

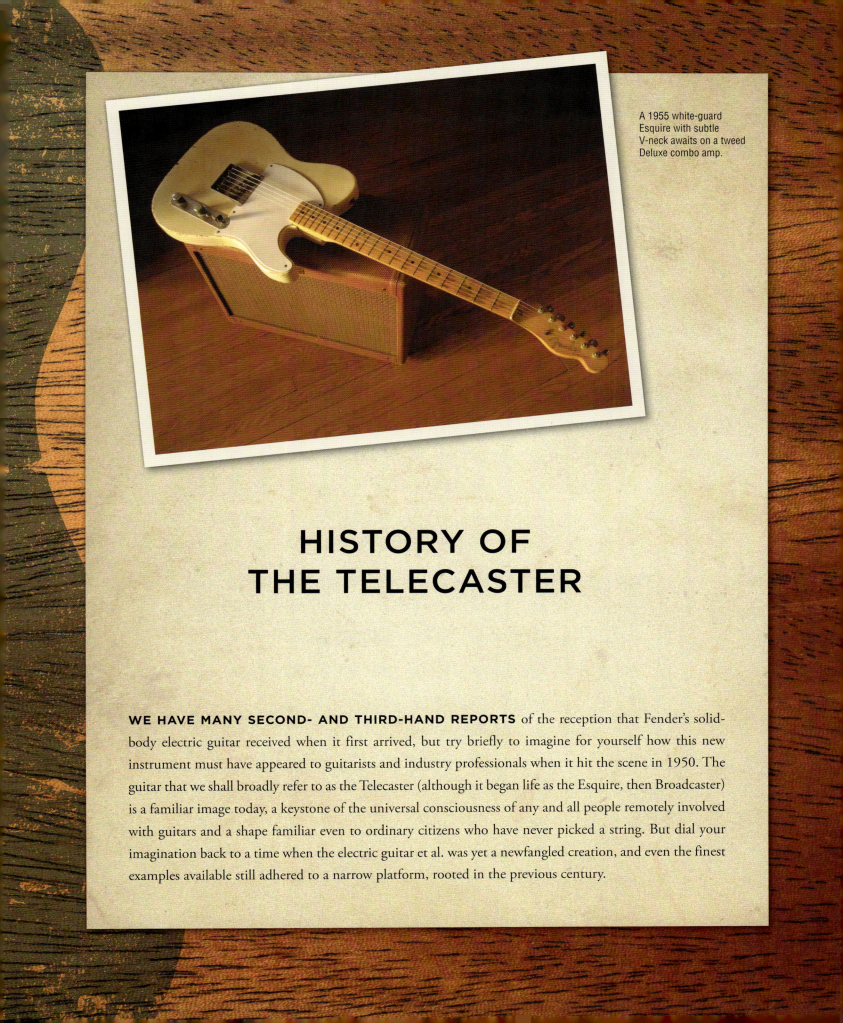

A 1955 white-guard Esquire with subtle V-neck awaits on a tweed Deluxe combo amp.

HISTORY OF
THE TELECASTER

WE HAVE MANY SECOND- AND THIRD-HAND REPORTS of the reception that Fender's solid-body electric guitar received when it first arrived, but try briefly to imagine for yourself how this new instrument must have appeared to guitarists and industry professionals when it hit the scene in 1950. The guitar that we shall broadly refer to as the Telecaster (although it began life as the Esquire, then Broadcaster) is a familiar image today, a keystone of the universal consciousness of any and all people remotely involved with guitars and a shape familiar even to ordinary citizens who have never picked a string. But dial your imagination back to a time when the electric guitar et al. was yet a newfangled creation, and even the finest examples available still adhered to a narrow platform, rooted in the previous century.

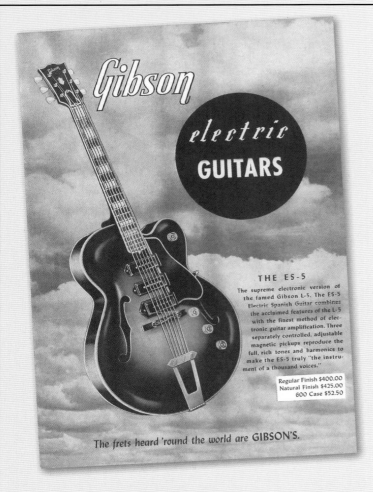

Upon its debut in 1949, Gibson's three-pickup ES-5 was the premier guitar of the day. Still, the ES-5 was truly just an acoustic guitar with pickups screwed on.

In the mid-1940s, when Gibson returned to production after the war effort, the most advanced electric guitars from this market leader were still just standard hollow-body archtop acoustics with added pickups, and efforts from Epiphone, Gretsch, and most others were not much different. Even Gibson's major electric breakthroughs of the late '40s—the two-pickup ES-350 of 1947, followed by the three-pickup ES-5 and laminated-bodied ES-175 of 1949—were but marginal adaptations of the acoustic guitar. The Fender guitar, though, was different, and not simply because it was made of solid wood with a bolt-on neck. Sure, it was basic, crude even, and easily derided as a "canoe paddle," a "baseball bat," or simply a "plank" (all of which were leveled at it by musicians and competitors alike). And yet, we can imagine the industry naysayers must have been quaking in their boots just a little bit, too, wondering, "Could this be the future of the guitar?" Oh, it most certainly could. Far more than just an electric guitar, a trick that had already been done, Fender's instrument was a total redrawing of the blueprint, virtually a

surrealist reinvention of what "the guitar" even was, whether electric or not, and therein lay the brilliance of it. It retained the six strings and it retained the tuning, and that was just about it. It was a plank, and if you wanted to, you could probably whack a baseball or paddle a canoe with it, and very likely even play it afterward . . . once you let it dry out again. This was an entirely new tool, and it offered barely a nod over its shoulder to whatever had come before.

Fender's new instrument embodied a brave new amplified world of music for the guitarist, and, as it would happen, for the listener, too. It would not only fill a very real need, but also would change the course of popular culture in doing so. The humble design and appointments might seem to have been superceded in the design stakes by plenty of guitars and gizmos that followed, whether we credit the Gibson Les Paul, Fender's own Stratocaster, the Floyd Rose vibrato, or even self-tuning, synth-ready, and USB-enabled guitars of the twenty-first century. But the Telecaster's form and function remain so seminal, so standard-setting, that it is still the clear template for every solid-body that followed, however radical. Not just a "new model" of guitar, the Telecaster, and its arrival in 1950, is a clear demarcation between *then* and *now*, before and after. It's a "guitar," sure, but—as a player might have put it on the eve of that sixth decade of the twentieth century—not as we know it.

HAWAIIAN TO WESTERN SWING TO JAZZ: MAKING IT LOUDER

The fact that Leo Fender's inroads into the musical instrument business revolved so heavily around the lap steel guitar gives some insight into the development of that quirky creation that came to be known as the Telecaster. Evolving from a Hawaiian music craze that spread like wildfire in the 1920s and early '30s to the burgeoning Western Swing and country scenes that ignited in the late '30s and through the '40s, the lap steel guitar, played with a solid steel bar, or slide, was really the most popular "electric

An unidentified Hawaiian band circa 1930 playing a range of Rickenbacker electric lap steel and Spanish guitars and Spanish tenor guitars. Rickenbacker's solidbody Hawaiian, lap, and Spanish hollow-body guitars pioneered electric-guitar technology.

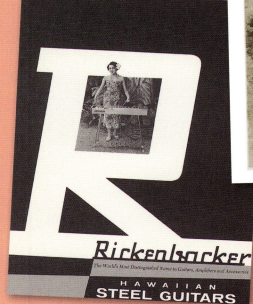

guitar" of the era. Part of its prominence can be attributed not merely to the music that it suited so well (and helped to inspire), but also to the fact that it was more effective as a lead instrument, and therefore more capable of putting "guitarists," in the broad sense, in the spotlight. Players of what we now view as "conventional" guitars had been seeking the same sonic advantages for two decades by the mid-'40s and—the playing achievements of artists such as Charlie Christian, Eddie Durham, Alvino Rey, and others on boomy, feedback-prone archtop electrics not-withstanding—a satisfactory solution to the difficulty of being heard amidst a big band had yet to be found. The bright, clear, steel guitar, on the other hand, cut through the mix like a searchlight through the California night.

While makers like Gibson, Epiphone, Gretsch, and other traditional acoustic guitar manufacturers had, or thought they had, the vehicle for the electric guitar in hand, Leo Fender knew by the latter edge of the mid-'40s that he had the sound fairly well defined in his "mind's ear," as confirmed by the musicians who provided so much feedback to the cause, and that he had the electronic means of creating it. Essentially, the guitarists with whom Fender was fraternizing wanted, even craved, the sound that steel players were already finding in production instruments, but in a guitar that could be played in the Spanish style. Essentially, the sound, and the means of achieving it, came first; as for the guitar it would be bolted to, that could be pure function over form.

Paul Bigsby's electric guitar was one of the first solidbodies built, but was only made in small numbers. Still, the Bigsby guitar is believed to have had a profound influence on Leo Fender's own creation. In particular, Bigsby's six-on-a-side tuners configuration was a novel and clever route to get straight string runs. This 1948 Bigsby was made for country picker Merle Travis. *Outline Press Ltd.*

PROTOTYPING THE FENDER SOLID-BODY ELECTRIC GUITAR

To begin to get a handle on Leo Fender's approach to the task in hand circa 1948, we need to revisit his own stated goals in developing electric instruments. As he told *Guitar Player*, "I guess you would say the objectives were durability, performance, and tone." That's it, in a nutshell. Expounding upon this, however, as he did on several occasions, Fender extrapolates the components within each of those three objectives, painting a bigger picture of what went into achieving them.

We have already discussed the tone as having descended from the lap steel guitar, and Fender's pickup designs for those instruments were already evolving toward the seminal Telecaster bridge and neck pickups by the late 1940s. His use of six individual magnets, one for each string, which passed vertically through the horizontal coil, helped to enhance clarity in the unit's response. Fender himself noted another advantage of the design: "I think that perhaps I was the first person to use separate magnets, one for each string," he told *Guitar Player* magazine in May 1978. "That way, I found that the notes didn't seem to run together—you could get more of an individual performance off of each

string." The narrow coil and tight magnetic field also contributed to a bright tone, another boon to the guitarist's effort to "cut through the band."

Ask any player to discuss components that differentiate the Telecaster from other electric guitars (Fenders such as the Stratocaster and Jazzmaster included) and they are likely to mention the bridge and the bridge pickup. Even before the Esquire and Broadcaster hit the scene, these are the very elements of the design that Leo Fender sought to protect. Via a patent application filed on January 13, 1950, and granted a little over a year later, Fender sought to protect his new "Combination Bridge and Pickup Assembly," displayed in drawings that clearly show the very recognizable Tele bridge plate with three saddles and pickup

suspended beneath, all mounted on an extremely rudimentary guitar that lacks even a cutaway, and carries a three-per-side headstock. As iconic as the Telecaster body shape has become, this mating of hardware and electronics in one simple and ingeniously functional design really is what defines the Telecaster.

This design also fulfills Fender's desire to provide guitarists with a more versatile bridge than previously available, and although the three saddles atop the steel base plate of the classic vintage-Tele design might seem crude by today's standards, the configuration appeared wonderfully versatile in its day. At the time, electric guitars from the major manufacturers almost universally carried a "floating" bridge, a two-piece design that encompassed a wooden base with a single wooden saddle mounted on two bolts with thumbscrews. It was adjustable for height, and for approximate intonation settings by sliding the entire unit back and forth (or angling it one way or the other), but that was about it. Fender's new design provided height adjustment for each individual string, and more precise intonation adjustment for the strings in pairs, in addition to the sustain-enhancing properties of metal saddles. As such, it was a big step forward.

Regarding the overall design of the guitar in general, Leo was driven largely by his long-standing goal that it should be easy to service. Following from this, as he told *Rolling Stone* in 1976, "The design of everything we did was intended to be easy to build, and easy to repair. . . . If a thing is easy to service, it is easy to build." To that end, the use of a screwed-on neck (usually, though errantly, referred to as "bolt-on") addressed several objectives. The neck itself wasn't necessarily easier to manufacture than one that would be glued into a guitar's body in the traditional way—other than its lack of additional fingerboard—but the steps of attaching and correctly aligning it were greatly simplified. The "easy-to-service" side of the goal was fulfilled, too, in that the player could simply bolt on a replacement if necessary, or re-align the original more easily than he or she could a glued-in neck. Several reports also indicate that Leo felt the bolt-on neck would be useful because, rather than having to re-fret the guitar, a new neck could simply be added by the player in the field, armed only with a Phillips head screwdriver.

The guitar's body was conceived to be just as functional, and just as easy to produce. A slab-style body made from swamp ash, or even pine, as were some early prototypes, was clearly much cheaper and easier to manufacture than a hollow body of any quality, or even a carved or contoured solidbody. Its electronics and hardware could obviously be added, and accessed for repair, much more easily, too. Beyond the ease of manufacture, though, the solidbody offered performance and tonal characteristics that elevated it above the obvious "well, it's cheaper" criticism. Its lack of the acoustic resonance of a hollow-body guitar was actually a positive, given Fender's aims, since this reduced feedback howl exponentially, making it much easier to use the instrument on stage at any significant volume levels. Tonally, the solid wood was also a boon to both sustain and clarity, making the new guitar a superior instrument for lead playing.

As for "features," well, that was about it. So simple was the initial design that it can be summed up in just a few short paragraphs, as we have done here. And to Leo Fender's mind, as well as those of the thousands of players who would latch on to the Telecaster year after year, that simplicity was a definite plus.

MOVING FROM PROTOTYPE TO PRODUCTION

While continuing to turn out steel guitars and amplifiers, Fender worked through much of 1949 to produce a viable Spanish electric prototype. Electronics and component design were mainly the provenance of Leo himself, while George Fullerton was tasked with designing the body. Fullerton was born in 1923 in Hindsville, Arkansas (and, ironically, had no familial connection to Fullerton, California), and moved to California before the war to work in a plant manufacturing aircraft parts. Fender

hired him in 1948 to repair radios in the shop, and, shortly after, charged him with servicing warranty returns of Fender amplifiers and steel guitars. As Fender's business expanded through the late '40s and early '50s, both conceptually and physically, Leo brought Fullerton more and more into the design and manufacturing fold.

Exercising a long-standing interest in art that would work hand in hand with his technical abilities, Fullerton set about drawing a simple and subtly elegant solid-wood guitar that could stand alongside the best of mid-century modern design. The result, embodied in the first real Esquire/Broadcaster prototype of 1949, clearly displays the iconic Telecaster body shape, hardware, and electronics, with a few crucial differences when compared to the production model that would follow:

- In place of the familiar post-1950 Tele pickguard that runs beneath the strings, the prototype has a pickguard more like that of other electric guitars of the era, protecting only the treble side of the body, from the controls to the cutaway.

- The control plate is shorter and installed at an angle between output jack and bridge, and carries volume and tone pots only for the single pickup, with no tone selector switch.

- Perhaps most notably of all, the headstock is a conventional, symmetrical three-a-side type as used by most makers of the day—Gibson, Epiphone, and Gretsch included—carved to what is often referred to as a "snakehead" shape.

- The neck plate is a little longer than would be conventional for production guitars, at 2⅝ inches.

- The body is made from pine and finished in an opaque white.

- Also less obvious from any front views of the instrument, but discernable from the lack of "skunk stripe," the solid-maple neck has no truss rod. It is also wider than normal for an electric Spanish guitar, at nearly two inches across the nut.

Even with these elements accounted for, the prototype still represents all of the crucial design points that would make the Telecaster eventually, if not immediately, such a successful instrument. In addition to the visible links to the final form of the instrument post-1950—such as the bridge and pickup

Custom Shop 60th Anniversary Esquire. *Fender Musical Instruments Corporation*

1954 Esquire.
Fretted Americana

assembly, narrow control plate, body shape, and bold-on maple neck—the prototype's 25½-inch scale length would become a standard of Fender's most popular instruments, too, including the Stratocaster and Jazzmaster after the Telecaster. Responsible in great part for the Telecaster's shimmering harmonic content and firm, punchy, low end (ingredients of the classic "twang" sound), the scale length was perhaps something of a random occurrence, rather than the result of the kind of hard-graft R&D that Fender would normally be known for. From Forrest White again, writing in his book *Fender: The Inside Story*: "Leo told me the scale and fret placement had been copied from a Gretsch archtop guitar. This is why it was 25½ inches from the nut to the bridge." Many big-bodied jazz guitars had traditionally been made with 25½-inch scale lengths, although several Gibsons of the day, including some of the more advanced electrics designs such as the ES-175 with laminated body woods and built-in (rather than "floating") pickups, were made to a shorter 24¾-inch scale, and most standard steel guitars had scale lengths that were shorter still.

Other prototypes followed, and as 1949 rolled toward 1950, the guitar would approach its now-classic state. Before getting there, however, its development would encounter a few hiccups that, in some instances, Fender was strangely slow in correcting. One of the most significant of these revolves around the lack of a truss rod in the first prototypes, and an apparent debate over the necessity of this feature versus the production expense and effort of including it.

Reports indicate—and appear to be validated by Forrest White—that Fender sales manager Don Randall took two prototypes to the National Association of Music Merchants (NAMM) show in New York City in the summer of 1949, and that the guitars stirred some interest, but were largely criticized for their lack of truss rods. White tells of meeting Valco founder Al Frost in the late 1950s, and being told that Frost advised Randall not to manufacture the guitars in that condition, or they could expect warranty headaches further down the road. Although he apparently thought the maple necks would stand up fine without added support, Leo clearly bowed to informed opinion and tooled up for the feature, which was included in the official-release guitars

displayed at the Chicago NAMM show one year later. Before making the truss rod an official part of the formula, however, Fender seems to have manufactured several pre-production Esquires without them—some as final-phase prototypes, perhaps, and others as custom-order guitars sold directly to local musicians—several of which still exist today.

Many of these Esquires also have the pine bodies of the 1949 prototypes, but even before their manufacture, Leo appears to have settled on the six-in-line headstock for which the Telecaster has always been known. Whether he was influenced by the Merle Travis/Paul Bigsby guitar or by accounts of Croatian instruments, as he himself claimed, Leo Fender had sound engineering reasons for using the asymmetrical headstock. "My main reason," he told *Guitar Player* magazine in May 1978, "was that it put all the strings in a straight line to the tuners—right straight through the nut to the peg. I didn't want to fan out the strings like you have to with pegs on both sides." What Fender seems to be alluding to, without entirely saying, is the tuning issues from which Gibson, Epiphone, Gretsch, and guitars with similarly designed three-a-side headstocks can sometimes suffer, caused when the strings get caught up in the nut slots due to the relatively sharp break angle from nut to tuner.

Already in the habit of testing out new ideas on musicians and folding their feedback into reiterations of the design, Leo Fender sought professional opinions from several notable players during the prototyping stages. In 1984 he told *Guitar Player* of taking a guitar to the Riverside Rancho Dance Hall in Riverside, California, for Jimmy Bryant to try out. Bryant took the guitar up on stage with Little Jimmy Dickens and his band and started playing, and, as Leo told it, "Pretty soon the band stopped, everybody on the dance floor stopped, and they all gathered around Jimmy when he played."

In his own "Recollections" in the *John Edwards Memorial Foundation Quarterly* of the fall of 1979, Merle Travis recounted testing out a guitar that Leo brought with him when returning the Travis/Bigsby solidbody he had borrowed for a week. "I thought it was a fine instrument, and I told him so," Travis wrote. "He asked me to try it out, which I was pleased to do." But not all early tests, it would seem, went as well as these. There are also

The headstock of a 1950 Broadcaster.
Steve Catlin/Redferns/Getty Images

1950 Broadcaster.
*Geoff Dann/Redferns/
Getty Images*

stories of Dale Hyatt, then working as the manager of the shop at Fender's Radio Service, taking guitars to Northern California for other players to try out on the bandstand, only to have three in a row fail due to pickup wires that had pinched between the bridge plate and pickup base plate and shorted out. Given these minor setbacks, and the derisive comments about being a "canoe paddle" or a "toilet seat" that the prototypes received from other quarters, it's clear that it was not all smooth sailing for Fender and company. With that in mind, it's impressive that the team went from prototyping in mid-1949 to an official release by the spring of 1950, no more than a year later.

Murky with the fog of time, the order in which the late prototypes and early production models were produced, the numbers of them, and the precise dates of release are difficult to confirm. In his popular history, *The Fender Telecaster* (Hal Leonard, 1991), A.R. Duchossoir writes that trade magazines of the day reported that only the single-pickup Esquire was displayed at the Chicago NAMM show in July, 1950. This guitar had an opaque black finish and white pickguard (possibly concealing a body made of pine, like those of the prototypes) and an unusual push-button tone switch where the three-way selector switch would later be positioned. The same guitar, or one of very few rare early siblings, appears in Fender's spring catalog of 1950, as well as in early trade advertisements.

Forrest White tells, on the other hand, of being told by Leo and Don Randall alike that a dual-pickup guitar was ready for summer NAMM of 1950. "The guitar that made the show that year was a two-pickup version with truss rod," he writes. "Leo and Don called it the Broadcaster." Meanwhile, Esquires with two pickups and the more familiar blonde finishes were also made early in 1950, as evidenced by photographs and existing examples. Running slightly contrary to all of this, Leo told *Guitar Player* magazine in 1984, "Randall wanted us to come out with the single pickup design and wanted to call it the Esquire. That may be why it showed up in that catalogue and price list and the Broadcaster or Telecaster didn't. But the Broadcaster was the first one we built."

Whatever the truth, the idea that any kind of official Broadcaster or Telecaster was issued as early as 1948 is purely fiction. Fuelled largely by CBS-owned Fender's ads of the early '70s featuring a 1972 Telecaster beside a "1948 Telecaster," this was a misfire from a company that had lost touch with its roots, or just a marketing department brainstorm that slipped through without level-headed assessment from the powers that might usually approve such promotional efforts. Whatever the case, nothing more than very early workbench and drawing board efforts of a Fender electric Spanish existed in 1948, with the first even vaguely Tele-ish prototypes being produced around mid-1949, and no production guitars until 1950.

A lot of the confusion over what was introduced then was apparently caused by the occasional butting of heads between Leo Fender, as designer and manufacturer, and the reps at Radio & Television Equipment Company (RTEC), exclusive distributor of Fender Electric Instruments from 1946 to 1953. Fender clearly leaned toward the full-featured two-pickup instrument, an even more innovative design for the time, while RTEC salespeople wanted to get in on the ground with the more affordable single-pickup Esquire and promoted that in their literature in early 1950 in an effort to do so. Don Randall, as Fender sales manager (and having come to Fender via a similar position with RTEC), appeared to be wedged between the two parties. It's easy to see how, given the rough reception that the "plank" was receiving in some quarters, the more affordable Esquire might have seemed an easier sell—or less likely to get an RTEC rep laughed out the door, at least.

Despite the sparring between models, by the latter part of 1950 Fender was clearly leading with the two-pickup Broadcaster with so-called blonde finish—and starting to produce a decent number of them, too—with the single-pickup Esquire settling in as the entry-level model. Although Leo's own account tells us that Randall was pulling for the simpler one-pickup Esquire, and he the two-pickup version, it was apparently Randall who named the Broadcaster, for the vast popularity of radio and fledgling television. Once they were established as official models, the Esquire carried a list price of $139.95 and the Broadcaster $169.95, plus $39.95 for the optional case for either model. (At roughly 25 percent of the cost of the guitar itself, it was a pricey case for its day.)

LAUNCHING THE "NEW ELECTRIC STANDARD"

There are tales of several early Esquires without truss rods, but these are very likely apocryphal. However many were produced, Fender was clearly ramped up for truss rod installation by the time of the guitars' official releases, and the first-generation specs were pretty much settled by the latter part of 1951. An insert to the RTEC sales catalog entitled "New Fender Electric Standard—'Broadcaster Model'" boasted of the truss rod, as well as several other features that have come to define this ground-breaking guitar. Among these, with explanatory details, were:

- Micro-Adjustable Bridge
- Adjustable Solo-Lead Pickup
- Adjustable Rhythm Pickup
- Adjustable Neck Truss Rod
- Neck Anchor Plates
- Tone Control
- Volume Control
- Lever Switch
- Modern Cutaway
- Modern Styled Head

The ingredients of the "Telecaster tone" will be investigated more thoroughly in Telecaster Tone and Construction (see page 131), but one of these features—not yet mentioned—bears just a little discussion here. Fender's "lever switch," standard on so many dual-pickup guitars today, was originally wired to an archaic and rather puzzling circuit. On top of that, the so-called "tone control" really wasn't a tone control at all, by conventional standards, until after 1952. When the Broadcaster was first released, the settings accessed by the switch, from forward, to middle, to rear, were (1) "deep rhythm," achieved with the neck pickup wired through a tone capacitor; (2) neck pickup alone (no tone control); and (3) both pickups, with the "tone" control used as a blender control to add the neck pickup to the bridge pickup as desired. Most who have tried a Broadcaster or Telecaster with original wiring will attest to the fact that this deep rhythm sound—dull, muted—is very nearly useless.

Later in 1952 the wiring was changed to offer the same bassy sound from the neck pickup at the forward switch setting, neck

pickup with conventional tone control in the middle, and bridge with tone control at the rearward position. Rather incredibly, the Telecaster wouldn't receive the logical neck/both/bridge pickup selections, all with tone control in-circuit, until 1967, even though countless players were rewiring their switches for these options long before then. Leo did feel, however, that the tone control itself was revolutionary enough to warrant a patent of its own: He filed for such on July 31, 1953, and it was granted on March 12, 1957. Even prior to this, though, Leo had sought his second patent related to the new Fender electric guitar, a design patent filed April 23, 1951, and granted August 14, 1951. Offering front, side, and rear views of the Telecaster as we know it today, this patent represents the only effort to protect the overall shape and look of the instrument, which has nevertheless been copied in near-exact detail for several decades.

Two features not mentioned in the RTEC catalog insert were the Broadcaster's transparent blonde finish, now standard in place of the opaque black seen in the first advertising insert of earlier that year, or the change in body wood beneath it. The blonde, or "limed," finish had become standard, as had the ash body, which had replaced the pine used in several early examples many months previous. Which came first is difficult to say, but they went hand in hand: the blonde finish gave the guitar a look that was more distinctive in the black-and-white world of the day, and which also jibed better, aesthetically, with the limed Scandinavian-style finish of the predominant modern furniture of the era. And, while plenty of players credit the tone of the early pine-bodied Esquires, the ash itself—in the form of light, resonant swamp ash in particular—would become a classic of the tonewood library thanks primarily to its use in Fender guitars of the 1950s.

TEST PILOTS: EARLY FENDER ENDORSEES

Even with the early hiccups cured, the wrinkles ironed out, and the Esquire and Broadcaster officially on the market, Fender faced a rough road, acceptance-wise, in the early days of the new solid-body guitars. Many players had been asking for just such an instrument, in theory anyway, but the majority proved a traditional and conservative lot, and took some winning over.

1950 Broadcaster. *Steve Catlin/ Redferns/Getty Images*

Virtually hand in hand with the official release of the new solid-body models, Fender was ramped up to promote its innovative new instrument with several prominent artist endorsements. The guitars' acceptance radiated outward in ever-expanding circles from the epicenter of the Western Swing and country scene, conveniently located in Southern California at the time, alongside a growing entertainment industry that was making Los Angeles its headquarters.

Bandleader Spade Cooley was one of the most significant Western artists of the day, and his steel player Noel Boggs, a Fender steel guitar and amplifier endorser, was a major star on the scene, too. Right alongside Boggs, guitarist Jimmy Wyble was himself a rising star, and one of the first artists to promote Fender's new solidbody in print. In an advertisement first published in May of 1950, Wyble is shown playing an Esquire with a black body and white pickguard—a guitar that might have been an early pine-bodied example, or might simply have been the victim of a photo touched up in production to show a black guitar like that which would appear in the first NAMM flier two months later.

Fender's real coup, though, came with landing an endorsement from Jimmy Bryant. Bryant was celebrated as one of the fastest players in the Los Angeles area, and one of the most skillful, in a scene that wasn't short of hot pickers. Skills aside, Bryant's own back-story—his Depression-era childhood, war service, and "go west, young man!" journey to join the entertainment industry—reads like the perfect mid-century Americana bio, and made him the ideal endorsement for Fender's newfangled guitar. For a few years in the early '50s, Bryant belonged to Fender. Along with steel guitarist Speedy West, who would also later endorse Fender instruments, Bryant recorded many of the stand-out electric sides of the '50s and proved an invaluable beacon for the Fender electric Spanish guitar in general.

On the heels of Bryant's endorsement, plenty of others followed: Bill Carson, a guitarist with the Eddy Kirk Band; Hank Thompson and His Brazos Valley Boys, who would shortly after be instrumental in testing and helping to develop the Stratocaster; Arthur Smith, Leon Rhodes, Charlie Aldrich, and several others.

In addition to the six-string stars willing to fly the flag, Fender's deeper and longer-standing roots in the steel community certainly

Tawnee Hall plays lead on an early Broadcaster guitar for Lefty Frizzell on October 26, 1952. *Scotty Broyles/courtesy Deke Dickerson photo archive*

helped to establish credibility for the solid-body electric Spanish, too. Even before the release of the Broadcaster and Esquire midway through 1950, barely four years into the company's existence, Fender was regarded as one of the leading manufacturers of steel guitars and the amplifiers that went with them.

BROADCASTER TO NOCASTER TO TELECASTER

In February of 1951, just as the Broadcaster was gaining some tentative footing in the guitar world, RTEC received a letter from Gretsch stating that the well-established Brooklyn company owned the trademark to the model name. Gretsch "Broadkaster" banjos and drums (with a "k" in place of the "c") had been on the market since the 1920s, and a drum kit of that name was still available at the time of the Fender Broadcaster's release. Eager to avoid conflict so early in the game, Don Randall urged Fender to pull the Broadcaster name from the headstock and from all advertising immediately, and Leo conceded. The event marks the end of the short-lived model, in name at least. With no reliable company records remaining, accounts differ on how many

Broadcasters were produced from around the spring of 1950 to February of 1951. *Gruhn's Guide to Vintage Guitars*, by George Gruhn and Walter Carter, estimates three hundred to five hundred, although several accounts indicate that the tally could even total fewer than two hundred guitars.

For a few months, Fender produced its two-pickup solid-body electric with no name on the headstock other than the company logo. This run of guitars, which came to be known as "Nocasters," represents another exceedingly rare and collectible Fender. Precise production dates for any of the three—Broadcaster, Nocaster, and early Telecaster—are difficult to trace because necks and bodies were often dated after coming off the assembly line and stored on shelves for weeks or even months before being used in a completed guitar. For this reason, a Nocaster might have a neck date from firmly within the Broadcaster era, or a Telecaster a neck dated within the Nocaster era, and so forth. It's a situation that can be confusing to the historian hoping to pin down Fender's evolution with any precision, but one that most collectors have just come to accept.

By April of 1951, Don Randall, who had named the Broadcaster little more than a year before, took Fender from the radio days straight into the age of television by coining the name "Telecaster." Fender added the Telecaster model name to the two-pickup guitar later that month, or certainly by early May of 1951, and it has stayed that way for sixty years and counting. Television was the big thing in the early 1950s and throughout that decade, so Fender's new name couldn't have hurt the product in the least. A simple guitar, with simple contrasting colors—it's almost as if the Telecaster was designed to look good on the grainy, low-definition, black-and-white TV sets of the day, and would even be identifiable amidst the typical snowstorm while you jiggled the rabbit ears seeking better reception. Funny enough, the look of the guitar on television would itself inspire Leo to make a physical change in the Telecaster later in the decade, but the model's specs would evolve in other subtle ways before that point arrived.

(continued on page 62)

Above: Billy F Gibbons with a brace of Esquires in 2005. *David Perry (davidperrystudio.com)*
Right: Billy F Gibbons played this 1952 Broadcaster with ZZ Top on "Jesus Just Left Chicago" in 1973. *David Perry (davidperrystudio.com)*

Jimmy Bryant

Custom Shop Jimmy Bryant Tribute Telecaster in white blonde. *Fender Musical Instruments Corporation*

Thanks to his Johnny-on-the-spot associations with Leo Fender and the pre-production development of the Broadcaster, Jimmy Bryant will forever be thought of as "Mister Telecaster." Even if he weren't hanging out in So-Cal to take up a prototype Fender solidbody and display its capabilities for the masses, this fleet-fingered country, jazz, and Western Swing soloist would deserve some attention for the sheer gymnastics of his playing.

Bryant was born in 1925 to a hardscrabble farming family in Moultrie, Georgia, and despite the encroaching Great Depression, he received a comprehensive musical education from his musician father, Ivy. He played the violin early on and was a skilled fiddler even as a young child, playing on street corners at the tender age of five and performing at two World's Fairs with his father. Soon hailed as a fiddle prodigy in rural Georgia, Bryant's career on the violin was cut short when he was drafted into the army at the age of eighteen and shipped out to the European front. He suffered a head injury from a grenade blast in Germany and he picked up the

guitar during his long recuperation. Following his discharge, Bryant packed up his larger git-fiddle and headed west to Los Angeles, to get in on the burgeoning Western Swing scene.

Bryant's impressive guitar skills—blending country swing with a little be-bop influence and a clear love of Django Reinhardt-style hot jazz—helped him make a name on the circuit rather quickly. He was already something of a phenomenon when Leo Fender asked him to test out one of his early Telecaster prototypes. Bryant was a member of Roy Rogers's band The Sons of the Pioneers, and he was hired for the band for Cliffie Stone's *Hometown Jamboree*, broadcast live on the radio and then on local television. While playing on the session and movie scene around LA, Bryant teamed up with steel-guitar whiz Speedy West to back a string of country artists, and eventually the duo were signed to Capitol Records as artists in their own right. Together, they cut more than fifty "sides" between

1951 and 1956, including the showpieces "Stratosphere Boogie," "Speedin' West," "Bryant's Bounce," and "Frettin' Fingers."

Throughout the early '50s Bryant played and promoted the Broadcaster, then Telecaster, sporting a standard black-guard example early on, but replacing this with a custom-engraved white pickguard before that color became standard for the model. Bryant was purportedly a rather surly character, and difficult to work with. This attitude, it would seem, would lose Bryant his Capitol Records contract in 1956 and trigger his early departure from other prominent steady gigs. In the 1960s Bryant moved over to record production more than performing, and even moved from Fender to be an endorser for Vox guitars for a time in the late '60s. Bryant relocated to Nashville in the mid-'70s and reunited with former musical collaborator Speedy West in 1975. Bryant, a lifelong smoker, died of lung cancer in 1980.

Paul Burlison

The Rock 'n Roll Trio at New York City's Pythian Temple during the band's May 7, 1956, recording session for Coral Records. Even in this photo, the bandmates seem to have a hard time keeping still.

The Rock 'n Roll Trio at New York City's Pythian Temple during the band's May 7, 1956, recording session for Coral Records. Even in this photo, the bandmates seem to have a hard time keeping still.

> "I bought that Les Paul model Gibson, the first one they came out with—you know, that gold one? I bought it, but I didn't keep it for but six months. . . . I never did like it, so as soon as that Fender came out, I traded it for a Fender."
>
> —Paul Burlison

As a founding member of the Rock 'n Roll Trio, Paul Burlison was at the epicenter of the rock 'n' roll boom of the mid-'50s. He secured his place in history as a godfather of rockabilly, but the guitarist never achieved the wider fame that such eminence might be expected to bring. Even so, he was one of the first true rock 'n' rollers to ply his trade on a Telecaster (or originally, in his case, an Esquire), and he left an indelible mark on popular music.

Burlison was born in Brownsville, Tennessee, in 1929, but his musical conscience was really formed by Memphis, the city to which his family moved in 1937. Burlison enlisted in the Navy in 1946 at the age of seventeen, where he earned an all-navy runner-up boxing title as a welterweight a year later. Upon his return to Memphis in 1949 he met brothers Dorsey and

Johnny Burnette through the local Golden Gloves boxing association. In addition to boxing, the Burnettes shared Burlison's interest in music, and, in particular, the blend of country and Beale Street blues that was then bubbling up around Memphis. While learning a trade as an electrician, Burlison pursued his interest in the guitar. In 1952, the three formed The Rhythm Rangers. Burlison also played with other groups around town, backing Howlin' Wolf briefly, and even working as a studio guitarist at Sun Records before Elvis Presley joined the label.

In 1956, Burlison and the Burnette brothers left their wives and young children behind and hit the road for New York City, ostensibly to find union work for Paul and Dorsey, the electricians of the group. But their guitars came with them, and they found musical success. An audition for the *Ted Mack Original Amateur Hour* show on ABC-TV affiliate WHBQ in New York—where they were briefly billed as the Rock 'N' Roll Boys of Memphis—landed three successive wins when the trio's performance of "Tutti Frutti"

consistently slammed the applause meter into the red. Band leader Henry Jerome signed them to a management contract, and the group signed to Coral and was renamed the Rock 'N' Roll Trio (often billed as "Johnny Burnette and . . ." for the singer and rhythm guitarist).

Although he briefly played a 1953 Gibson Les Paul prior to the big move east to NYC, Burlison's main instrument throughout his time with the Rock 'N Roll Trio was a white-guard Fender Esquire, most likely made in late 1954 or early '55. In a 1978 interview with *Guitar Player* magazine's Jas Obrecht, Burlison said, "I never did like [the Les Paul] because I got bad feedback . . . so as soon as that Fender came out, I traded it for a Fender." Early studio sessions in the spring of 1956 at the Pythian Temple in New York resulted in the singles "Midnight Train," "Tear It Up," "Oh Baby Babe," and "You're Undecided," and although none topped the charts, they achieved reasonable commercial success. Burlison's style on the Esquire, defined by boogie lines behind the rhythm guitar, and driving single-note and double-stop solos, are clear precursors of the style that would soon

after be known as archetypal rockabilly, and certainly seminal rock 'n' roll by any standards.

After tiring of the road late in 1957, Burlison headed back home to Memphis, and aside from a brief jaunt to California to join the Burnette Brothers (as Johnny and Dorsey were now calling themselves), that was essentially the end of the Rock 'N Roll Trio. "I enjoyed it, but the main thing was I missed my family," Burlison told Obrecht in 1978. "I enjoyed the playin', but I enjoy playin' just sittin' around. I really do. And the fame—or whatever you want to call it—I don't really think it ever affected me at all. I was really wanting to make enough money out of the thing to come home and open up an electrical supply company." When he got there, that's exactly what he did. For some twenty years Burlison played music only "on the side," for the fun of it, and concentrated on his electrical business. In the 1980s he revived his career and performed and recorded with several other artists, although the deaths of Johnny Burnette in a boating accident in 1964, and of Dorsey Burnette of a massive coronary in 1979, meant the Rock 'n Roll Trio would never ride again.

James Burton

James Burton and his Telecaster back Ricky Nelson in this classic Fender advertisement.

Rick Nelson and James Burton play

Fender MUSICAL INSTRUMENTS

Burton played this Paisley Tele with Elvis Presley, Gram Parsons, and Emmylou Harris. It now resides in the collection of actor Steven Seagal. *Rick Gould*

From making TV appearances on one of the nation's most popular shows while still in his teens, to being first-call sideman for massive stars from Elvis to Emmylou, James Burton was born to twang, and he was a Telecaster player right from the start. Born in 1939 in Dubberly, Louisiana, Burton expressed his musical drive early on. He took up the acoustic guitar while he was still in the single digits and first fell in love with a solid-body electric as a fourteen-year-old—at about the same time he turned professional—when he saw a new '53 Telecaster hanging on the wall of J&S Music in Shreveport, Louisiana.

Although he was younger than most significant players on the scene in the mid-1950s, Burton soon found himself right at the front edge of the rock 'n' roll boom. Shortly after turning pro, Burton was asked to join

A young James Burton added his defining Louisiana swamp riff to Dale Hawkins's rockabilly classic "Susie-Q."

DALE HAWKINS   Checker Recording

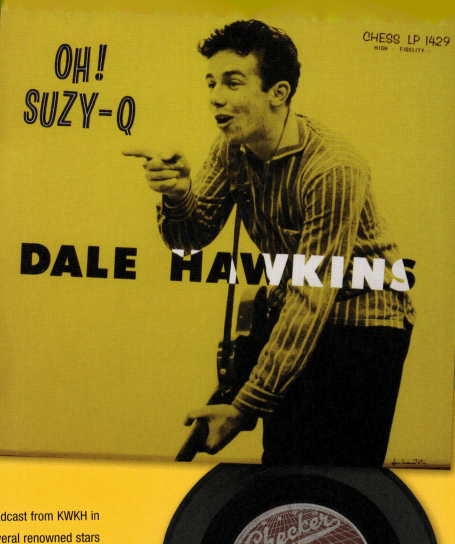

OH! SUZY-Q

DALE HAWKINS

CHESS LP 1429
HIGH · FIDELITY

the house band for the *Louisiana Hayride*, broadcast from KWKH in Shreveport, Louisiana, on which he backed several renowned stars and began to make a name for himself as a reliable sideman. In 1955 he joined Dale Hawkins's band and started developing his rock 'n' roll chops more fully. Playing his own distinctive style, using both a flatpick and a fingerpick on his middle finger, with light-gauge banjo strings on his Tele's D through high E for easy bending, the youngster was soon displaying one of the more distinctive sounds of the period. Together Hawkins and Burton cut the hit song "Susie-Q" at the KWKH studio in 1957, featuring an archetypal rock 'n' roll lick penned by Burton himself. Shortly after, Burton left Hawkins's band to form rockabilly wailer Bob Luman's backing band the Shadows, who scored minor hits with "My Gal Is Red Hot" and "A Red Cadillac and a Black Moustache" before heading west to appear in the 1957 Roger Corman film *Carnival Rock* (in which the eighteen-year-old Burton can frequently be seen squeezing out pyrotechnical riffs on a custom-colored Telecaster with a black guard sporting "James" in white script). The film itself has largely disappeared in the annals of B-movie mediocrity, but Burton's Hollywood debut brought him to the attention of Ricky Nelson and, soon, a much more long-lasting dose of national fame.

In joining Ricky Nelson's band—first as rhythm guitarist to Joe Maphis's lead, then as lead guitarist himself—James Burton found himself periodically in front of the camera on *Ozzie and Harriet*, one of America's most popular TV shows of the 1950s and early '60s,

James Burton

James Burton's country guitar licks were an essential part of Emmylou Harris's famed Hot Band in the late 1970s.

RICKY SINGS AGAIN

EMMYLOU HARRIS

JAMES BURTON
POLK SALAD ANNIE
FIRE AND RAIN
DELTA LADY
MISTERY TRAIN

Burton Signature Telecaster. *Fender Musical Instruments Corporation*

as well as performing on numerous hit recordings, and he even lived with the eponymous Nelsons (a real family) for two years before finding his own digs in Tinseltown. Burton stayed with Ricky Nelson until 1967, but continued to play with Luman's band, as well as making more and more studio appearances as a first-call LA studio player. In 1968, Elvis Presley tapped Burton for his famous "Comeback Special." Burton remained Elvis's guitarist until Presley's death in 1977, although he found time between tours and recordings to make country-rock history first with Gram Parsons, then as a member of Emmylou Harris's original Hot Band (in which he frequently sported a Paisley Red Telecaster from the late '60s). A lifetime Telecaster player, Burton is an uncontested entry into the original solidbody history book and even boasts a decorative signature model from the contemporary Fender company.

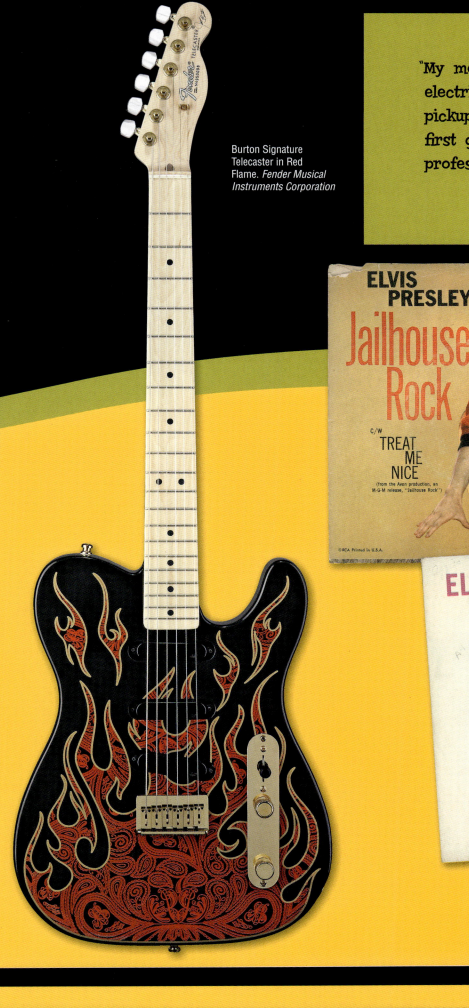

Burton Signature Telecaster in Red Flame. *Fender Musical Instruments Corporation*

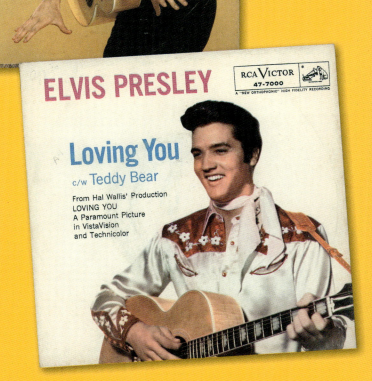

James Burton followed Scotty Moore as Elvis's main guitarist, adding his rockabilly licks to many No.1 hits.

1952 Telecaster. *Guitar courtesy of Elderly Instruments/photo Dave Matchette*

(continued from page 51)

TWEAKING THE FORMULA

Fender made a number of changes to the Telecaster in 1954, many of which were minor in the sense of structure and performance, but were often noticeable nonetheless. The only changes in the first couple of years were the move from three steel bridge saddles to three brass saddles around the fall of 1950, a change from 43-AWG wire to 42-AWG wire for winding the bridge pickup sometime around the move from Broadcaster to Nocaster (the smaller neck pickup continued to be wound with 43-AWG wire), and the rewiring of the Telecaster switching circuit to include a genuine tone control early in 1952. In addition, the look of the Kluson tuners changed slightly, from units that were stamped "Kluson Deluxe" in a single line along the center of the back up until mid-1951, to unbranded Klusons (a.k.a "no-line") from mid-1951 until 1957.

Less obvious to the eye, but evident to the left hand of any player who picked up the guitar, the shape of the back of the neck, known as the "neck profile," changed from a thick "V" on the earliest Esquires and Broadcasters, to a more rounded but still very full "D" shape around 1951. This approximate shape would remain, although thinning out some, through the course of the early 1950s, until a thinner "V" profile would reemerge around 1955 and remain for a couple of years. Although neck shapes tend to be tied fairly closely to different eras of the model, there is never a precise link between shape and date, because all of these necks were hand-shaped anyway, and displayed considerable variables, whatever period they were produced in.

Toward late 1954, several other changes were brought to the Telecaster, many of which were more noticeable, and thus constitute a demarcation point of sorts between the early guitars and those of the latter half of the decade. The most visible alteration was the move from a black fiber pickguard to a white plastic pickguard, a change that signals the end of the "black-guard Tele," as the pre-1955 guitars are so often called. Around the same time, Fender ceased stamping the guitars' serial numbers on the bridges' base plates, stamping them instead on the neck plates on the backs of the guitars, while the three string saddles changed back to solid steel, though of a smaller diameter than the earliest steel saddles. After 1955, a new—and repositioned—string retainer was used on the headstock, with a thin metal "butterfly" clip replacing the original round retainer. It was moved from its original placement near the G-string tuner to a position adjacent to the A-string tuner, and the Fender logo was moved further up the headstock, to the other side of this string retainer, as a result.

Through the course of the '50s the Telecaster's finish also evolved in a few subtle but noticeable ways, all of which were considered "blonde," the model's standard color. Broadcasters, Nocasters, and some of the first Telecasters had a finish that exhibited what might be called a very light beige hue, a color generally referred to now as "Butterscotch Blonde," which also showed off the distinctive grain of the ash used for the bodies. Toward the early part of the mid-'50s, the color took on more of a pale yellowy blonde look, then evolved toward a whiter (and slightly less transparent) blonde by the late '50s and early '60s.

All the while, Fender was willing to finish a guitar in a different "custom color" for any player who requested it, and after the mid-'50s, was willing to pay the additional 5 percent upcharge. Early nonstandard finishes were known to have been done for a handful of

An early white-guard 1954 Telecaster.
Guitar courtesy of Elderly Instruments/ photo Dave Matchette

players who were regulars of the local scene, but custom-colored Telecasters from the early '50s are extremely rare nonetheless. A.R. Duchossoir's *The Fender Telecaster* shows a 1952 Esquire finished in copper, 1956 Esquire and Telecaster in pale green and red respectively, and a 1957 Telecaster in two-tone Stratocaster-style sunburst, all of which are highly prized collector's items today. The open-ended offer to finish your Telecaster in a custom color was established in the 1957 Fender catalog, and by the late '50s, the most common of these "standard custom" colors, if you will, were Black, Lake Placid Blue, Fiesta Red, and Shoreline Gold.

The Telecaster and Esquire varied less from its standard color in the 1950s than would the Stratocaster (which came in sunburst as standard, with blonde being a custom color), but the factory upgrade would become a more popular option in the early '60s. The shift toward bolder colors probably had something to do with Fender's official publication of its first custom color chart in 1961, which offered fourteen different colors, in addition to blonde and sunburst.

ACCEPTANCE BROADENS, COMPETITION INCREASES

By the mid-1950s and shortly after, the Telecaster and Esquire were finding their way into the hands of many more star players than those of the little circle of Western Swing artists who had formed Leo's original "test bed" of sorts. Fender's debutante solid-bodies would be the choice of several players of the new breed of music soon known as rock 'n' roll, initially transported there, perhaps, by the crossover from country to rockabilly to straight-out rock. Luther Perkins with Johnny Cash, Paul Burlison with the Johnny Burnette Rock 'N Roll Trio, James Burton with Ricky Nelson, and Russell Willaford with Gene Vincent and His Blue Caps were all blazing the trail. Soon-to-be Elvis Presley guitarist Scotty Moore even played an Esquire with his country outfit, the Starlite Wranglers, before moving over to Gibson electrics, a transition that early Tele-wielding bluesers Clarence "Gatemouth" Brown and B.B. King would also make.

Gibson's entry into the arena in 1952 had perhaps helped to legitimize the concept of the solid-body guitar somewhat, although this long-standing company had its teething troubles

1956 Telecaster. *Guitar courtesy of Elderly Instruments, photo Dave Matchette*

with the format, too. A collaborative design between guitar star Les Paul and Gibson president Ted McCarty, the Les Paul Model exhibited many traditional features in character with Gibson style and construction, but it was an entirely solid instrument. The body was made from mahogany, to which a maple top—carved into an arch—was glued. Unlike Fender's guitars, there was binding around the body top and fingerboard, the neck was glued in, and the pickguard was of the raised types used on archtop guitars. For all this effort, Gibson included a significant design flaw in the Les Paul Model as initially released: A shallow neck angle required that the strings be wrapped under rather than over the bridge bar, resulting in a somewhat awkward playing position for the picking hand, which also had difficulty "palm muting" the strings.

(continued on page 70)

Luther Perkins

Johnny Cash tells it like it is. The faithful Luther Perkins was always at his side, armed with his favored Esquire. Cash, the failed door-to-door appliance salesman, and Perkins, the auto mechanic, were a perfect pair and teamed with bassist Marshall Grant. *GAB Archive/Redferns/Getty*

Luther Perkins's signature playing was far from the "hot Tele" style of other early solid-body electric guitar heroes, but he was no less influential on the country guitar genre and possibly backed more hits than the incendiary work of plenty of faster players. Not quite Travis picking, you could instead call it "Perkins picking," the alternating boom-chicka-boom-chicka-boom-chicka-boom riff that Luther Perkins laid down behind so many Johnny Cash songs—and which became an instant

tell that the Man in Black was about to strut his stuff on your radio. Upon hearing the twangy opening strains of "Folsom Prison Blues," "Get Rhythm," or "Cry, Cry, Cry," anyone who knows the remotest thing about the guitar will identify Perkins's tone as coming from a "Telecaster." But Perkins was a simple player, and his choice of guitar was even simpler. Throughout his career, he never actually played a Fender Telecaster, but instead preferred its single-pickup sibling, the Esquire.

Born in Memphis, Tennessee, in 1928, Luther Perkins was raised mostly in Como, Mississippi, but returned to Memphis as a young adult in 1953 to work as a mechanic at a dealership called Automobile Sales Company. The head of his service department was one Roy Cash, older brother of Johnny Cash. Perkins—who had taught himself a little rhythm guitar and some simple lead licks a few years earlier—started playing on the side with coworkers Marshall Grant and Red Kernodle, who would pull out their guitars back in the dealership's service department to pass the time when work was slow. When Johnny Cash was honorably discharged from the service in 1954, he followed his older brother Roy to Memphis, found work as an appliance salesman, and discovered a ready-made trio at Automobile Sales Company to back him. Kernodle would fall away before the outfit's first audition with Sam Phillips of Sun Records, but Grant and Perkins—as the Tennessee Two—would back Johnny Cash for his history-making early recordings, and Perkins would be his right-hand man for a decade and a half. On record after record, hit after hit, Luther Perkins's

Luther Perkins

Luther Perkins on stage with Johnny Cash and bassist Marshall Grant for the WSM Grand Ole Opry tour in 1956. *Michael Ochs Archives/Getty Images*

boom-chicka-boom rhythm work and simple single-note leads provided the instrumental foils to Cash's distinctively rich, deep vocals, while the guitarist himself—famously dry, deadpanned, laconic—served as straight man to many an on-stage quip from the singer.

Perkins went through several Esquires in his early days with Cash, trading up to acquire guitars whose condition, looks, or tone he preferred. The first, bought used in 1954, was a black-guard Esquire with some body damage and a volume control that was stuck on full. In 1956 Perkins acquired first a new white-guard Esquire with red custom finish (the instrument believed to have been used on "I Walk the Line"), and later purchased a white-guard Esquire finished in black that he customized with the initials "L.P." on the upper bout. In 1958, though, he stepped up to

his favorite Esquire of the bunch, and the most archetypal example of its kind: a standard blonde white-guard model with maple neck. Heard on just about everything he did with Johnny Cash up until the mid-'60s, this late '50s Esquire remained Perkins's number-one guitar, despite Fender's gift of an early Jazzmaster (which Perkins did use on the famous *Live from Folsom Prison* concert and other mid- to late '60s performances).

Luther Perkins died on August 5, 1968, two days after suffering severe burns and smoke inhalation after a fire in his home, started when he fell asleep on the living room couch with a lit cigarette. Although Johnny Cash went on to record several hits without Perkins, many fans consider the 1955 to '68 period, with Perkins on guitar, to be the Man in Black's golden era.

Muddy Waters

Muddy Waters sings the blues, circa 1960. *Michael Ochs Archives/Getty Images*

Muddy Waters Telecaster replica. *Fender Musical Instruments Corporation*

One of the true greats of the blues, Muddy Waters had the ability to sound like, well Muddy Waters, whatever guitar he played, and in whatever gig he played it. Waters certainly played a range of acoustic and semi-acoustic electric guitars early in his career, including models by Gretsch, Stella, and Harmony. He was famously photographed in the early 1950s with a Gibson Les Paul Goldtop with P-90 pickups, too, but from the late '50s onward, Muddy was a Tele man—and that Tele became an icon of his timeless breed of electric blues.

Generally thought of today as more of a country or bare-bones rock 'n' roll instrument, the basic, slab-bodied Tele isn't associated with the blues as much as its sibling, the Fender Stratocaster, or Gibson's ES-335 and Les Paul, but in the hands of Muddy Waters this simple, two-pickup, bolt-neck guitar epitomized the raw, wiry, and emotive voice of this artist's instrumental side. The real magic in the Tele sound occurs at the bridge pickup, and although this might generate the definitive country lead guitar sound, it easily segued into gritty, emotive blues tones when played aggressively with the raw, unique style of a master such as Muddy Waters.

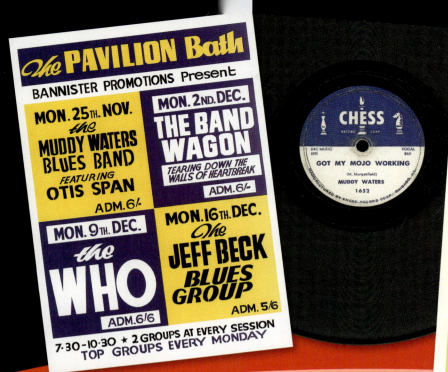

Water's first Telecaster appears to have been a white-guard example from 1957, which he took to England for his famous tour of 1958 and played at the Newport Jazz Festival of 1960. He is far and away most associated, however, with a red Telecaster that became his mainstay from the early '60s until his death in 1983, a guitar that was distinguished by its black plastic Fender amp knobs, but otherwise appeared largely stock. This is the dark-bodied guitar in several photos from the '60s and beyond, and the guitar on which Fender's Muddy Waters Artist Series Telecaster was based. The original is often reported as having been a Telecaster Custom from 1962, as its headstock logo and Candy Apple Red finish might seem to imply—but the body lacks the Custom's binding. It is likely that this guitar is actually the same blonde Tele from 1957, refinished and repaired with a circa-'62 Tele Custom neck. Other modifications included an extra screw hole to hold down a warping single-ply plastic pickguard and Waters's replacement of the standard knurled metal Tele knobs with black, numbered Fender amplifier knobs. Sometime in the mid- to late-'70s, he also added a brass six-saddle bridge in place of the guitar's original three-saddle bridge.

As with any great artist, there's far more to Muddy's tone than just the guitar-and-amp combination, and Waters had an unusual playing style that has become a benchmark for a particular genre of electric blues. He picked the bass notes on the lower three strings with a thumb pick, while strumming upwards with bare fingers on the three treble strings for his melody and lead lines, which he frequently executed with a small steel pinky slide. Waters strung his Tele with heavy .012–.056 gauge strings but often played in open G tuning, taking a little tension off, and he frequently used a capo, too. To hear the best of Muddy Waters's fluid yet frenetic electric style, seek out live recordings of his great tunes such as "Mannish Boy," "Rollin' and Tumblin'," "Hoochie Coochie Man," and "Rock Me."

(continued from page 63)

Left uncorrected until later in 1953, at which time a more functional stud-mounted "wraparound" bridge was introduced, this flaw in the Les Paul couldn't have hurt the easy-playing Telecaster's reception any. Soon, however, the new Gibson solidbody was proving a genuine rival to Fender, with more than two thousand sold in 1953, and it wasn't the only competition hitting the scene. Gretsch launched its first volley with the Duo Jet, released late in 1953. Francis Hall also had his Electro-String Music Corporation ramping up toward production. In 1954, the company released its first solid-body electric, using the now-familiar brand name that Hall had acquired in purchasing the company the year before: Rickenbacker.

TOP-LOADERS AND ROSEWOOD 'BOARDS

About midway through 1958, Fender adapted elements of the bridge design used on the Precision Bass to the Telecaster, dispensing with the through-body stringing and back-loaded steel ferrules for a Telecaster bridge that simply had six holes drilled along the base plate's back "lip," into which the strings would be fed on their way over the saddles. This change altered one of the major elements of Telecaster construction, and, therefore, tone, which apparently didn't sit well with players; late in 1959, bowing to popular demand, Fender returned to the original through-body string-loading design.

As much as it might not seem "classic Tele," however, plenty of notable players will attest that these "top-loader" Telecasters, as they have come to be known, can sound perfectly good. Noted Telemaster Jim Campilongo, for one, has a '59 top-loader that he has played for nearly twenty years, and upon which the Fender Custom Shop Jim Campilongo Signature Telecaster was based. As good as they might be, though, top-loader Teles and Esquires made from late '58 to late '59 are generally slightly less desirable to players and collectors today, given that deviation from the blueprint.

Another, more lasting alteration to the Telecaster came in 1959, when Fender began to use a glued-on rosewood fingerboard atop the maple neck. The new Fender Jazzmaster model

1960 Telecaster with accompanying "case candy."
Guitar and photo courtesy of Rumble Seat Music

that had debuted at the summer NAMM show the year before had proved a successful test bed for the rosewood fingerboard. While Fender perhaps felt the more traditional-looking and -feeling neck was a necessity on any guitar with pretensions toward jazz and the more traditional musicians who played it, it seems that many Fender dealers, and hence the reps at Fender Sales, had been inquiring about the availability of a rosewood 'board on the Tele and Strat for some time. The darker neck would ally Fender guitars with more traditional instruments, and therefore make for easier acceptance in corners that were still reticent to embrace the "plank." Simultaneously, it would do away with the detrimental image of the smudged, poorly wearing maple fingerboards that were being seen everywhere by this time, nearly ten years into the life of the solidbody.

One story, possibly apocryphal, goes that Leo Fender saw a Telecaster in the hands of a performer on TV with dark, worn patches on its maple fingerboard, and was swayed to take up the rosewood option out of dismay at this grimy look. The truth is, maple is virtually as hard as rosewood, but unlike rosewood, maple 'boards were finished with a clear coat of nitrocellulose lacquer to seal the light wood and prevent it from absorbing dirt. The grimy patches on these fingerboards eventually appeared once the finish was worn away beneath the strings and the players' fingertips, and once that coat of finish was gone, dirt, sweat, and grease took hold and began to discolor the exposed wood.

Whatever the impetus, the rosewood fingerboards brought a new look to the Telecaster and Esquire, as well as other Fenders, and would serve as a demarcation point between the guitars of the '50s and those of the early '60s. For about the first two and a half years, these separate fingerboards were sawn with a flat underside and glued to a flat neck face, a style that has since been dubbed the "slab board" for its thick, flat-bottomed appearance. Part of the way through 1962, Fender introduced the practice of radiusing the face of the maple neck as well as both sides of the fingerboard, enabling the use of a thinner piece of rosewood and creating what is now often referred to as a "laminated" or "round-lam" fingerboard. (By request from the mid-'60s, and as an official option from 1967, maple fingerboards would again be available, but until 1969 such necks were made much like the rosewood fingerboards, with a separately milled piece of maple glued to the face of the neck, a construction now known as a "maple cap" neck.)

Regarding Telecasters and Stratocasters alike, many players have expressed a preference for the earlier slab-board necks, usually in the belief that the thicker piece of rosewood is somehow superior. In a discussion about all things vintage Fender, however, Fender Custom Shop Master Builder Chris Fleming expressed a preference for round-lam rosewood 'boards. "Somebody asked me why I thought Leo decided to do round lams," Fleming explained, "and although I can't know for sure, I think it was for a couple of reasons. One is that he liked the idea of the maple being more of a majority of the wood, and he liked the idea that it was kind of a custom way to do it, it was proprietary. And I'd also like to think that he liked the sound of it. I feel like the slab 'board was the way that they did it because they had to figure out how to do it quickly. Then they had to tool up to make the rounded 'board and never turned back."

Considered in this light, it's clear that the thinner, rounded rosewood 'board used after mid-1962 took more work to produce, and the earlier flat-bottomed 'board never encompassed so thick a piece of rosewood that it would have been costlier, from a lumber-supply perspective, than the thinner board. In any case, Fleming, for one, declares the tonal difference between the two to be negligible, if detectible at all.

As it happens, the Jazzmaster that had introduced the rosewood fingerboard didn't make much of an impression on jazz guitarists in general, other than perhaps a few onto whom Fender pushed the model for promotional purposes. The Telecaster, on the other hand, has had a longstanding place in the jazz world, and, playing against type, has proved a surprisingly good fit for several prominent jazz artists. Ted Greene, Ed Bickert, and Jim Mullen are noted Tele enthusiasts, Joe Pass used one on several of his early recordings, and later players such as Mike Stern and Bill Frisell are also devotees. As for the Jazzmaster, it seemed to strike a chord with many players on the burgeoning surf scene of the late '50s and early '60s, then became a favorite of many punk and indie-rock players from the late '70s onward.

THE TELECASTER GOES CUSTOM

Early in 1958 Fender began making plans for a line of Telecasters and Esquires with deluxe appointments. Named the Esquire and Telecaster Custom upon their eventual unveiling at the summer NAMM show of 1959, the original Customs are typically characterized by a rosewood fingerboard, a sunburst finish trimmed with a traditional white body binding (some top only, some "double bound" with binding around both the top and the back), and a three-ply white/black/white pickguard made from nitrate. According to Forrest White, the first three renditions of what would become the Telecaster Custom were made in 1958 for country star Buck Owens and his guitarist Don Rich. Rather than the sunburst finish, those Teles were painted with a lacquer to which ground glass had been added to produce a "sparkle" finish. They were also made with the one-piece maple necks still in use at the time. This rendition of the birth of the "Custom" seems unlikely, however, since by most accounts Buck Owens and the younger Don Rich first met in 1959 and didn't return to Bakersfield to make music together until 1960. Regardless, these guitars, essentially "custom Customs," would become visual trademarks for Owens and Rich and would help to popularize this variation of the breed.

While sunburst was standard for the Custom models, several would be finished, by request, in a variety of custom colors, proportionally more so than would standard Telecasters and Esquires. While Teles were generally less often ordered in custom colors than were Strats, Jazzmasters, and the new Jaguar of 1962, it seems that players willing to break tradition and play a Telecaster with a bound body were also more likely to be enticed by the custom-color option.

Meanwhile, beneath those custom-color and sunburst Telecaster and Esquire Customs, a new timber option was in evidence. In use on sunburst

Stratocasters since 1956, alder was making its first regular appearance in Telecaster bodies, signaling, if not an entirely new direction, an alternative at least.

Relatively light, resonant swamp ash is the wood most associated with the Telecaster, and its broad, attractive grain is a big part of the classic look of the instrument, as well as a key ingredient in its sound. With Fender production hitting unforeseeable heights in the late '50s, however, good, lightweight ash was proving harder to come by on a consistent basis, and alder provided a good alternative, particularly in guitars where the finish concealed the grain. Alder is also a good, resonant tonewood for guitar construction, and alder-bodied Teles still sound very much like Teles (see Telecaster Tone and Construction for a more in-depth examination of tonewoods), but its use does change the character, and the look, of the guitar ever so slightly.

Through the course of the '60s, an increasing number of Telecasters would be made in alder. By the '70s, ash stocks would prove significantly heavier, resulting in many very weighty Teles. As much fuss as discriminating players make over tonewoods today, Fender didn't even publish the type of wood used in the guitars' bodies in the 1950s and '60s (nor, for that matter, did it widely publish specs such as fingerboard radius, nut width, neck profile and thickness, and so on).

MULTI-PLY PLASTICS AND ARTISTS PROLIFERATE

Midway through 1959, Fender added three more screws and repositioned the original five used to affix the pickguard on the Telecaster and Esquire to correct the minor warping that was occurring with many of the original single-ply white 'guards, which would noticeably lift along the upper edge between the bridge and the neck in particular. Then, late in

1960 Custom Telecaster. *Fretted Americana*

1963 Fender altered this minor adornment further by adding the three-ply nitrate pickguard of the Custom and custom-colored models to all Telecaster and Esquire guitars. Early in 1965, however, these flammable nitrate 'guards, often called "green 'guards" for their faint green hue, would be superseded on all models by three-ply plastic pickguards. Less likely to burst into flames in the warehouse, these pickguards would also prove resistant to the warping and shrinkage that would plague original nitrate 'guards, albeit not for quite a few years yet, in most cases.

By the front edge of the mid-'60s, Tele love had already spread well beyond the country scene that had first embraced it. Blues legend Muddy Waters was plying his trade on a Telecaster, while Steve Cropper was using a rosewood 'board Tele to churn out countless hits with the Stax Records house band, better known as Booker T and the MGs. Bob Dylan chose a white-guard '58 Telecaster in his controversial decision to go electric at the 1965 Newport Folk Festival, while Mike Bloomfield played a '64 Tele in the band behind him. Across the pond, the use of a Telecaster or Esquire at one time or another by all three Yardbirds guitarists—Eric Clapton, Jeff Beck, and Jimmy Page—was evidence of its proliferation on the British scene. And back in the United States, of course, more and more country players were continuing to prove that the Tele was the preeminent king of twang from Nashville to Austin to So-Cal, including Roy Nichols and Merle Haggard, as well as former Buddy Holly sideman-gone-solo-artist, Waylon Jennings, with his '53 Tele with tooled-leather cover.

At Fender itself, though, an event of far bigger import was in the works as the middle of the decade approached—a transition that would, for many hardcore Telecaster fans at least, draw a line under the Fender that they knew and loved.

(continued on page 92)

1960 Custom Telecaster.
Fretted Americana

Albert Collins

ALBERT COLLINS   Frank Scott, Personal Manager

Buffalo Booking Agency
2807 Erastus Street
Houston 26, Texas

Promotional photo of Albert Collins, circa 1960. *Michael Ochs Archives/Getty Images*

Albert Collins Signature
Telecaster in natural
finish. *Fender Musical
Instruments Corporation*

Appropriately known as the "Iceman" for his blistering treble-heavy tone, bluesman Albert Collins also wore the honorary a.k.a. "Master of the Telecaster," a tribute to his association with the debutante Fender solidbody that he made very much his own. Born in Leona, Texas, in 1932, Collins was actually led to the Telecaster by his love for the playing of fellow Texan Clarence "Gatemouth" Brown, an early Telecaster proponent who would be better known in later years for his use of a Gibson Firebird. In emulation of Brown—with whom Collins had performed on stage at the age of fifteen, during both players' pre-Tele years—Collins capoed his own Telecaster high up the neck and developed a boppy, horn-lick-inspired blues style that was one of the most distinctive in the genre.

At the age of seventeen, Collins formed his own band, the Rhythm Rockers, which made a name for itself in Houston's Third Ward before he jumped ship to record and tour with a string of other artists, including Big Mama Thornton and Little Richard (where he filled Jimi Hendrix's rather large shoes). In the late-1950s Collins had the first glimmer of solo success in the form of a single called "The Freeze." The Iceman theme gained momentum with a million-selling single, "Frosty," in 1962, followed by his first major

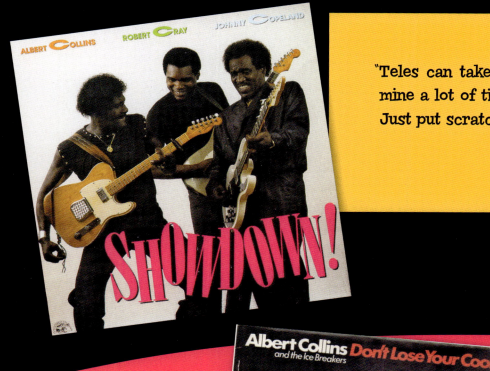

solo album, *Truckin' With Albert Collins*, released on Blue Thumb Records in 1965. Appearances at the Newport Jazz Festival in 1969, the Filmore West in 1971, and the Montreaux Jazz Festival in 1975 further solidified his status, however, as did the Grammy Award-winning album *Showdown*, recorded at the peak of his career in 1985, with Robert Cray and Johnny Copeland.

In the early '50s, unable to afford the object of his desires, Collins had put a Fender Telecaster neck on the body of a lesser make of electric guitar. He bought his first proper Fender Telecaster in the late '50s, but was ultimately best known for his use of a 1966 Telecaster Custom with a maple-capped neck and a Gibson humbucker added in the neck position, the guitar on which the Fender Custom Shop Albert Collins Signature Telecaster would be based. Always a dazzling live performer, Albert Collins was known for his interactive approach to the stage as much as for his frenetic, electrifying playing style and searing tone. Using an extra-long cable between his Telecaster and his amplifier up on stage (a blisteringly loud Fender Quad Reverb from around the mid-'70s onward), Collins would strut down into the audience while still playing, or even leave the stage at the end of the set while the band still played, without dropping a lick. Collins became ill while on tour in Switzerland in the summer of 1993, and he died the following November at the age of sixty-one.

Steve Cropper

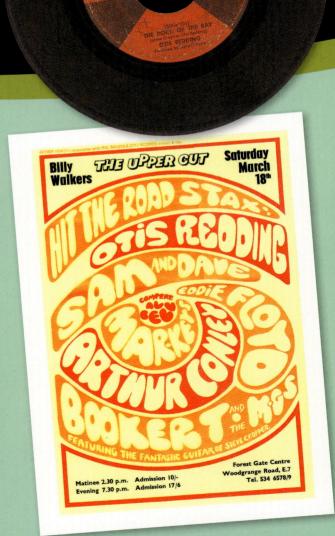

Steve Cropper of Booker T. and the MGs coaxes a soulful riff from his Telecaster, circa 1965. *Pictoral Press Ltd./Alamy*

Chalk this one up in the columns for "tasteful chops" and "playing for the song." A shred-meister he is not, but Steve Cropper has authored some of the most distinctive guitar parts, both solo and rhythm, in all of popular music. What Cropper might lack in flash he makes up for in an abundance of cool taste. Witness the sleek, spare licks on everything from Sam & Dave's "Soul Man," to Otis Redding's "(Sitting on the) Dock of the Bay" (which Cropper co-wrote) and "I've Been Loving You Too Long (To Stop Now)," to Booker T. and the M.G.s' instrumental classic "Green Onions," and you'll instantly hear what players in the know have been talking about since Cropper laid down these cool sounds in the early to mid-'60s. You don't have to play a flurry of notes to be a genius on the guitar—and when you want to keep it simple, there's arguably no better instrument than the Fender Telecaster.

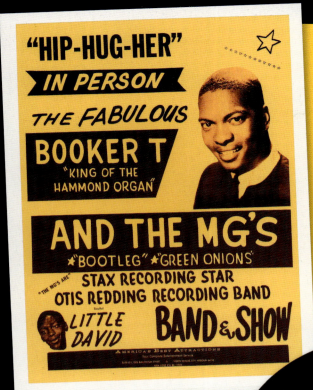

"I had heard some Telecasters in the music shop, and I had an opportunity to buy a used Esquire. I remember stripping it and sanding it down, then I went to Western Auto and bought a can of what they called Candy Apple Red spray, and with the brown wood, it sort of turned out a purplish color. That's the guitar I used on 'Green Onions' and a bunch of other stuff. I wish I still had it."

—Steve Cropper

On those early Stax recordings, including 1962's "Green Onions," Cropper is known to have played a 1956 Fender Esquire, the single-pickup version of the Telecaster. In 1963, however, he acquired the blonde Telecaster with rosewood fingerboard that he played on the majority of the many hits to which he contributed and used in most of his live performances for many years. Both were simple, solid, roadworthy working-man's guitars, and both sounded roughly similar, especially in Cropper's very able hands. Cropper served as the guitarist for Booker T. and the M.G.s, the Stax Records house band, in the label's Memphis studio and out on tour throughout the 1960s. In this role, Cropper and that blonde '63 Tele contributed their lithe, slightly countrified R&B licks to an unprecedented number of hits by other artists, including Sam & Dave, Otis Redding, Carla and Rufus Thomas, Wilson Pickett, Johnnie Taylor, Eddie Floyd, Albert King, The Staple Singers, and several others. In the course of doing so, Cropper and his bandmates helped lay the foundations of soul music.

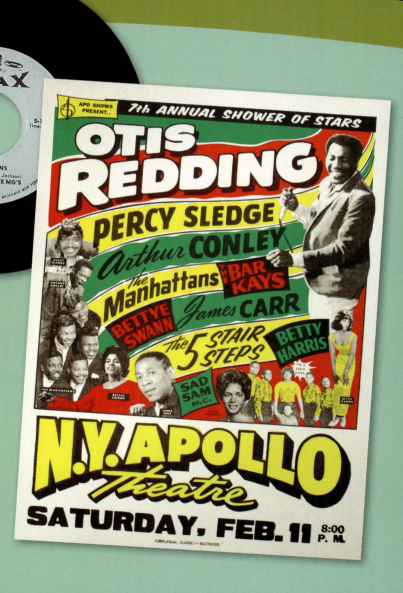

Michael Bloomfield

Bloomfield and his white-guard Telecaster back Bob Dylan at the 1965 Newport Folk Festival. *David Gahr/Getty Images*

Blues master Michael Bloomfield is perhaps most associated with "fatter" sounding Gibson Les Pauls, but his first ascent to worldwide fame was made with a Fender Telecaster in hand—and one performance in particular is firmly etched in the annals of rock history (and folk music infamy). When Bob Dylan boldly "went electric" before a raging crowd of folk purists at the Newport Folk Festival in 1965, a Telecaster was his weapon of choice. And right behind him, wailing on a matching white-guard Tele, was his lead guitarist, Michael Bloomfield.

Born in Chicago, Illinois, in 1943, Michael Bloomfield was first drawn to the guitar at the age of thirteen by the sounds of seminal rock 'n' rollers such as Elvis Presley and his guitarist Scotty Moore. Soon, however, Bloomfield was tapping into Chicago's booming blues, hanging out in the clubs on Chicago's South Side, listening to legends such as Otis Spann, Howlin' Wolf, and Muddy Waters. While still only in his mid-teens,

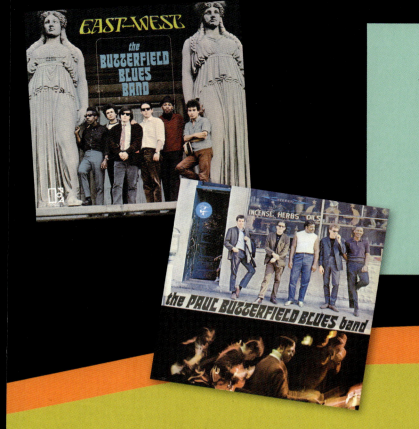

EAST-WEST
the
BUTTERFIELD
BLUES
BAND

the PAUL BUTTERFIELD BLUES band

"I saw Bob Dylan at a few parties and then out of the clear blue sky, he called me on the phone to cut a record, which was 'Like a Rolling Stone.' So I bought a Fender, a really good guitar for the first time in my life, without a case—a Telecaster."

—Michael Bloomfield

Bloomfield himself became a stand-out as one of a few white youths in the crowd at the predominantly Black establishments—and even harder to miss once he started hopping up on stage, guitar in hand, and asking to sit in with the greats (often digging in without awaiting the "yes" or "no" reply).

Bloomfield became widely accepted in Chicago, and soon beyond, as a musician in his own right. He performed and recorded with blues originators such as Big Joe Williams, Sleepy John Estes, and Little Brother Montgomery, and drew the attention of legendary blues producer John Hammond, who signed him to a contract with CBS in 1964. With his initial CBS recordings languishing unreleased, however, Bloomfield joined the Paul Butterfield Blues Band, providing an able foil for the singer and guitarist's own talents.

Although a Fender Duo-Sonic first accompanied Bloomfield into his professional career, in late 1964 or early '65 he acquired an "L" serial number white-guard Telecaster with rosewood fingerboard, which would be his main squeeze until Les Paul fever won him over in 1966. In that brief time, though, the young blueser made some major noises with his Tele. Between fiery exchanges with Butterfield in the Blues Band—including the 1965 release *The Paul Butterfield Blues Band* and the more experimental,

psychedelic-leaning *East-West*—Bloomfield and his Tele trucked east for much of the summer of 1965. In June, he put the Tele to work recording the first batch of New York sessions that would become Bob Dylan's *Highway 61 Revisited*. Then, after joining Dylan in Newport, Rhode Island, to be booed off the stage by the sandals-and-beards crowd on July 25, he returned to NYC for another week of sessions to complete the famous album. Legend has it that Bloomfield dragged the Telecaster from gig to gig without a proper case to put it in, the journey taking its toll in the wear and tear soon evident on the guitar.

Even after revising his sound with the Les Paul in the late '60s, Bloomfield remained fond of the Telecaster and occasionally dragged one back on stage. Photos of the band Mike Bloomfield and Friends performing live in 1973 show him wielding another old white-guard Tele with rosewood fingerboard, first unmolested, then later in the year updated with a crude psychedelic paint job. In the late '70s, he also occasionally played a later Tele with a maple fingerboard, his legendary Les Paul having been surrendered in Vancouver, Canada, in compensation for an abandoned performance date. Michael Bloomfield was found dead in his car, having suffered an apparent drug overdose, on February 15, 1981.

1964 Telecaster in faded Sonic Blue finish with
Parsons-White B-Bender. *Outline Press Ltd.*

1963 Telecaster in a Charcoal Frost
custom color. *Outline Press Ltd.*

1963 Telecaster in Fiesta Red.
Outline Press Ltd.

Roy Buchanan

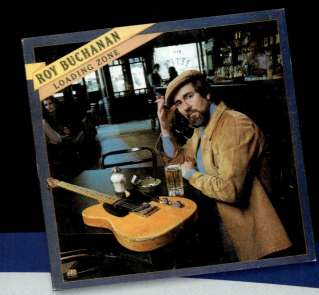

Roy Buchanan makes his Telecaster, Nancy, sing at Alex Cooley's Electric Ballroom in Atlanta, Georgia, in June 1975. *Tom Hill/WireImage/Getty Images*

Far better-known guitar stars have logged time on iconic pre-CBS Telecasters, perhaps, but the 1953 Telecaster that Roy Buchanan called "Nancy" is widely considered one of the most iconic vintage Teles in existence. Many factors contribute to Nancy's status, not least of which was Buchanan's raw skill as a Tele-meister. Another factor is Nancy's condition. Where the Telecasters and Esquires of Keith Richards, Bruce Springsteen, and others were hacked, chopped, and modified over the years to suit their owners' requirements, Nancy remained largely original, barring some necessary routine maintenance and one bungled modification.

Buchanan got his start in the early days of rock 'n' roll, record-ing and touring with Dale Hawkins in 1958, then with Dale's cousin Ronnie Hawkins's group, which, with young Robbie Robertson alongside him on guitar, would eventually morph into The Band. Dissatisfied with life on the road, however, Buchanan settled in the greater Washington, DC area, where he built a reputation as one of the hottest players on the scene. He eventually gained some fame as "the world's foremost Tele master," upon the broadcast of a 1971 PBS television documentary entitled *The Best Unknown Guitarist in the World*. With Nancy by his side, he came to be known as a gui-tarist without parallel in any genre, his haunting pinched harmonics, faux-steel bends, and lightning-swift single-note runs unequaled by any other player in the jazz, blues, or country worlds. But he failed to gain the recognition that players and fans in-the-know were con-vinced he deserved—or the adequate financial compensation that might have come with it—before his death in 1998.

Aside from its heavily worn finish and beautifully played-in neck, Nancy remains in much the same condition as when it left the Fender factory in 1953. In addition to natural distress, Nancy displays Buchanan's name etched into its back and three friction marks behind the bridge. Nancy also appears to have had jumbo frets installed at some point and carries a hole that was drilled right through the headstock, piercing the "n" of the Fender logo, pur-portedly a botched effort by Buchanan to install a B-bender of his own devising (though he would often tease interviewers with the tale that he had "drilled that hole so he could hang Nancy up on a nail in the wall"). Nancy is currently in the collection of Mac Yasuda and has been displayed on loan to the Fullerton Museum Center in Fullerton, California.

Waylon Jennings

Waylon Jennings picks his trusty Telecaster at the Palomino Club in Los Angeles on August 16, 1973. *Michael Ochs Archives/Getty Images*

We think of him today as one of the original "country outlaws"—alongside anti-Nashville rebels such as Johnny Cash, Willie Nelson, and Merle Haggard—but Waylon Jennings's career has its roots in seminal 1950s rock 'n' roll. A native of Littlefield, Texas, Jennings played bass in Buddy Holly's band for what would be the star's final tour in late 1958 and early '59. When the band booked a small airplane to take them between shows mid-tour, Jennings famously gave his seat up to J.P. "The Big Bopper" Richardson, and therefore avoided the crash that took the lives of Holly, Richardson, and teen idol Ritchie Valens.

Jennings laid low in the early '60s, moving to Phoenix, Arizona, to work in radio and put Holly's death behind him.

He slowly made his way back into recording and live performance. By the mid-'60s he had developed his songwriting chops alongside his own inimitable singing and playing styles, catching the attention of the prevailing music scene. When he started to get serious about performing again, his bandmates decided he needed a good Telecaster and purchased a used 1953 Tele that they had adorned with a custom-fitted, tooled-leather cover before presenting it to Jennings. Considered necessities by some, due to the hard knocks that guitars received on the road in those pre–flight case days, leather covers had been seen in country circles before. But Jennings's eventual fame, and the unmistakable look of that black leather cover with white floral work, helped

establish these erstwhile protective devices as badges of honor for country pickers everywhere.

With his new country persona firmly in place, Jennings signed first to the newly formed A&M records, but his contract was bought out by RCA, and in 1965 he traveled to Nashville to begin a long and successful recording career. He developed an instantly recognizable, spanky-twang style of guitar playing. Using a light touch that often incorporated bare thumb-and-finger playing for rhythm work and a pick for lead runs, Jennings combined driving low-string hammer-on and pull-off riffs with evocative upper-fret double stops, making frequent use of the modulation effects of which he was fond (tremolo in the early days, then phaser pedals after these units reached the market)—all of which gave his hallowed 1953 Telecaster a sound like no other guitar on the scene.

Beneath the cover, Jennings's secondhand black-guard Tele remained largely unadulterated for years. In the early '80s he did eventually swap its original three-brass-saddles bridge for a '70s six-saddle Tele bridge, and EMG pickups finally replaced the thirty-plus-year-old Fender single-coils. But through it all, the guitar never lost that fluid, slappy, swirly twang that was so recognizable as the "Waylon sound."

1956 Esquire. *Fretted Americana*

Roy Nichols & Merle Haggard

Haggard's role on the Telecaster most often covered rhythm duties. Here, he performs in Anaheim, California, circa 1980. *George Rose/Getty Images*

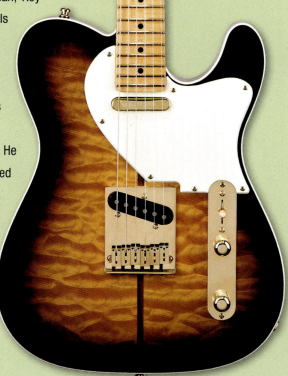

Merle Haggard Signature Telecaster. *Fender Musical Instruments Corporation*

Not unlike Buck Owens and Don Rich, Merle Haggard and his trusty sideman, Roy Nichols, formed a Tele-wielding duo that will forever be interlinked in the annals of country music, tagged as the "Outlaw" kin to the hard-twanging Bakersfield sound.

Although Merle Haggard's name would achieve wider fame, giving Roy Nichols his own greatest fame by association, Nichols was an established guitarist with a good reputation on the country scene long before Haggard. He even gave his would-be boss a leg up in the industry shortly after his release from prison.

Born in Chandler, Arizona, in 1932, Nichols grew up mainly in Fresno, California. He learned to play the guitar at the age of eleven, and just three years later, he played at local dancehalls to supplement the family income. Shortly before his sixteenth birthday, Nichols hit the road with the hillbilly band The Maddox Brothers and Rose—the first truly professional gig in a career that would land him jobs with Johnny Cash, Cliffie Stone, Wynn Steward, Lefty Frizzell, and other significant names on the country circuit in the 1950s and early '60s. From the late '50s onward, Nichols was best associated with a white-guard '57 Telecaster, although he also played several others.

"The Telecaster was not for the timid; you had to be a bulldog to play a Telecaster, because it's hard to play. It doesn't respond like a lot of guitars, so you have to play it with a different attitude, and that makes the results different."

—Merle Haggard

Merle Haggard was born in 1937 in Oildale, California, a suburb of Bakersfield, to parents who had come west from Oklahoma looking to escape the Dust Bowl during the Great Depression. The death of his father in the mid-'40s seemed to tip Haggard toward delinquency and petty crimes that landed him in one juvenile facility after another. During one stint on the outside, Haggard attended a Lefty Frizzell show and, after singing along to several numbers from his seat, was asked to join the artist on stage. This taste of the limelight launched his efforts to make it in the music business, and Haggard was soon performing at venues around Bakersfield. In 1957, however, Haggard was arrested for attempted robbery of a bar in Bakersfield and was sentenced to three years in San Quentin Prison.

His stay in the notorious adult facility showed Haggard the error of his ways. After his release in 1960 he set about walking the straight and narrow. A trip to Las Vegas, Nevada, later that year took Haggard to a show featuring Wynn Stewart and Roy Nichols, and what would be a life-changing meeting. "Roy wanted to get off and go to the restroom or something," Haggard told the Associated Press in 2001. "He said, 'Here, play this thing,' and handed me his guitar. I sung 'Devil Woman' and Wynn Stewart saw me and hired me on the spot. . . . Because of Roy, my career commenced. He was the stylist that set the pace." Haggard played bass with Stewart for a time, with Nichols on guitar, while also working on his dream of a solo career. In the early years of this effort, he scored a minor hit with Wynn Stewart's "Sing a Sad Song" in 1964, and a Top 10 the following year with Lynn Anderson's "(My Friends Are Gonna Be) Strangers." In 1965 he formed the band Merle Haggard and the Strangers for his first U.S. tour, hired Nichols on guitar, and hit the ground running. The Tele-totin' outlaws would work together until 1987, scoring thirty-eight number one songs on the *Billboard* Country Chart, including "I'm a Lonesome Fugitive," "Mama Tried," "Okie From Muskogee," and "The Fightin' Side of Me."

While Haggard was a mean picker himself, his role on the Telecaster more often covered rhythm duties (which he frequently handled on an acoustic guitar, too). Nichols, on the other hand, was a consummate twang artist, and one of the early pioneers of hybrid picking, a style that employs both a flat pick and the middle and ring fingers of the right hand. He was also adept at slick faux-steel bends, licks that have become staples of the country guitar style, often pre-bending notes before picking them to create effective pedal-steel sounds.

Buck Owens & Don Rich

Buck Owens and The Buckaroos. From left: Bob Morris, Don Rich, Buck Owens, Willie Cantu, and Tom Brumley.

As creators of "The Bakersfield Sound," Buck Owens and his sidekick Don Rich virtually defined "twang" as understood by many country Telecaster players today. Alvis Edgar "Buck" Owens Jr. was born in 1929 in the small town of Sherman, Texas, on the Oklahoma border. At the height of the Great Depression, when Buck was eight years old, his family moved to Tempe, Arizona, in search of jobs, and the young Owens himself worked at a range of laboring jobs before and after school—pursuing his growing love of music in what little spare time remained—before dropping out of high school altogether. He married at the age of eighteen, and, not long after, set his sights on Bakersfield, California, after passing through the town on his trucking route and deciding he liked what he heard in the music clubs there. In 1951, Owens packed up his young family, moved to Bakersfield, and set about becoming a central figure not only in the local scene, but, eventually, in country music in general.

Given the location, the sound, and the images of both, it's as if Buck Owens was made for the Telecaster, or the Telecaster was made for Buck Owens. By the late '50s, he was making a name for himself in Bakersfield, further afield in California, and soon beyond, playing a working-class breed of country—more urban, blue-collar than the cowboy country that had largely preceded it—and doing so with the ultimate blue-collar electric guitar in hand: a Fender Telecaster. The Bakersfield Sound was virtually driven by the Tele's low-E string, that growly, bent twang that practically defined the genre and suited Owens's own vocal twang so well.

In 1958, Buck left Bakersfield for a suburb outside Tacoma, Washington, where he had bought a share in the small local radio station KAYE. His own radio appearances led to spots on local TV, where, early in 1959, Owens was introduced to a talented young fiddle player named Donald Eugene Ulrich. Born in Tumwater, Washington, in 1941, Ulrich had learned the fiddle as a child, but also

Owens signed one of his signature red-white-and-blue metalflake Telecasters to Dick Clark and wife Kari Wigton. The guitar was sold at auction in 2011. *Courtesy Julien's Auctions (juliensauctions.com)*

played a mean guitar—something the rest of the world would soon understand when he was heard wielding his distinctive Telecaster licks right alongside Owens, using his new nom de twang Don Rich. Back in California, Owens recorded a series of sides for Capitol Records, including "Under Your Spell Again," which eventually rose to number four on the *Billboard* Country Chart. In 1960, Owens returned to Bakersfield—taking Don Rich with him—where the pair formed the band the Buckaroos and set about becoming a fixture in country music. Beyond his Tele-pickin', Rich lent perfect close harmonies to Owens's lead vocal throughout their time together, their voices merging so sympatheti-cally that it was often difficult to tell who was singing harmony and who was singing lead.

From the early 1960s, Rich and Owens had distinctive sil-ver, gold, and eventually red-white-and-blue sparkle Telecaster Customs made by Fender, while Buckaroo bassist Doyle Holly often played a matching sparkle Jazz Bass. Together, the sparkle Teles and the sharp "urban western" suits that the band wore on stage defined the aesthetic edge of Buckaroo fever, fueled by hits like "Love Is Gonna Live Here" and "Act Naturally" in 1963, the first of what would be twenty-one number one singles on the *Billboard* Country Chart.

Beginning in 1969, Buck Owens joined Roy Clark as host of TV's country music and comedy show *Hee Haw*, a leap to greater fame that, conversely, diluted the Buckaroos' appeal to country pur-ists. After a day spent in the recording studio in July 1974, Don

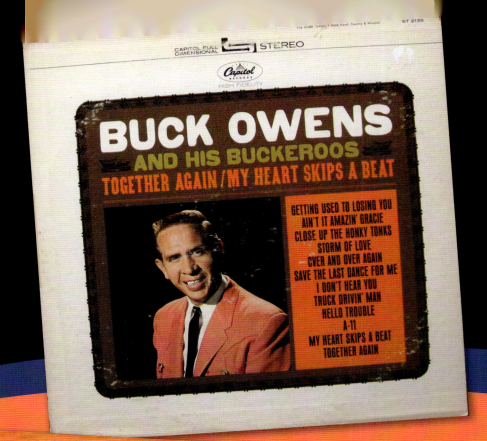

Rich headed home on his motorcycle and suffered a fatal crash near San Luis Obispo, California. The loss of his close friend and musical companion was a major blow to Owens, although he continued to fulfill his *Hee Haw* hosting duties until 1986. After several years of retirement from the performance stage, Owens was lured back into the spotlight in the late '80s by the "new country" singer Dwight Yoakam, whom he joined for several live appearances and the duet "Streets of Bakersfield" on Yoakam's 1988 album *Buenas Noches from a Lonely Room*. On the evening of March 25, 2006, Buck Owens gave his final performance—at his own Crystal Palace restaurant and club in Bakersfield—and died in his sleep that night, of an apparent heart attack.

DECLINING QUALITY

On January 5, 1965, Fender Musical Instruments was officially sold to Columbia Broadcasting System, Inc. Fender aficionados mark CBS's acquisition of the company as the start of a decline—at first gradual, then more pronounced—in the quality of Fender guitars. As such, the term "pre-CBS" has come to stand as the demarcation point between the more valuable and collectible vintage Telecasters (and other Fenders) and the less desirable later examples, although many collectible Teles were produced throughout the mid to late '60s as well.

Given that the changes brought to the Telecaster format occurred gradually, and were largely superficial at that, the guitars built in the mid '60s—during the first few years of CBS ownership—still very much followed the standards set out in the golden years of production under Leo Fender's supervision. In February of 1965, just a month after the CBS takeover was made official, the clay dots on the rosewood fingerboards of both Stratocasters and Telecasters were replaced by slightly larger pearloid dots, and plastic pickguards took over from nitrate on all models. In 1967 the "maple-cap" neck was officially introduced (maple necks made with a glued-on maple fingerboard, rather than being a one-piece maple neck as used on guitars of the '50s). This option

1966 Telecaster in Lake Placid Blue.
Fretted Americana

gives plenty of late-'60s Teles more of the look of those made from late 1954 to mid '59, although these lacked the dark wood "teardrop" behind the nut and the "skunk stripe" at the back that filled the routes where the truss rods were installed, since the truss rod was installed in these two-piece necks from the front before the maple fingerboard was glued on.

Among the more detrimental changes of the late '60s, however, was the move to polyester finishes around 1968. This "thick-skinned" finish, with its resilient, plasticky feel, was achieved with as many as ten to fifteen coats of polyester paint, and is believed by many players to severely choke the resonance—and therefore the tone—of any guitar that carries it. Even beyond these points, more significant issues of declining quality control, driven by increased production and an eye more on raw sales figures than the quality of the instruments, were beginning to take their toll on Fender quality by the late '60s, and certainly the early '70s.

NOTABLE POST-CBS TELECASTERS

Whatever individual players and collectors feel about the decline of Fender guitars under CBS, several worthy Telecasters were nevertheless produced in the late '60s and early '70s, many of

1970 Telecaster in Candy Apple Red.
Outline Press Ltd.

which even pique the interest of serious collectors. Some of these were merely alternative cosmetic treatments, while others represented an entire redrawing of the sonic blueprint.

As the late '60s approached, Fender found stocks of ash and alder getting heavier and heavier, and sought ways to relieve the weight. Some early efforts included removing additional

(continued from page 73)

1968 Telecaster in a rare Teal Green custom color. *Doug Youland/Willie's American Guitars*

wood from the body beneath the area covered by the pickguard, resulting in a rare breed of guitar known as the "smugglers Tele." Then in 1968, turning this concealed effort into a virtue, Fender introduced the Telecaster Thinline. Using bodies of ash or mahogany—the latter previously seen in a limited number of Mahogany Telecasters in the early '60s—Fender routed three chambers into the wood from the back, then carved an f-hole on the bass side of the body front to advertise this semi-solid construction, and capped off the work with a solid fillet of wood glued to the back. To further distinguish the model, Fender also designed an elongated pearloid pickguard for the Thinline, to which the volume and tone controls and selector switch were mounted, in addition to the neck pickup. Otherwise, the Telecaster Thinline was equipped exactly like the standard Telecaster, although its chambers altered the resonance of the body somewhat, and therefore introduced a slightly rounder, more scooped tone to the Telecaster template.

(continued on page 104)

Clarence White

White and his famous B-Bender perform with the Byrds at Carmichael Auditorium, Chapel Hill, North Carolina, 1971.
Ric Carter/Alamy

Perhaps as well known, if not better known in the relevant circles, for his work on a Martin dreadnought acoustic guitar with an enlarged soundhole, Clarence White was nevertheless a central figure in the electric-folk boom of the mid- to late '60s and helped to calcify the country-rock scene in the early '70s. Not only did he frequently strap on a Telecaster for these adventures, but he also proved a major innovator and co-inventor in the process.

He was born Clarence Joseph LeBlanc in Lewiston, Maine, in 1944 to French-Canadian parents who had emigrated from New Brunswick. When he was ten years old, the family moved west to California, and soon after, Clarence and his brothers Roland and Eric Jr. formed the Little Country Boys. After several early recordings and appearances on the *Andy Griffith Show*, the Little Country Boys evolved into the Kentucky Colonels in 1962—but the encroachment of rock 'n' roll on the folk scene brought a new direction to White's music, and the Colonels disbanded in 1965.

White established himself as a session player in and around Los Angeles, appearing on recordings by the Monkees and founding Byrd Gene Clark. He soon found inroads into the fledgling folk-rock scene of the mid-'60s, which was based largely around the revolving-door roster of the Byrds, and, Telecaster in hand, White introduced a solid electric country element to music that had previously leaned more toward psychedelic folk. White played sessions on several Byrds records from 1966 to 1968 (including the influential *Sweetheart of the Rodeo* with Gram Parsons in his short-lived stint as a Byrd), and was asked to be a permanent member in 1968, following the departure of Gram Parsons and Chris Hillman.

Prior to this point, though, while working recording sessions with drummer Gene Parsons around 1965 (who would join the Byrds alongside White), and playing together in the seminal country band Nashville West at night, White and Parsons began developing ideas for a string-bending device that could be used with the

The home-cooked route cover on the back of the original B-Bender.
Rusty Russell

Clarence White

The mechanism machined by Parsons and installed in a route in White's 1954 Tele bends the B string a whole tone sharp when the guitarist pushes a lever that replaces the upper strap button. *Rusty Russell*

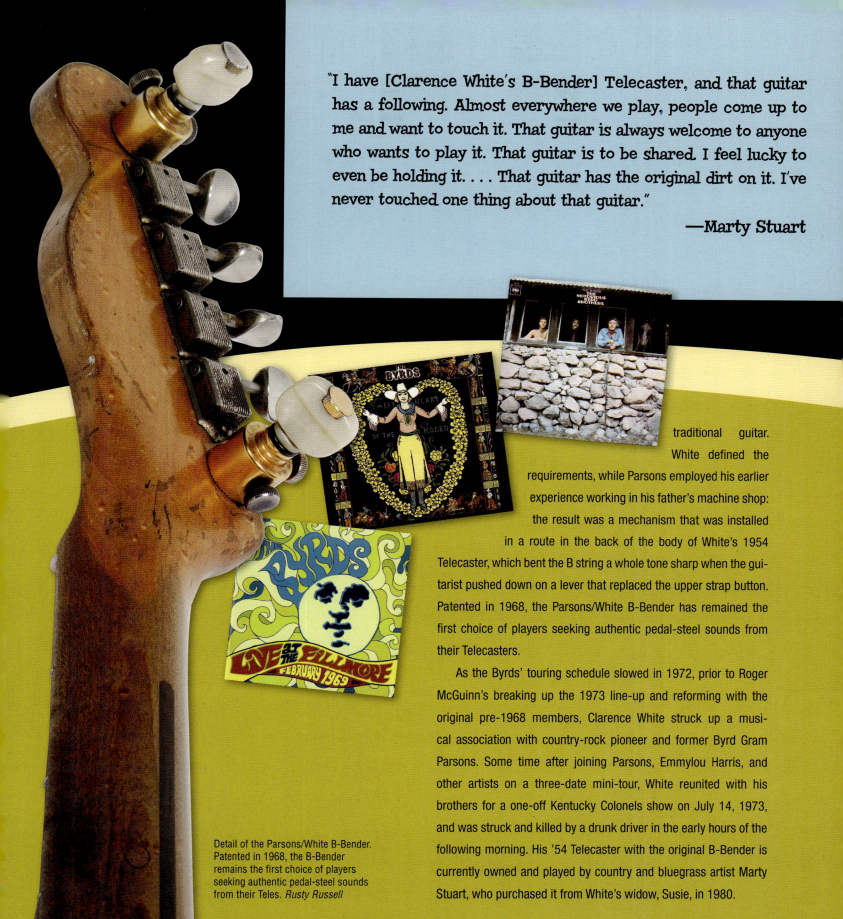

"I have [Clarence White's B-Bender] Telecaster, and that guitar has a following. Almost everywhere we play, people come up to me and want to touch it. That guitar is always welcome to anyone who wants to play it. That guitar is to be shared. I feel lucky to even be holding it. . . . That guitar has the original dirt on it. I've never touched one thing about that guitar."

—Marty Stuart

traditional guitar. White defined the requirements, while Parsons employed his earlier experience working in his father's machine shop: the result was a mechanism that was installed in a route in the back of the body of White's 1954 Telecaster, which bent the B string a whole tone sharp when the guitarist pushed down on a lever that replaced the upper strap button. Patented in 1968, the Parsons/White B-Bender has remained the first choice of players seeking authentic pedal-steel sounds from their Telecasters.

As the Byrds' touring schedule slowed in 1972, prior to Roger McGuinn's breaking up the 1973 line-up and reforming with the original pre-1968 members, Clarence White struck up a musical association with country-rock pioneer and former Byrd Gram Parsons. Some time after joining Parsons, Emmylou Harris, and other artists on a three-date mini-tour, White reunited with his brothers for a one-off Kentucky Colonels show on July 14, 1973, and was struck and killed by a drunk driver in the early hours of the following morning. His '54 Telecaster with the original B-Bender is currently owned and played by country and bluegrass artist Marty Stuart, who purchased it from White's widow, Susie, in 1980.

Detail of the Parsons/White B-Bender. Patented in 1968, the B-Bender remains the first choice of players seeking authentic pedal-steel sounds from their Teles. *Rusty Russell*

Jimmy Page

Jimmy Page's heavily decorated Telecaster, seen here in Copenhagen in 1969, was perhaps most famously employed on the solo in "Stairway to Heaven" in 1971—a solo that no doubt sent countless would-be guitar heroes mistakenly in search of Gibson Les Pauls. *Jan Persson/Redferns/Getty Images*

stairway to heaven

Although he attained some success as a professional musician before either Eric Clapton or Jeff Beck, particularly as a working session guitarist on London's busy studio scene, Jimmy Page was the last of the three to take up guitar duties with the Yardbirds. As it would come to pass, however, Page made more significant use of a Telecaster throughout his career than either Clapton or Beck, and he never entirely discarded the model, even though he became more commonly associated with the Gibson Les Paul and, occasionally, the EDS-1275 doubleneck.

Born in Heston in West London in 1944, and raised mainly in Epsom, Surrey, essentially another London suburb, Jimmy Page found much the same path to the guitar as his fellow London six-stringers, listening to records by bluesers such as Buddy Guy and B.B. King, but he was arguably more influenced by rock 'n' rollers like Elvis sidemen James Burton and Scotty Moore. Page's early fluency on the instrument landed him in several up-and-coming cover bands, which transitioned to a burgeoning studio career. By the mid-1960s he was one of the first-call session aces on London's pop and blues-rock scene.

The first time the Yardbirds knocked on the door to ask him to join the band (replacing the departed Eric Clapton), Page declined, and passed the job along to friend Jeff Beck. Less than a year later,

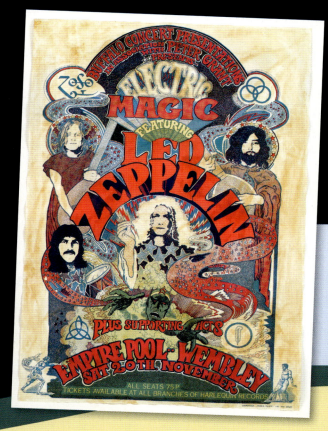

"The 'Stairway to Heaven' solo was done when I pulled out the Telecaster, which I hadn't used for a long time, plugged it into the Supro. . . . That's a different sound entirely from the rest of the first album. It was a good versatile setup."

—Jimmy Page

"It's more of a fight with the Telecaster, but there are rewards."

—Jimmy Page

however, in the summer of 1966, he was again approached, this time to fill the shoes of departing bassist Paul Samwell-Smith until rhythm guitarist Chris Dreja could learn the instrument. This time, Page agreed, and took up the bass for upcoming Yardbirds dates, segueing to guitar once Dreja had come to grips with the four-string. The Telecaster Page played for much of his tenure in the Yardbirds was one given to him by Jeff Beck, the '59 white-guard model with rosewood fingerboard that Beck had acquired from a pre-Yardbirds bandmate. Page soon covered the guitar in reflective metal discs, perhaps an homage to the Esquire played by Syd Barrett of The Pink Floyd, then repainted the guitar in psychedelic colors with a large dragon graphic to match the mood of the times. He used this Tele alongside Beck's guitar work on the only real Yardbirds hit of the Page/Beck era, "Happenings Ten Years Time Ago," as well as on the song "Stroll On," recorded for the Yardbirds' appearance on the seminal Michelangelo Antonioni film *Blowup*.

After Beck's firing from the band midway through a U.S. tour in October 1966, Page was the sole Yardbirds guitarist until the demise of the band, and more and more he used it as a test lab for musical ideas that he would explore further with his next venture. When two more original Yardbirds, singer Keith Relf and drummer Jim McCarty, departed in 1968, he soldiered on as the New Yardbirds, hiring singer Robert Plant and drummer John Bonham to avoid reneging on contractual obligations for a Scandinavian tour. Growing further and further from what the Yardbirds had been just a year before— with more intensive adventures into its own blend of psychedelic rock mixed with heavy electric blues and some acoustic folk—this line-up was clearly an entirely different band. The addition of bassist John Paul Jones calcified the new direction. Page dropped the New Yardbirds name and dubbed the outfit Led Zeppelin.

The heavily decorated rosewood-board Tele remained a major part of Page's arsenal in Led Zeppelin. He employed it on the band's first album, Led Zeppelin, but perhaps most famously pulled it out for the seminal solo in "Stairway to Heaven" in 1971, a performance that no doubt sends countless thousands of wannabe guitar heroes mistakenly in search of the Gibson Les Pauls that Page was often seen playing on stage by that time, or the double-neck that he used to perform the song live, playing the intro on the upper 12-string neck, and the solo on the lower six-string neck. During the remainder of the Led Zeppelin years Page would acquire and play a handful of other Telecasters, but the '59 or '60 Tele with the dragon graphics would always be considered "the one" in the minds of Zeppelin fanatics.

Syd Barrett

Syd Barrett performs with The Pink Floyd at London's UFO Club in 1967, wielding his Esquire.
Andrew Whittuck/Redferns/Getty Images

Way back when Pink Floyd was The Pink Floyd, guitarist and singer Syd Barrett was the man at the helm of their spontaneous art-rock hijinks, and he pioneered British psychedelia on the most unlikely of instruments: a Fender Esquire. Born Roger Keith Barrett in Cambridge, England, in 1946, he got into the local music and arts scene at an early age and adopted the nickname "Syd" as a play on the name of drummer Sid Barrett. Barrett displayed considerable avant-garde leanings—long before there was such a thing as "psychedelic rock"—and he was already making a name for himself on the local bohemian scene while he was in his teens.

After he moved to London to study at Camberwell Art College, momentum toward Barrett's creative zenith developed quickly. In 1964, the fragmentation of a band formed by bassist Roger Waters (in which he occasionally played lead guitar), which also included would-be Floyd drummer Nick Mason and rhythm guitarist (later keyboardist) Rick Wright, offered Barrett an opening in a London-based outfit. The four evolved quickly from students to part-time musicians to happening artists on the scene, and by late 1965, they were going by the name The Pink Floyd—a name chosen by Barrett, derived from the first names of American bluesmen Pink Anderson and Floyd Council. Through the course of 1966, The Pink Floyd developed their chops as a live band, spurred on by Barrett's drive to produce spontaneous, original performances with "songs" that generally extended into unstructured psychedelic improvisation. As such, they quickly became prominent fixtures on the underground music scene in the early days of "swinging London" and acted as a "resident band" of sorts at clubs such as UFO and the Roundhouse, performing long sets that were as impressive for the lights and special effects—genuine performance art, in other words—as they were for the music.

Barrett's Esquire was most likely a 1964 model, and had a white pickguard, rosewood fingerboard, and of course the single bridge pickup characteristic of the breed. Shortly after the formation of The Floyd, he repainted the guitar, then covered it in silver plastic sheeting and stuck several reflective metal discs on the front. The epitome of the psychedelic stage prop, it was, for a time, the most notable guitar among those of all the bands in London's burgeoning

acid-rock scene. For a basic, workmanlike instrument more at home churning out low-string twang or lean country picking, the Esquire served Barrett's experimental sonic explorations surprisingly well.

In 1967 the band signed to EMI Records and released two hits—the only hit singles of their career—"Arnold Layne" and "See Emily Play," along with a debut LP *The Piper at the Gates of Dawn*. Much of this recorded work hints at Barrett's on-stage Esquire antics, although the full dose really required The Floyd live experience. As an embodiment of this, perhaps, the disparity between the expectations of the commercial music industry and Barrett's creative muse gradually alienated him from the direction in which the band was heading, while his purported excessive indulgence in psychedelic drugs was simultaneously making him more difficult to deal with on a personal level.

Barrett left The Pink Floyd (now just Pink Floyd) in 1968, with the intention of maintaining a solo career under the wing of the band's management company, Blackhill Enterprises, and EMI offshoot Harvest Records. The solo albums *The Madcap Laughs*, recorded in 1969 and released in January of 1970, and *Barrett*, recorded soon after and released in November of 1970, both completed with help from his former Floyd bandmates, were considered creative and critical successes, but they were the last original work of Barrett's career. As the '70s rolled on, rumors abounded that Syd Barrett had either fried his mind on acid or was in fact dead, although he was often simply living in near-seclusion in Cambridge. Other than the sporadic studio work of his first two years post-Floyd, Barrett remained virtually inactive musically from 1968 onward, discounting occasional, largely aborted studio efforts of the early '70s. Barrett told *Melody Maker* magazine's Michael Watts in March of 1971, in regard to his fitful musical efforts, "I feel, perhaps, I could be claimed as being redundant almost. I don't feel active, and that my public conscience is fully satisfied." Later that same year, Barrett told Mike Rock of *Rolling Stone* magazine: "I never felt so close to a guitar as that silver one with mirrors that I used on stage all the time. I swapped it for the black one [a late-'60s Telecaster Custom], but I've never played it." Syd Barrett died of pancreatic cancer in July of 2006.

This 1969 Paisley Red Telecaster was part of Fender's bid for the hippie crowd in the late sixties. The paisley red finish was only offered in 1968 and 1969. *Fretted Americana*

(continued from 93)

Also in 1968, Fender made a blatant bid for favor with the Haight-Ashbury scene with the release of the Paisley Red and Blue Flower Telecasters. Equipped with maple-capped necks to accent the bright decorative treatments, both were standard Telecasters other than the application of pinkish-red paisley or blue floral stick-on wallpaper front and back. The guitars' body edges were finished to match the color of the appliqué, the entire thing was sprayed in a clear coat to protect the effort, and each was topped off with a clear Plexiglass pickguard.

While your hippie of the day was perhaps still more likely to choose a Stratocaster, these guitars did eventually appeal to a few major stars of the country scene, including James Burton during

1972 Custom Telecaster in rare black finish.
Doug Youland/Willie's American Guitars

his stint with Emmylou Harris's Hot Band, and, later, rather inevitably, lick-slinger Brad Paisley. Bluegrass and country artist Marty Stuart is also an avid collector of original Paisley Telecasters. Having sold poorly in their day, though, the Paisley and Flower Teles were dropped from the catalog after 1969, making original examples quite collectible, despite their post-CBS pedigree.

The Rosewood Telecaster, available in extremely limited numbers from 1969 to 1972, is another post-CBS oddball that has become something of a classic. The design was first seen in two proto-types made in 1968 by Fender master builder Roger Rossmeisl, formerly of Rickenbacker, and Phillip Kubicki, later a respected custom guitar maker in his own right. The guitars had a solid rosewood neck and a rosewood "sand-wich" body with maple center section. One of the original pair was given by Fender to George Harrison late that year, and used prominently on the recording of The Beatles' *Let It Be* and other sessions, as well in the famous "rooftop concert" atop the Apple building in London in 1969, The Beatles' last live performance. Production Rosewood Telecasters were initially made with solid bodies, but these were later chambered to relieve the extreme weight of this hard, dense wood. Otherwise, the Rosewood Telecasters had standard Tele specs and appointments, and three-ply black plastic pickguards. The extreme rarity of this model, along with George Harrison's association with the guitar, makes it another highly collectible post-CBS Telecaster.

The final changes to Telecaster models that might still be considered "vintage" came largely at the hands of a significant new Fender pickup. In 1967 Fender hired former Gibson engineer Seth Lover—famous as the main man behind the humbucking

1968 Blue Flower Telecaster.
Guitar and photo courtesy of Rumble Seat Music

pickup introduced by Gibson some ten years before—and by 1970, he had developed a humbucker for Fender, too. This pickup, known as the Fender Wide Range Humbucking Pickup, looks outwardly somewhat like a Gibson PAF-style pickup, but its six adjustable pole pieces are staggered with three on the treble side of one coil and three on the bass side of the other, with six more non-adjustable poles hidden beneath the cover. Also under the cover is quite a different design from Lover's Gibson humbucker, too: rather than the single Alnico bar magnet mounted beneath and between the two coils as on Gibson's "PAF," the Wide Range pickup uses individual pole pieces made from cunife magnets, which are a blend of copper, nickel, and ferrite.

Although these pickups definitely have characteristics of humbuckers, the use of magnets within the coils, something seen in all significant Fender pickup designs, also helps them retain characteristic Fender clarity and "twang." They were relatively "hot" pickups for their day, but still enabled Fender guitars to sound like Fenders, while giving players a version of the humbucking pickup that was such a popular component by this time in the history of the electric guitar.

The first production model to be given the Wide Range Humbucking Pickup— two, in fact—was the revamped Telecaster Thinline of 1971. In 1972, the Telecaster Custom was reconfigured with one humbucker at the neck position and a new four-control layout and toggle-style pickup selector switch, á la many Gibson guitars, while at the same time losing the body binding that had defined the model since 1959. Many blues, rock, and jazz players had been modifying Teles for years by adding a Gibson humbucker at the neck position for a thicker, warmer tone, and the update of the Custom was clearly a bid to appeal to that market.

That same year, the Telecaster Deluxe was introduced, with the same switching array as the revamped Custom, humbucking pickups in both neck and bridge positions, and an enlarged Stratocaster-style headstock. The Custom and Deluxe also sported telltale signs of further Fender "innovations" that the standard Tele would otherwise escape. Each had the new "bullet" style headstock-positioned truss-rod adjustment nut, along with the three-screw "Tilt Neck" attachment with neck-angle adjustment bolt, two new features of all Stratocaster guitars from 1971.

Promoted as beneficial new features at the time, the three-bolt neck and bullet-head adjustment nut have, together, long been regarded as the most obvious outward demarcation point between "the good" early CBS Stratocasters and the, well, not so good ones. Their use on these Telecaster models also rendered them less desirable among traditional Tele players for many years, although these solid, versatile, early humbucker-loaded Fenders now retain a certain cache with rock, blues, and roots players. The Telecaster Deluxe was also available for a time with a '70s-style Stratocaster vibrato unit, making it the first Fender Tele to be produced with a proprietary vibrato, rather than with a rendition of the Bigsby vibrato. Quirky, a little cumbersome looking, and certainly rather dated in the mahogany-brown finish that many such models wore, the Deluxe and Custom models, along with the updated Thinline—alongside their still-breathing predecessor, the standard Telecaster of the early '70s, of course— are all generally very functional and good-sounding guitars.

1976 Telecaster Deluxe. *Outline Press Ltd.*

Keith Richards

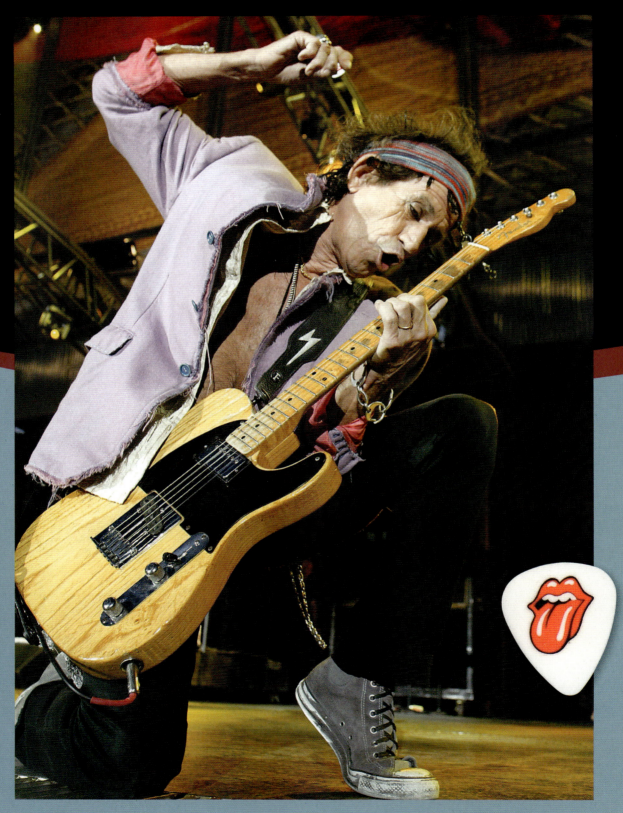

Keith Richards performs with the Rolling Stones at Velodrome Stadium in Marseilles, France, in July 2003. *Gerard Julien/AFP/Getty Images*

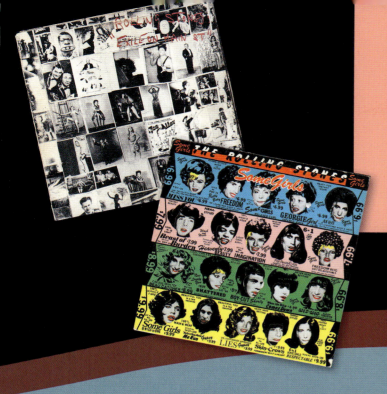

"There's no reason for my guitar being called Micawber, apart from the fact that it's such an unlikely name. There's no one around me called Micawber, so when I scream for Micawber everyone knows what I'm talking about."

—Keith Richards

Much like Eric Clapton, Jeff Beck, or George Harrison, Keith Richards has played a wide variety of different guitars over the years—Gibson Les Pauls, ES-335s, ES-345s, and ES-355s, Fender Stratocasters, Ernie Ball/Music Man Silhouettes, a Dan Armstrong Lucite guitar, and a Zemaitis—but he is far and away most associated with the modified early '50s black-guard Telelecaster that has remained his signature instrument since 1972's *Exile on Main St.* Indeed, Richards can be viewed as one of the players who took the Tele from country and blues into mainstream rock (where it had rarely been used since the '50s), and it has remained a major player there ever since.

Named "Micawber" by Richards, after a character from Charles Dickens's novel *David Copperfield*, this Telecaster is understood to be a 1952 or '53 model that retains its original body and neck (with their original, heavily road-worn finishes), and knurled knobs and control plate, but has been modified in many other ways. Most notable among these alterations is the Gibson PAF humbucking pickup that Richards installed in the neck position (backward, with the adjustable pole pieces toward the bridge) early in his ownership of the guitar. The neck pickup is often considered the "weak link" of the Telecaster, tonally speaking, and a humbucker modification is one of the more popular options for improving this setting. Micawber was also updated with a latter-day, six-saddle brass bridge, from

which Richards has removed the block-style saddle from the low-E position to better accommodate his preference for using only five strings when playing in open-G tuning, as he always does with this Tele. Other notable details include its modern, diecast tuners and the white Strat-style switch tip in place of the original black barrel switch tip. Known for its cutting yet meaty tone, Micawber can be heard on too many classic Stones recordings to mention. Richards also habitually uses it in live performances of "Brown Sugar" and "Honky Tonk Woman."

On tour, Richards carts several backup Telecasters that are also usually used on specific songs. Most distinctive among these are "Malcolm," a blonde 1954 Telecaster, and "Sonny," a sunburst 1966 Telecaster. Both also have humbuckers added in the neck position and six-saddle brass bridges with the low-E saddle removed. Although countless guitarists happily maintain six strings when playing in open G (which, as such, runs D-G-D-G-B-D, low to high), Richards has often mentioned that the low D just isn't necessary to him, and it gets in the way of his own playing and the bassist's parts, too. To complete his rich, gnarly, rock-and-roll tone, Richards rams his guitars through a pair of vintage late-'50s "high- powered" (80 watt) tweed Fender Twin amplifiers on stage, while frequently blending large and small amps in the studio.

Wilko Johnson

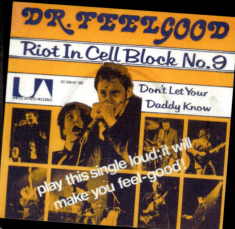

Johnson performs with Dr. Feelgood at Hammersmith Palais, 1975. *Ian Dickson/ Redferns/Getty Images*

With his shaggy bowl haircut, black clothes, herky-jerky stage presence, and frenetic playing style, Wilko Johnson was considered by many to be the heart and soul of Dr. Feelgood, the band he cofounded in 1971. His black Telecaster with red pickguard was as much a part of his image as anything, and an even bigger force upon the music, given its punchy tone and the energy it injected into this seminal London pop-rock outfit.

The guitarist was born John Wilkinson in 1947 in Canvey Island, a seven-square-mile island just off the southern corner of Essex, England, that is known mainly for its large oil depot

and flat, swampy land. Inverting his name to create his better-known stage moniker, Wilko Johnson launched his music career shortly after graduating from the University of Newcastle upon Tyne with an English degree. Settling back home in Essex, he met up with two old acquaintances: singer Lee Collins (soon Lee Brilleaux) and bassist John Sparkes, whose group the Pigboy Charlie Band had just lost its guitarist. Johnson hopped aboard, and local working drummer John "The Big Figure" Martin was roped in to fill out the quartet, which opted to mark the personnel change with a name change. The new name—Dr. Feelgood—seems to have originated

Wilko Johnson's famous "red-guard" Tele takes a break. *Andrew Lepley/Redferns/Getty Images*

INTERVIEWER: "I know you're a fan of the Telecaster guitar. Have you used any other makes of guitar?"

WILKO JOHNSON: "No."

INTERVIEWER: "Why have you stuck with Telecasters?"

WILKO JOHNSON: "Because Mick Green [of Johnny Kidd and the Pirates] had one."

INTERVIEWER: "I understand you never use a plectrum—that must be hard on your fingers?"

WILKO JOHNSON: "They used to bleed a lot, but they are all right now."

from a song by bluesman Piano Red, which was covered by English rock 'n' rollers Johnny Kid and the Pirates, although it is also the name given to any doctor on the rock scene who was willing to dole out "feel good" meds.

From the start, the members of Dr. Feelgood considered it an R&B band, but the tag might be misleading to R&B purists. Blending blues, rock 'n' roll, R&B, and something distinctly London into their own original sound—buoyed by an electric stage presence in live shows—Dr. Feelgood became the central fixture of what would be known as the London pub-rock scene of the 1970s. Including bands like Ducks Deluxe, Brinsley Schwarz, Chilli Willi and the Red Hot Peppers, and Nick Lowe, and later the likes of Ian Dury, Joe Strummer's 101ers, The Stranglers, and Elvis Costello, pub-rock stood out as a back-to-basics reaction of sorts to the phoniness and glitz of the booming glam-rock scene. Pub-rock is also credited as the breeding ground for the riotous punk-rock scene that followed.

Johnson bought his first Telecaster from a shop in Southend, Essex, in 1965 for £90 (around $150). In 1974, after Dr. Feelgood

signed its first record deal, he bought a second Telecaster. Originally a sunburst model from 1962 with rosewood fingerboard and white pickguard, the new guitar was painted black, and a red pickguard was added once Dr. Feelgood got rolling so it would match his favorite black-and-red shirt. The choice of a Telecaster had been inspired by its use by guitarist Mick Green with Johnny Kidd and the Pirates. As Johnson told Richard Flynn of *Guitar & Bass* magazine in the U.K. in September of 2011, Green also had an enormous effect on Johnson's playing style. "I can remember discovering him and being intrigued by the way he played," said Johnson. "The thing that hit me was his style. It was so American. It was a rhythm and blues style, and it didn't sound like what most people were doing over here. One of the many things that intrigued me was when I found out the Pirates didn't have a rhythm guitarist. It was all one guy, and I thought that was great and

Wilko Johnson

Wilko Johnson plays his trademark black Telecaster with red pickguard during a 2009 show. *Jon Gardner/Alamy*

I started learning how to do it. . . . But I worked out a way of doing it, which of course was wrong—it's not the way he did it. So if you like, I've ended up with my own style." A big part of that "own style" also revolves around the fact that Johnson is a natural left-hander but plays guitar right-handed, while also using his bare fingers and thumb rather than a pick.

Dr. Feelgood was on tour in the United States in 1976 when punk hit it big in the U.K. Upon their return, they found a drastically altered scene, one in which they were a little less welcome than they had been in the years before. This, and increasing animosity between Johnson and signer Lee Brilleaux, led to Wilko's disenchantment with the band. In 1977, after several modest hit singles, three successful studio albums—*Down by the*

Jetty, *Malpractice*, and *Sneakin' Suspicion*—and a 1976 live album, *Stupidity*, that reached number one on the U.K. album chart, Wilko Johnson left Dr. Feelgood. Johnson continues to record and tour with his own band, figured largely in the award-winning pub-rock documentary *Oil City Confidential* (2009), and played the part of the mute executioner in the HBO TV series *Game of Thrones*. He still owns his original black Telecaster but has retired it from the road. A Wilko Johnson Signature Telecaster was developed by Fender in 2013. Dr. Feelgood pressed on in the late '70s with replacement guitarist John "Gypie" Mayo, who has been replaced by three successive guitarists in the intervening years. Brilleaux died of cancer in 1994. The band is still performing today, although none of the founding members remain.

In 1964, like many British teenagers I was learning to play the electric guitar—my hero was the great Mick Green of Johnny Kidd and the Pirates, who chopped out his fantastic riffs on a Fender Telecaster. There was a blonde Telecaster in the display window of the local music shop—it was beautiful as a dream and just as unattainable. The price tag of £107 was way beyond the means of a Canvey Island schoolboy and all I could do was gaze at it through the glass.

Came the day when the shop put on a sale and dropped the price to £90. I had to have it. My mum would never allow me to buy anything on credit, so I went into the shop, put down a small deposit, and asked if I could pay by weekly installments while they retained the guitar. Every Saturday I would go to the shop with my payment book and hand over all the money I had scraped together that week, and they would bring out the guitar and let me spend the afternoon playing it. At closing time the Tele went back into the storeroom and I walked home. Eventually I made the final payment and triumphantly carried my Fender Telecaster out of the shop. Walking through the crowded streets I felt like a king.

1975. Working hard with Dr. Feelgood I wanted another guitar to use on the road. I found a 1962 Tele in the small ads in *Melody Maker* (£180!). This was a sunburst model—I customized it with a black spray job and a red scratch plate and I've used it for almost every gig and recording session I ever played since.

I still have both these guitars—fifty years old now and playing as good or better than ever. I also have the chrome "ashtray" tailpiece covers, both in shining never-used mint condition. There must be thousands of these things stashed away in the backs of cupboards and drawers, the Telecaster's one concession to 1950s Detroit-style streamlining and the most unused piece of hardware in history.

I'm still on the road and so is my Tele. Every hotel room I check into, the first thing I do is take the Telecaster out of its case and lean it against the wall. It looks so good—just like in that shop window all those years ago.

—Wilko Johnson, 2012

Bill Kirchen

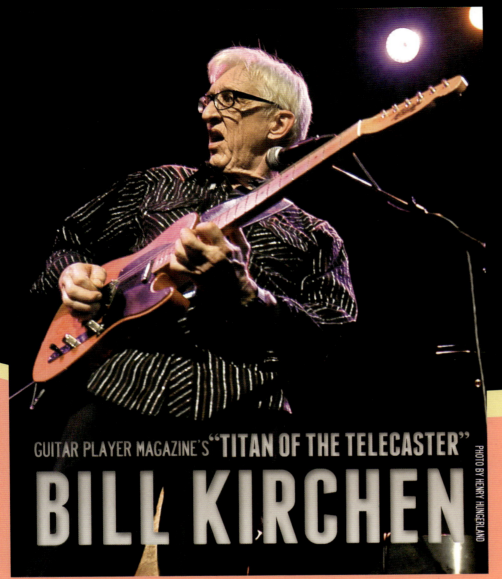

GUITAR PLAYER MAGAZINE'S "TITAN OF THE TELECASTER"
BILL KIRCHEN

PHOTO BY HENRY HUNGERLAND

"T itan of the Telecaster," Dieselbilly originator, lead guitarist with Commander Cody and His Lost Planet Airmen—Bill Kirchen has worn plenty of labels, but beneath all of them he has stayed true to his slab-bodied paramour, the Fender Telecaster. Kirchen was born in Ann Arbor, Michigan, in 1948 and raised on a diet of folk and classical music, which he played before discovering the rock 'n' roll, country, blues, and rockabilly that he would eventually twist into something all his own. Having been hipped to rock 'n' roll in the early '60s by the first Beatles records, Kirchen migrated toward country twang through the course of the decade and formed psychedelic country-rock-bluesers

Commander Cody in 1967 with fellow Airmen George Frayne, Andy Stein, John Tichy, Billy C. Farlow, Lance Dickerson, Bobby Black, and Paul "Buffalo" Bruce Barlow.

After acquiring his first guitar, a Gibson SG, from fellow Cody guitarist Tichy, Kirchen pretty quickly realized that what he really needed was a Telecaster. Less than a year later, in 1968, he practically stumbled into one: a chance meeting with a Tele-toting stranger on a bus resulted in an even swap, the fruits of which is a somewhat enigmatic instrument that has been with him ever since. "That's the same Tele that I've played just about every day since," Kirchen relates, "whatever the hell year it is . . . sunburst, you know. When I got it the serial number on the bridge plate was 2222, but it had a seven-screw pickguard and no neck date. No one could figure out, because it didn't have a big fat [early] '50s neck, it had a thinner neck, so we thought it might have been a factory refinish, who

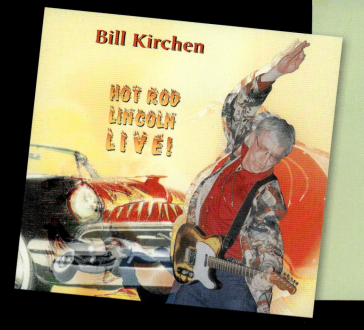

Bill Kirchen

HOT ROD LINCOLN LIVE!

knows. But then, mind that in '68 there was no real value in counterfeiting; however you cut it, it was a hundred-dollar guitar."

Hundred-dollar guitar in tow, Kirchen and Commander Cody headed west to San Francisco in 1969 just in time to join the likes of the Byrds, Gram Parsons, the Grateful Dead, and others in a ripe country-rock scene. They signed with Paramount Records in 1971, released the debut album *Lost in the Ozone*, and shot the single "Hotrod Lincoln" into the *Billboard* Top 10 in 1972, propelling Kirchen's hotrod Tele licks into the national consciousness along with it. After signing to Warner Brothers in 1975, Cody et al. found themselves butting heads with the new label's efforts to turn them into the next Eagles. After sticking true to its harder-edged roots for a time, the Lost Planet Airmen disbanded in 1976, with singer George Frayne retaining his Commander Cody stage persona as a solo artist from 1977 onward.

Post-Cody, Kirchen toured and recorded with Nick Lowe for a time (along with his other San Francisco–area band, the Moonlighters), then based himself in Washington, DC, for many years, where he fit in well with fellow hot Tele-meisters like Roy Buchanan, Tom Principato, and Danny Gatton. With his band Too Much Fun, Kirchen released several acclaimed albums and toured widely, returning to his DC base before relocating first back to the West Coast, then to Austin, Texas.

More than four decades after virtually stumbling upon it, Kirchen still has his own original hammer, although he leaves it at home these days, touring instead with Tele clones made by the likes of Big Tex and Rick Kelly. But, while the enigmatic '50s Telecaster that came to him in 1968 is laughably far from its original state, it remains "the one" in Kirchen's heart. "It's so far from original . . . the only metal left on there that's original are the six ferrules that the strings go through. Everything else on there I've changed one, two, three, four, five, times, just because it's a player. It was immaculate when I got it, just a few little scrub marks where somebody had grabbed ahold of an E chord, you know. Now where my little finger rests between the bridge plate and the volume-tone strip I've worn it down so far there's a hole about a half-inch deep just from my little finger resting there." And as precious as this instrument has been to him—truly the tool of a Telecaster original—its owner still can't tell us when the thing was born. "I never really knew, and the other thing was that I figured I wasn't going to sell it. I figured when I got done with it I was going to pound it into my front yard and stick those trapezoid house numbers on it, you know; by now it's a moot point, I think."

Mike Campbell

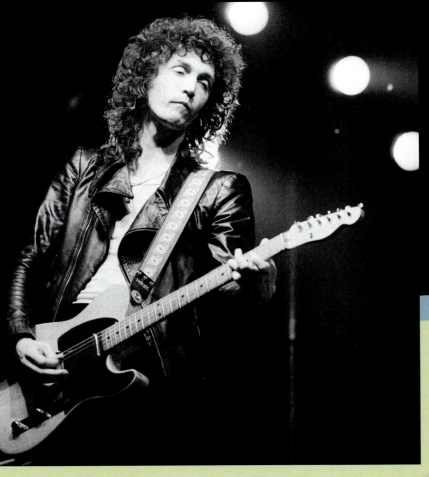

Campbell performs with Tom Petty and the Heartbreakers in London, early on in his ownership of his famed Broadcaster. *Estate of Keith Morris/ Redferns/Getty Images*

Mike Campbell was first introduced to fellow Floridian Tom Petty in Gainesville in the early 1970s when mutual friend Randall Marsh, drummer for Petty's band Mudcrutch, recommended him to fill a vacancy on lead guitar. In 1974 Mudcrutch moved from Florida to Los Angeles, signed a deal with Shelter Records, and recorded an album that was never released. In 1976, however, out of the wreckage of the Mudcrutch implosion, Campbell and Petty formed the band that would forever after be known primarily for its lead singer's name. Along with old Gainesville pal Benmont Tench on Hammond organ, plus Ron Blair on bass and Stan Lynch on drums, the pair regrouped as Tom Petty and the Heartbreakers and soon started rolling out the hits.

The self-titled debut album on ABC Records yielded only a minor hit in "Breakdown," which reached the Top 40, while "American Girl," now considered a Heartbreakers classic, failed to make a dent in the charts. The follow-up album, *You're Gonna Get It*, did at least go gold, while the band's

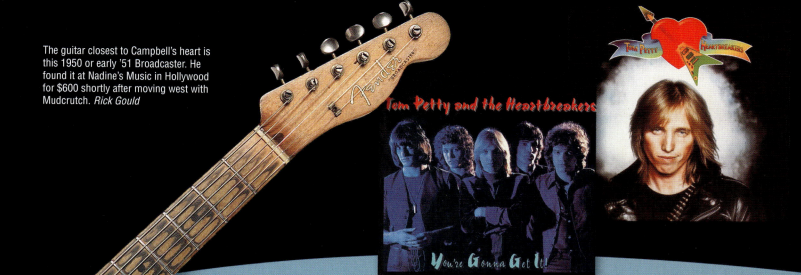

The guitar closest to Campbell's heart is this 1950 or early '51 Broadcaster. He found it at Nadine's Music in Hollywood for $600 shortly after moving west with Mudcrutch. *Rick Gould*

third outing, 1979's *Damn the Torpedoes,* finally shot them into the big time. After that, Tom Petty and the Heartbreakers logged numerous hits, including nineteen Top 10s. The band received myriad awards, a star on the Hollywood Walk of Fame, and induction into the Rock and Roll Hall of Fame.

A major fan and collector of guitars, Mike Campbell is known for the range of different models he plays on stage and in the studio, including Rickenbackers, Gretsches, Gibsons, and German-made Duesenbergs. But from the very start of the band, Campbell's signature guitar, and the one that is closest to his heart, was an early Fender Broadcaster. Shortly after moving west with Mudcrutch, Campbell found the 1950 or early '51 Broadcaster at Nadine's Music in Hollywood for $600. In the early days of Tom Petty and the Heartbreakers, the Broadcaster was the guitar for Campbell. Used on the recording of the band's debut single "Breakdown," as well as notable tracks like "American Girl," "Hurt," "I Need to Know," and—in Petty's hands—"Mary Jane's Last Dance," its beefy, slightly gritty snarl is as definitively Heartbreakers as the twelve-string Rickenbacker jangle that often counterpoints it.

As such, not to mention its status as one of relatively few existing Broadcasters, this old black-guard became extremely precious to its owner. "I put it off the road many years ago because it became so valuable," Campbell told the author in 1999. "Then in rehearsal I brought it down one day and the soundman came running down saying, 'What was that!? You gotta take that out—it sounds better

than all your other guitars!' So I thought, why leave it at home? This is my sound, you know?" Inspired once again by the instrument's power, Campbell took the Broadcaster out on the 1999 summer tour following the release of the album *Echo* (having used it to record the album track "I Don't Wanna Fight," and others). In the years following, however, the vintage Fender was largely consigned to studio duties once again. In addition to the Broadcaster, Campbell also has a 1956 Telecaster with Parsons-White B-Bender, which can be heard on the occasional Heartbreakers track and in "Lover of the Bayou," a 2008 track from Mudcrutch.

Throughout his work with Petty and others, Campbell has been known for being a consummate "song player," a guitarist driven to play to the benefit of the composition rather than for the sake of logging flashy riffs and solos. "The stuff that got me into guitar," Campbell explains, "the Stones, the Kinks, the Beach Boys, the Animals, all those '60s bands, had real simple guitar parts to go around the song as opposed to guitar solos that interrupted the song. That's the way our band's always been: the song's the most important thing."

In addition to his work with Tom Petty and the Heartbreakers, Campbell collaborated with several other notable artists, as guitarist, producer, and songwriter. He cowrote Don Henley's massive hit "Boys of Summer," produced four tracks on Roy Orbison's *Mystery Girl* album, and produced two of Petty's non-Heartbreakers albums, *Full Moon Fever* and *Wildflowers*.

Bruce Springsteen

Bruce Springsteen and his original Esquire with added neck pickup. *Michael Ochs Archives/Getty Images*

Bruce Springsteen's use of a Telecaster (or to be precise, an Esquire) is typical of this instrument's utility as a blue-collar rock 'n' roll guitar. It has also made his own Esquire one of the most recognizable guitars in all of rock music, thanks largely to its appearance on the covers of the *Born to Run*, *Live 1975–85*, *Human Touch*, and *Greatest Hits* albums. Springsteen's Fender Esquire has often been cited by techs and the Boss himself as a 1953 or '54 model, and most fans have been happy to leave it at that. Closer examination of this hallowed instrument, however, shows that there might be a little more going on under the hood.

In live concert footage from the mid-'70s, Springsteen states that he purchased the guitar in the early '70s from New Jersey–based luthier Phil Petillo, who also cared for the instrument in the early days of Springsteen's ownership. Other reports indicate that Petillo purchased the Esquire at a liquidation sale for a New York recording studio, and that the guitar was already somewhat modified when he acquired it, most notably having had a considerable amount of wood routed from beneath the pickguard to accommodate extra pickups in addition to the factory route for a future neck pickup that all Esquires carry beneath their pickguards. (The star's Esquire outwardly has the look of a Telecaster anyway, thanks to the

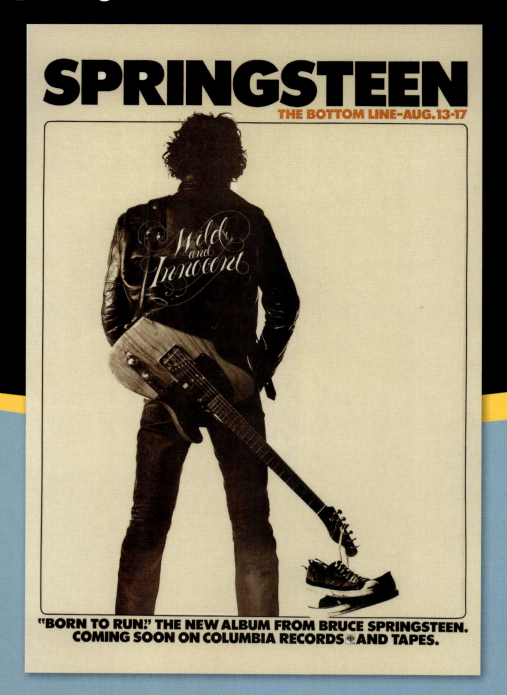

SPRINGSTEEN
THE BOTTOM LINE-AUG. 13-17

Wild and Innocent

"BORN TO RUN." THE NEW ALBUM FROM BRUCE SPRINGSTEEN. COMING SOON ON COLUMBIA RECORDS ● AND TAPES.

added pickup in the neck position.) The instrument's heavily worn Butterscotch Blonde finish and black pickguard uphold the '53 or '54 estimate, but the headstock wears a butterfly string guide for the B and E strings positioned roughly in line with the A-string tuner post; the butterfly guide didn't replace the earlier round guide (which was more distant from the nut) until mid-'56, a change accompanied by a move of the logo decal to the far

side of this guide. Myriad interviews also indicate that the neck has the soft-V profile that came back into fashion at Fender in late '55 and remained largely through '57 (early '50 and '51 necks were also V's, or "boat necks," but were thicker overall). All of these indicators point to a neck made after 1954, and the possibility that the entire instrument is actually a 1956 or 1957 white-guard Esquire with a swapped-in black guard.

Other later modifications are beyond speculation. The Esquire already has replacement tuners in the *Born to Run* photo, although it still wears a three-saddle '50s bridge with stamped-steel base plate. Later, it received a titanium six-saddle bridge from Petillo, along with a set of the luthier's own patented Petillo Precision Frets, a fret wire with an inverted V-shaped crown for precise intonation. Petillo also added hot rewound single-coil pickups, which the guitar retains to this day.

Ultimately, the fine points matter not. These were "Erector Set" guitars to begin with, and whatever kind of mutt of an instrument it is, it has been the driving force behind some of the most compelling rock anthems from the mid-1970s on. One listen to the searing solos from "Prove It All Night" or "Candy's Room" render the details moot.

Joe Strummer

Joe Strummer and his well-used Telecaster front the Mescaleros in July 2002, a few months before his passing. *Tim Mosenfelder/Getty Images*

The archetypal blue-collar guitar for hard-working country and blues players of the 1950s and '60s, the Telecaster transitioned well to the punk-rock ethos of the '70s. Less "posh" than a Les Paul, more straightforward than a Stratocaster, the Tele was a guitar adept at hammering out chunky power-chord rhythms or simple yet searing single-note solos, and it appealed to the burgeoning punk scene in a way that was almost primal. As such, the Telecaster was a natural choice for Joe Strummer, guitarist and singer with the Clash. As much as he might have tried to maintain the band's stance, however, and that of the entire genre, really, against the worship of material goods, it was clear that Strummer loved his 1966 Telecaster just a little bit. No, he never coddled the guitar—as evidenced by his slipshod modifications and rough treatment of the instrument— but he certainly respected it, and he turned to this Tele far more than any other guitar through the course of his entire career.

Strummer (born John Mellor) acquired this early-CBS Telecaster—with its transition "spaghetti" logo, rosewood fingerboard, three-ply white/black/white pickguard, and three-tone sunburst finish—in 1975 while playing with a London pub-rock band called the 101ers. He bought it used for £120, which is around $200, and a lot of money back in the day, and legend has it that he "earned" the sum by agreeing to marry a woman from South Africa so she could stay in the United Kingdom. In 1976, just as the punk movement was exploding in London, guitarist Mick Jones and bassist Paul Simonon persuaded Strummer to join their new band, the Clash, and the '66 Telecaster came with him. This was punk, though, and a serious statement had to be made. At the urging of the band's manager, Strummer and company took a selection of gear to a friend's body shop, where the guitar's sunburst finish—a custom color option, now highly prized among collectors—was shot with a coat of gray

primer and, finally, a thick coat of jet black paint. Strummer stenciled on the word "NOISE" in white and added the first of an evolving number of stickers to the front, this one reading "Ignore Alien Orders." With these overt statements of disrespect duly made, a punk legend was born.

Although he owned backup guitars, Strummer used the '66 Tele on the vast majority of his work with the Clash, and on much of his solo work in the years that followed. The instrument is equally responsible for the crunching, metallic strum that propelled so many of the band's ferocious early punk outings, including "White Riot" and "London's Burning," as well as the clever, playful rhythm work that underpinned Mick Jones's lithe lead playing on later, more nuanced songs such as "Rudie Can't Fail," "Spanish Bombs," and "Lost in the Supermarket." Strummer played the Telecaster

so hard that much of the black overspray was worn down to the gray undercoat, and even to glimpses of the original sunburst finish in places. Strummer took the faithful '66 Tele with him on the road again in late 2001 and 2002 before dying of a congenital heart defect in December of that year at the age of fifty. The guitar is believed to be in the possession of Strummer's family in England. In 2007, Fender released their Joe Strummer Telecaster, complete with worn gray/black finish and a selection of decals and stencils.

Safe to say some of the world's most unique custom Esquires reside in the collection of ZZ Top's Billy F Gibbons. The chartreuse Crop Duster Special was a gift from the Top's bassist, Dusty Hill, who played the EMG-equipped guitar on "Breakaway" from the band's 1994 album, *Antenna*. *David Perry (davidperrystudio.com)*

This piece from the Gibbons collection is a nod to the guitarist's love of country music and Tele pioneer Buck Owens. The guitar is one of a pair made for ZZ Top pals Dwight Yoakam and Pete Anderson. *David Perry (davidperrystudio.com)*

Gibbons's Snake and Bones Esquire is one of the most-valued guitars in his collection. The stacked humbucker and intricate fingerboard inlay are complemented by the work of famed Los Angeles silversmith Gabor. *David Perry (davidperrystudio.com)*

Right: Custom Shop LTD 50s Esquire. *Fender Musical Instruments Corporation*

Andy Summers

Andy Summers plays his Telecaster Custom with the Police at the Brøndbyhallen in Copenhagen, Denmark, in January 1982. *Jan Persson/Redferns/Getty Images*

Given his background in jazz, fusion, classical music, and psychedelia, Andy Summers might have seemed an odd choice as the third man in a British "punk" trio that was forming in 1977. He had already played with Eric Burdon and the New Animals, Soft Machine, and Zoot Money and the Big Roll Band, plus Kevin Coyne, Kevin Ayers, and Tim Rose; toured the USA with major acts; and found time to earn a BA in music from California State University, Northridge, in the early '70s. But there was something about this outfit—bassist/vocalist Stewart "Sting" Sumner and drummer Stewart Copeland—that promised more than just the rudimentary power-chord romps that punk had embodied so far, something that might just give Summers's eclectic, ethereal playing style room to breathe. Summers's hunch proved right, and the Police's blend of punk energy, psychedelic sonic explorations, and reggae-fusion rhythms proved not only the perfect foil for his own diverse explorations, but it also proved extremely popular to the world at large, taking the guitarist to the top of his field in the process.

Through it all, Summers played a beaten concoction of a vintage Telecaster that, seemingly against all odds, turned out to be the

Custom Shop Andy Summer Tribute Telecaster Custom. *Fender Musical Instruments Corporation*

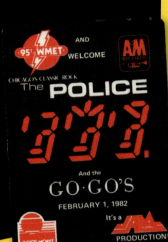

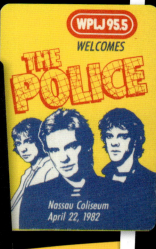

perfect guitar for this broad tonal palette. Summers bought the sunburst 1961 Telecaster Custom with maple neck from one of his guitar students for $200 in the early '70s while teaching to subsidize his studies. "There is a certain magic in life," he told *Guitar Player* magazine's Michael Molenda in 2007. "It was destiny that brought that guitar to me. It was a great guitar to play, and it had a wide range of tonal colors—from a typical clean Tele sound to a thick and creamy humbucker tone . . . and it sparked something that really came together when I joined a band with these two other guys. That Tele was the main guitar for almost everything the Police did."

The guitar already had extensive modifications, including the addition of a Gibson PAF humbucker in the neck position (later replaced by a Seymour Duncan after it failed on tour), a phase-reverse switch on the control plate, another switch above the control plate and a volume control below it that governed a preamp/overdrive unit mounted in the back of the guitar, and a brass replacement bridge with six individual brass saddles. The original single-coil bridge pickup was mounted into the ash body of the guitar, rather than suspended from the bridge plate, and in perhaps the biggest alteration of all, the maple neck was clearly not original to the guitar, which would have been born with a "slab board" rosewood neck in '61. Bearing the "Telecaster" model name rather than the "Telecaster Custom" that the bound, sunburst body of this guitar designates, the neck was clearly taken from a '50s Tele and updated with Schaller tuners and an extra string guide for the G and D strings. In addition to the Telecaster, Summers's Police tones were supplemented by a wide range of effects units, which expanded from the famous Boss Chorus Ensemble-infused riff of "Message in a Bottle" to include a Maestro Echoplex, a Mutron III envelope filter, and several fuzz, overdrive, and phaser units—all controlled via a Pete Cornish pedalboard in the original era of the Police, as well as a Bradshaw floor unit in later years.

Danny Gatton

Danny Gatton plays "slide" with a Heineken bottle while backing Robert Gordon at the Berkeley Square in Berkeley, California, on May 10, 1981. *Clayton Call/Redferns/Getty Images*

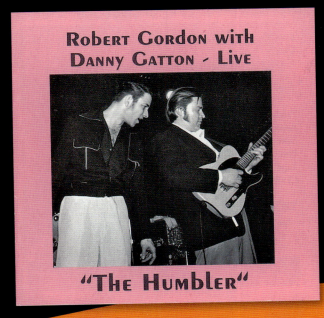

Robert Gordon with
Danny Gatton - Live

"The Humbler"

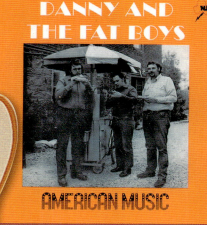

Just try making a list of "great Tele players" without including Danny Gatton. It's sometimes surprising to find that a player of Gatton's magnitude was so devoted to a guitar as "primitive" as the Telecaster, but there's something magical about a good Telecaster that seems to draw in virtuoso pickers. If one looks past the plank styling, it's clear that the Tele's blend of chime and bite, its ringing sustain, and its solid, bend-friendly construction are all major plusses for the players who pick it.

Born in Washington, DC, in 1945, Danny Gatton initially learned the guitar from his father, Daniel Sr., who had played professionally before stepping into the mainstream to raise a family. Gatton joined his first professional band, The Offbeats, in 1959 at the age of fourteen, where he made a long-time association with organist Dick Heintze. He followed countless hot young pickers to Nashville in the '60s, but ultimately returned to his native DC in the early '70s. The guitarist's reputation grew exponentially within the music community from the mid-'70s onward,

Danny Gatton Signature Telecaster in Frost Gold. *Fender Musical Instruments Corporation*

Danny Gatton

Danny Gatton's original '53 Telecaster, here fitted with the later Joe Barden pickups. Gatton played this Tele through most of the 1980s and 1990s; his Signature model was based on the guitar. *Steve Gorospe*

although he never really earned the broader fame and commercial success that such talent surely deserves. Often pigeonholed as a "country" or "rockabilly" player, due perhaps to the combination of his beat-up Telecaster and slicked-back "DA" hairstyle, Gatton could in fact turn his hand to any musical style, and incorporated elements of bebop, blues, Django-esque hot jazz, and others into his own playing. Asked "What kind of musical styles are you influenced by?" on camera in the 1980s by an anonymous—and rather curt—interviewer, Gatton replied, "Just about everything that happened in the '30s, '40s, '50s, '60s, '70s, and '80s." The interviewer clearly took it as the response of a precocious artist, but it was as honest an answer as could have been replied.

The music that Gatton made on his 1953 Tele was nothing short of phenomenal. Joe Barden, who worked as a self-appointed roadie while still in his teens and became Gatton's personal pickup maker toward the end of the guitarist's life, related the first time he experienced Gatton's stellar abilities: "It was one of the foremost moments in my life—I was completely transfixed. This was at a club called The Keg, in Georgetown, DC, on a snowy Sunday night. I was one of two paying customers, and there was a drunk passed out, leftover from the afternoon happy hour. I'm watching this short, stumpy little redneck, and he's covering everything . . . they were playing the most bizarre mix of shit, from straight-up 'Mystery Train' rockabilly to ancient chestnuts like 'Matilda' to slow blues. But none of this is 'normal' music at all. It's not rock and roll; it's not jazz. I thought I'd walked into a time warp or an alternative universe." Such was the power of Gatton's talent, which had reached far too few fans by the time he took his own life in 1995 at the age of forty-nine.

As much as Danny Gatton loved his Telecaster, he was often chasing a fuller, fatter tone than the model was born with, but he sought to attain it by modifying the instrument rather than by surrendering it entirely. For a time, he installed a large, cumbersome Gibson "Charlie Christian" pickup in the neck position of his Tele to bring that notoriously underpowered setting up to par. A more manageable solution eventually came in the form of the standard-sized, dual-blade pickups that Barden designed for him, which he took to using in both the bridge and neck positions from the early '80s onward. Gatton is believed to have sold his prized '53 Telecaster to a collector in 1990, after which he often played prototypes of Fender's Danny Gatton Signature Telecaster.

ALBERT COLLINS   Frank Scott, Personal Manager   Buffalo Booking Agency
                                                             2807 Erastus Street
                                                             Houston 26, Texas

Albert Collins displays his early white-guard Telecaster in a 1950s publicity photo.

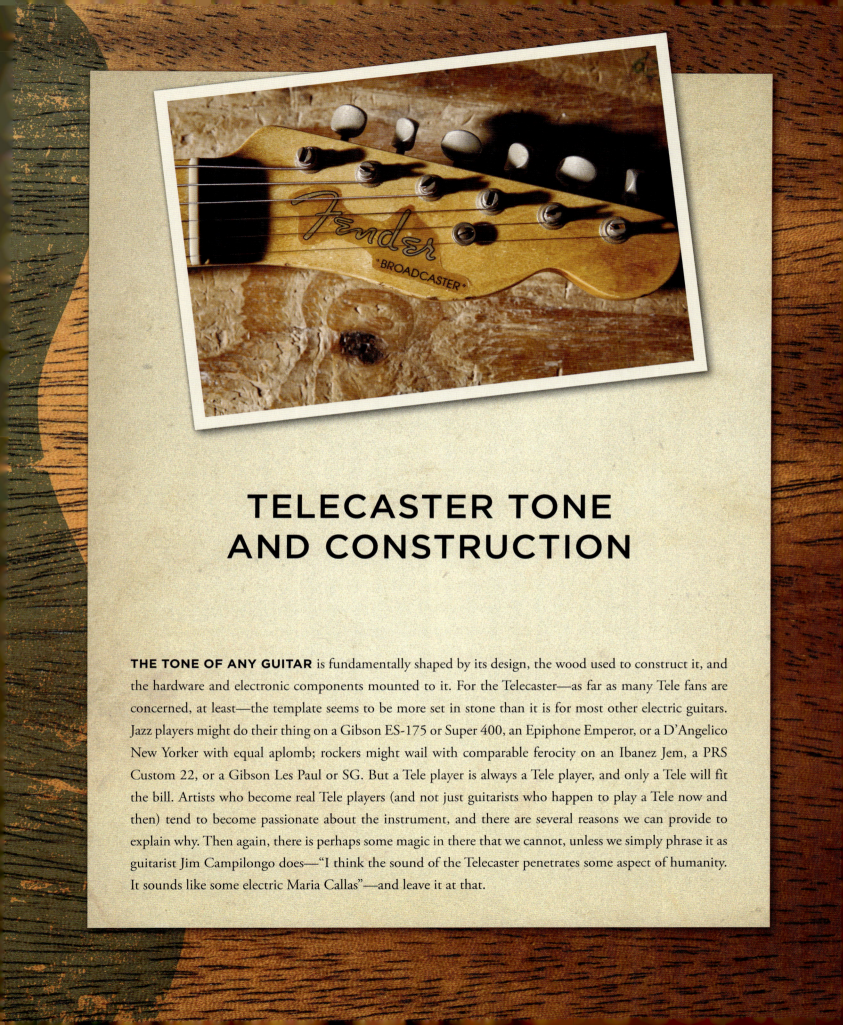

TELECASTER TONE AND CONSTRUCTION

THE TONE OF ANY GUITAR is fundamentally shaped by its design, the wood used to construct it, and the hardware and electronic components mounted to it. For the Telecaster—as far as many Tele fans are concerned, at least—the template seems to be more set in stone than it is for most other electric guitars. Jazz players might do their thing on a Gibson ES-175 or Super 400, an Epiphone Emperor, or a D'Angelico New Yorker with equal aplomb; rockers might wail with comparable ferocity on an Ibanez Jem, a PRS Custom 22, or a Gibson Les Paul or SG. But a Tele player is always a Tele player, and only a Tele will fit the bill. Artists who become real Tele players (and not just guitarists who happen to play a Tele now and then) tend to become passionate about the instrument, and there are several reasons we can provide to explain why. Then again, there is perhaps some magic in there that we cannot, unless we simply phrase it as guitarist Jim Campilongo does—"I think the sound of the Telecaster penetrates some aspect of humanity. It sounds like some electric Maria Callas"—and leave it at that.

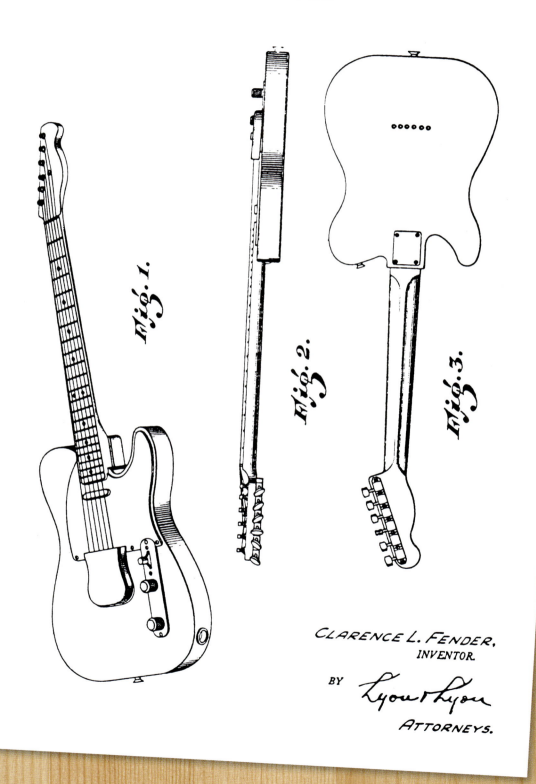

Aug. 14, 1951

C. L. FENDER

Des. 164,227

GUITAR

Filed April 23, 1951

Fig. 1.

Fig. 2.

Fig. 3.

CLARENCE L. FENDER,

INVENTOR.

BY

Lyon & Lyon

ATTORNEYS.

The Telecaster's unique sonic signature is formed by the combination of several crucial ingredients, many of which are indispensable to the recipe. You can change one or two of the lesser of these, perhaps, and a Tele still sounds like a Tele—or will be in the ballpark, at least. Certain parts of the formula, however, are crucial, unless you merely want "an electric guitar" that is shaped like a Tele. As such, the Telecaster really is a prime example of a design's whole being greater than the sum of its parts.

As I discussed in some detail in History of the Telecaster, the Telecaster truly represented a redrawing of the blueprint of the electric guitar. Looks-wise, it boiled down the lines of the traditional guitar to something that was extremely simple, while elegantly modernistic. More important, though, was the way in which it re-evaluated the function of the instrument, to produce an entirely new concept of "the guitar" that was aimed wholeheartedly at the goal of amplification. In chasing this objective, Fender would retain the fretted neck and the six strings traditionally tuned E-A-D-G-B-E, and little else. Fortunately, Leo and his cohorts did have a functional tonal template to work from, and one that he himself had put considerable effort into developing and advancing. The electric lap steel, or "Hawaiian," guitar was already the most successful electric stringed instrument, in sonic terms, available to the guitarist. It was bright, clear, well-defined, and resisted feedback at high volumes, none of which could be claimed in their entirety by the acoustic archtop electric guitars of the mid-1930s to late '40s. Since these qualities were already working for the steel guitar, Leo reasoned that they would also be successful with Spanish-style guitarists. This is the logic that led him down the road toward the Telecaster.

The key ingredients held over from Fender's steel-guitar designs were the solid body and the bright, clear pickup. Beyond these, two other primary design elements make a Telecaster a Telecaster: its highly functional and playable bolt-on maple neck (classically with maple fingerboard, but a rosewood 'board alters the formula

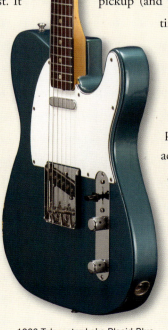

1966 Telecaster Lake Placid Blue.
Fretted Americana

only slightly), and its unusual bridge design, which incorporates a bridge base plate that doubles as pickup mounting plate on which three brass or steel saddles rest. In addition to these, one intangible ingredient—its 25½-inch scale length—also makes an impact on the guitar's final voice. Drastically alter any one of the above, and a Telecaster no longer sounds quite like a Telecaster, or the platonic form thereof, at least.

THE TELECASTER MYSTIQUE

Whereas incarnations of the electric guitar manufactured prior to 1950 were really born out of a popular music rooted in big-band jazz, the Telecaster was built to chase a different sonic ideal. As guitarist Bill Kirchen puts it, "Leo Fender was plying the waters of that fantastic country music scene on the West Coast in the late '40s and early '50s, and you know . . . it's kind of reverse engineering. Old country music sounds like a Telecaster, so it's hard to say 'why does a Telecaster sound like that?' Rather than being in a big horn environment where it was supposed to sound like a saxophone, it was supposed to more sound like a banjo or a guitar. So to me, it stayed more true to that particular sonic territory of the guitar."

The versatility of this electric guitar does come through, though, in the very different voice available from its neck pickup (and yet another voice heard in the in-between setting with both pickups on, when the guitar is wired for this). The neck pickup, somewhat different in sound and construction from the bridge pickup, comes closer to duplicating the sound of an acoustic guitar than does the bridge pickup, which really sounds very little like an acoustic instrument. "The Telecaster has a purity of sound," says Jim Campilongo. "And, for me, if you looked up the definition of 'electric guitar,' the neck position would be that. It just sounds like an acoustic guitar that's amplified. It's really beautifully organic, and any other variations, like the Strat for example, have a nasal overtone."

(continued on page 141)

Redd Volkaert

Redd Volkaert's 1951 Nocaster.
Courtesy Redd Volkaert

Every inch the Texan both in speech and in attitude, Redd Volkaert actually acquired his twang and drawl in rural Canada. Born in New Westminster, British Columbia, he left home at seventeen for Saskatoon, Saskatchewan, then various parts of Alberta before roving south and eventually ending up in Texas. Long before crossing the border, though, Volkaert was messing heavily with his '58 Esquire, and the music. Working on the latter, he forged his own breed of searing twang by melding his beloved country and the inevitable rock 'n' roll. On the former, he did what most kids did in the mid-'70s and hacked some wood

out of an otherwise pristine vintage instrument to wedge a fatter pickup into the neck position. "I ruined it early on," he confesses. "I wanted to be a rock god. . . . I took a screwdriver and a hammer, like a fourteen-year-old genius, and made a big old gaping hole under there." First in was a Gibson P-90, but after seeing Roy Nichols come through Edmonton playing with Merle Haggard with a Charlie Christian pickup in the neck position of his own Telecaster, Volkaert ripped a Christian from an old lap steel and popped it into his Esquire, where it has remained ever since.

Aspiring rock god-dom gave way to the country music that was proving to be his true love, and in 1981 Volkaert joined traditional outfit the Prairie Fire Band, moving over to Danny Hopper and Country Spunk (featuring fiddle virtuoso Calvin Vollrath) a few years after that. Volkaert headed to California in 1986, where he landed some significant gigs but ultimately struggled to stay afloat financially, before drifting the way of all serious pickers to struggle even more, initially, in Nashville. Hard work and hot licks eventually paid the dues, though, and Volkaert landed a residency job with the

Don Kelly Band at the Stage Coach Lounge, a gig that had proved a springboard other successful pickers. While the four-year run with Kelly would help to secure Vokaert's reputation, his own springboard to more significant success came in 1997, when a country music legend called to ask him to replace one of his own early heroes.

In his stint with Merle Haggard, Volkaert was often praised as the most Ray Nichols–like of the Nichols replacements. And as such, he wowed audiences in parts farther afield than he had ever traveled before. In 2000, tiring of the "bubble-gum" nature of Nashville's popular music scene, Volkaert—though still touring with Haggard—relocated to Austin. He relates, "The crowds in Austin seem to accept people for their musical ability more than their clothes or lack of, hair or lack of, hats or lack of. . . ." The Haggard gig aside, Volkaert took his solo career from strength to strength (with several solid releases since the move to Austin, after his 1998 solo debut *Telewacker*) while also landing him sit-ins with, perhaps, one of the longest lists of eminently droppable names in the business, including Al Cooper, Johnny Paycheck,

Redd Volkaert

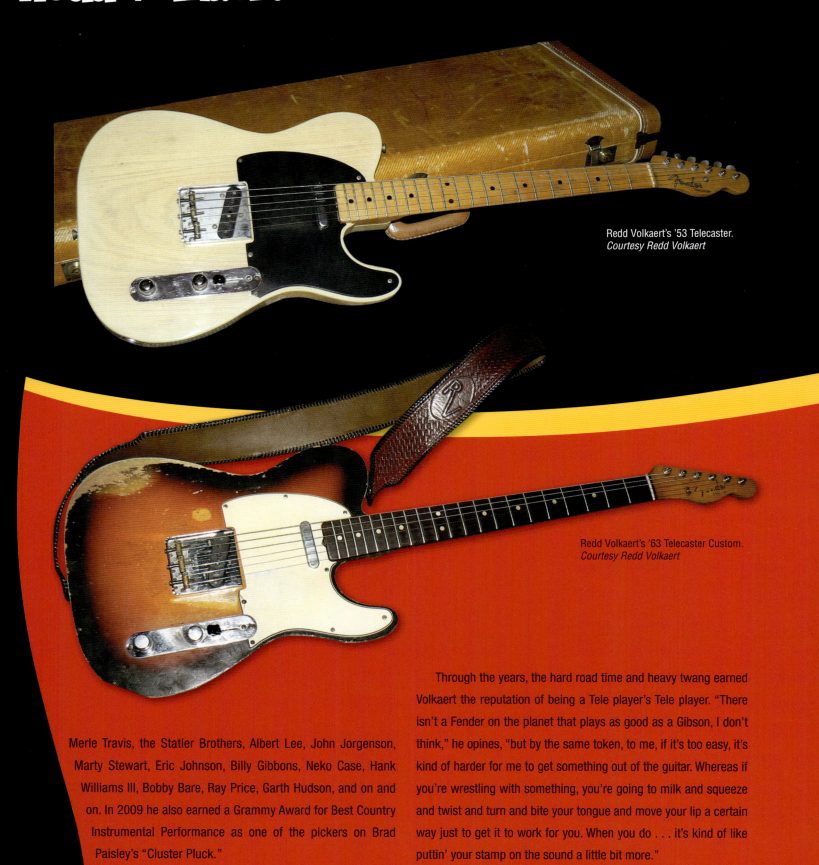

Redd Volkaert's '53 Telecaster.
Courtesy Redd Volkaert

Redd Volkaert's '63 Telecaster Custom.
Courtesy Redd Volkaert

Merle Travis, the Statler Brothers, Albert Lee, John Jorgenson, Marty Stewart, Eric Johnson, Billy Gibbons, Neko Case, Hank Williams III, Bobby Bare, Ray Price, Garth Hudson, and on and on. In 2009 he also earned a Grammy Award for Best Country Instrumental Performance as one of the pickers on Brad Paisley's "Cluster Pluck."

Through the years, the hard road time and heavy twang earned Volkaert the reputation of being a Tele player's Tele player. "There isn't a Fender on the planet that plays as good as a Gibson, I don't think," he opines, "but by the same token, to me, if it's too easy, it's kind of harder for me to get something out of the guitar. Whereas if you're wrestling with something, you're going to milk and squeeze and twist and turn and bite your tongue and move your lip a certain way just to get it to work for you. When you do . . . it's kind of like puttin' your stamp on the sound a little bit more."

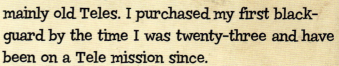

I've been accused of being born with a Tele in my hands. My mother says, "No, that's not the case"—although I wish I had, because I might be a better player having had it that much longer.

I got my first '58 Esquire when I was thirteen, and the hook went in! My dad brought it home one day and said, "I've got you a guitar like Buck Owens plays." Prior to that guitar, I had gotten a '58 Strat in a pawnshop with my paper route money.

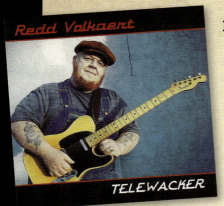

TELEWACKER

My dad made me make monthly payments on that Esquire (more paper route work) til I paid him for it. And to teach me about patience and staying mad at him, he let me play the guitar on Sundays for just twenty minutes. He said, "You can't take it anywhere til it's paid for, cause it's not yours yet, and if you lose it or break it, then I'm out all that money." He won it on a pool game, so I'd say he actually had zero in it.

After it was paid for, I used that guitar and didn't touch my Strat for at least ten years. I loved everything about that Esquire, even the hard edges of the body that made my arm sore after hours of practice every day.

After having the Esquire for a year, I cut a hole in the neck position with a hammer and a chisel to install a Gibson P-90. I dreamed I could sound like Don Rich and Roy Nichols—as well as Johnny Winter and Dickey Betts—with my new pickup!

From then on, any money I'd save, guess where it went? I left home at seventeen and moved 1,200 miles away to play six nights a week in a traveling bar band, so if I wasn't practicing, playing, or jamming, I'd be in the local music stores and pawnshops buying, selling, and trading, all the while trying to upgrade my gear and ultimately collect cool guitars—mainly old Teles. I purchased my first blackguard by the time I was twenty-three and have been on a Tele mission since.

Each Telecaster has a unique sound and feel to it, and to me, certain eras have a certain sound. I won't start a war by saying which era is best, but they definitely have distinct differences.

I believe Jimmy Bryant (the first Fender endorser), Buck Owens, and Don Rich, Mike Bloomfield, Muddy Waters, Roy Nichols, Jimmy Page, and James Burton were all on to something way back then. Even later on, folks like Roy Buchanan, Danny Gatton, and Bill Kirchen have all been bitten and smitten by the Tele bug. Just listen to any of these folks' recordings and you'll agree: the sound is exhilarating, exciting, and just cuts through the mix in an awesome way—never mind the mind-bending playing of all these Tele-nuts and hundreds more musicians that I could mention.

I think the Telecaster had a sound these guys loved, and they individually added a huge contribution to electric music.

Without the Telecaster, there would be a lot less music for the world to enjoy. There'd also be more crime on the streets from would-be guitar players who couldn't find the right guitar and turned to an alternative life on the dark side instead.

—Redd Volkaert, May 2012

Pete Anderson

Pete Anderson's 1959 Custom Esquire. This was one of Anderson's main guitars with Dwight Yoakam, used on many tours and played on at least four of Yoakam's early 1990s recordings. *Courtesy Pete Anderson and Kevin Sepriano*

In taking the crucial roles of both lead guitarist and producer on Dwight Yoakam's formative recordings and tours, Pete Anderson played a major part in bringing "real" back to country in the late 1980s and early '90s and beyond—and it's no surprise that he did it on a Telecaster. Anderson was born in Detroit, Michigan, in 1948, and first gained a love of music from the country and Elvis records that his father played at home. After graduating from college, Anderson played hardcore urban blues in several Detroit bands and eventually moved west in the early 1970s to pursue a career as a musician. Paying his dues around Los Angeles

and further afield with the band Hollywood Gumbo and others, Anderson drifted from the blues back to hard-twang country. In the early '80s, he met Dwight Yoakam and forged a partnership that became one of the most potent in the history of country music.

Yoakam had moved to Los Angeles after rejecting the pop-country pabulum that was the stock-in-trade of Nashville in the early '80s. He forged a Bakersfield-influenced sound infused with the hard-driving honky-tonk and authentic twang of artists such as Buck Owens and the Buckaroos, and found an able and willing compadre in Anderson. His first full-length release, *Guitars, Cadillacs, Etc, Etc,* of 1986, is widely hailed as having launched the "New Country" movement (alongside Steve Earle's *Guitar Town* of the same year), and it did so in large part by reminding listeners how powerful a few great Tele licks can be. Licks, for example, like Anderson's seminal playing on the title track.

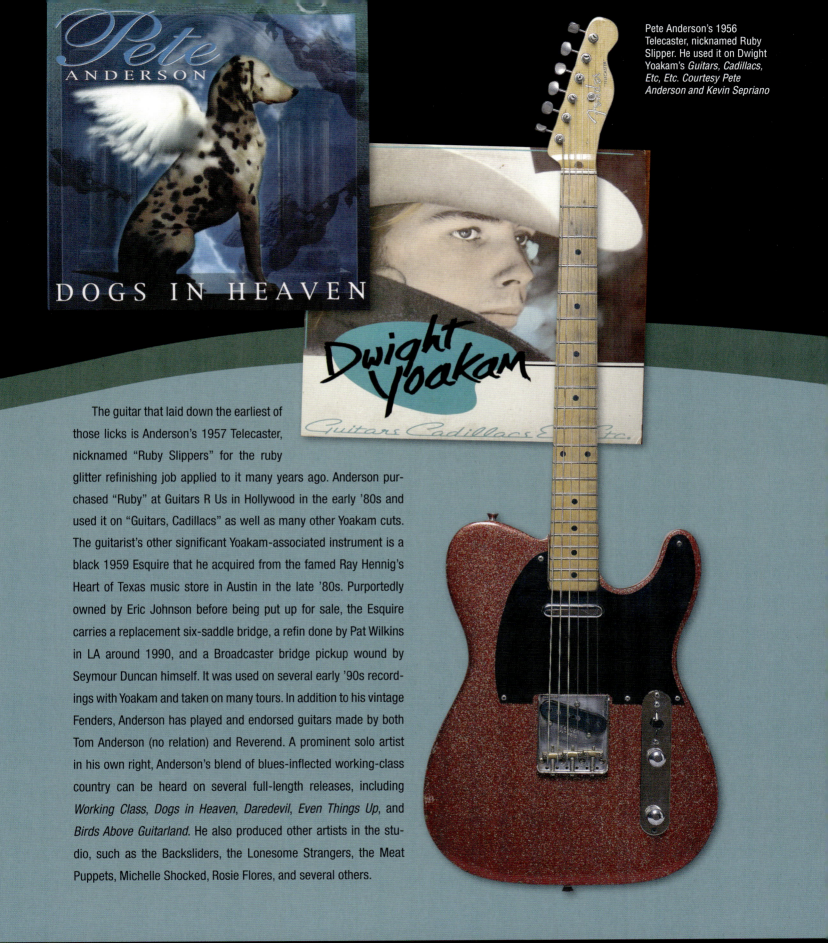

Pete Anderson's 1956 Telecaster, nicknamed Ruby Slipper. He used it on Dwight Yoakam's *Guitars, Cadillacs, Etc, Etc. Courtesy Pete Anderson and Kevin Sepriano*

The guitar that laid down the earliest of those licks is Anderson's 1957 Telecaster, nicknamed "Ruby Slippers" for the ruby glitter refinishing job applied to it many years ago. Anderson purchased "Ruby" at Guitars R Us in Hollywood in the early '80s and used it on "Guitars, Cadillacs" as well as many other Yoakam cuts. The guitarist's other significant Yoakam-associated instrument is a black 1959 Esquire that he acquired from the famed Ray Hennig's Heart of Texas music store in Austin in the late '80s. Purportedly owned by Eric Johnson before being put up for sale, the Esquire carries a replacement six-saddle bridge, a refin done by Pat Wilkins in LA around 1990, and a Broadcaster bridge pickup wound by Seymour Duncan himself. It was used on several early '90s recordings with Yoakam and taken on many tours. In addition to his vintage Fenders, Anderson has played and endorsed guitars made by both Tom Anderson (no relation) and Reverend. A prominent solo artist in his own right, Anderson's blend of blues-inflected working-class country can be heard on several full-length releases, including *Working Class*, *Dogs in Heaven*, *Daredevil*, *Even Things Up*, and *Birds Above Guitarland*. He also produced other artists in the studio, such as the Backsliders, the Lonesome Strangers, the Meat Puppets, Michelle Shocked, Rosie Flores, and several others.

Jerry Donahue

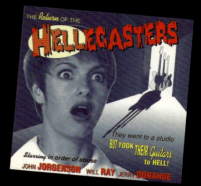

Although he has often played Tele-style guitars by other makers, notably his signature model Peavey Omniac JD and Fret-King Black Label model, as well as going against type on a modified Stratocaster, Jerry Donahue remains a formative, and formidable, Tele-slinger, and an undisputed entrant into the annals of hot-licks Telecaster players. He is accomplished in a wide range of playing styles, but Donahue is best known for his fast country, electric-folk, and country-rock playing, and particularly his slick tricks and acrobatic bends, both on the fingerboard and behind the nut. In short, Donahue's playing epitomizes what many guitar fans think of when "hot Tele" comes to mind, and he has blown the minds of many for the better part of four decades.

Donahue made his jump to the big leagues after he moved to England in 1970. He was often thought of as a British-based guitarist, but he's a Yank, born in Manhattan in 1946 and raised in Los Angeles. With big-band saxophonist Sam Donahue for a father and actress Patricia Donahue for a mother, Jerry was encouraged in his artistic endeavors right from the start and showed a prowess on the guitar from an early age. After moving from emulating players like Chet Atkins, Duane Eddy, and Hank Marvin in his teens, Donahue evolved his own amalgam of styles based on hot country and swing, with some Celtic and broader folk influences thrown in. He was right at home, therefore, with the British band Fatheringay, and his move to join the iconic folk-rockers Fairport Convention in 1973 seemed a natural progression. Donahue helped to maintain that band's instrumental prowess for four albums until Donahue moved on again after 1975's *Rising for the Moon*.

Post-Fairport, Donahue's career has included recorded and live performances with a stunning list of major artists, including Elton John, George Harrison, the Beach Boys, Roy Orbison, Nanci Griffith, and several others. Donahue's debut solo album, 1986's *Telecast-ing*, is a perennial entrant on critics' "best Tele recordings" lists, and was reissued as *Tele-casting Recast* in 1999, with added material. As if one blinding Tele warrior wasn't enough, Donahue formed the Hellecasters in 1990 along with Will Ray and John Jorgenson, unleashing three blinding, bending speed freaks on unsuspecting guitar fans.

(continued from page 133)

1952 Telecaster. *Fretted Americana*

Part of the Telecaster's tonal magic certainly springs from the player, and the fact that the instrument itself is a pure and uncluttered sonic template. The Tele's simplicity forces the performer to strive for a certain sonic versatility in their very playing style, achieving it with the fingers, pick, and other cornerstone elements of "playing the guitar."

"A lot of those guys—I call 'em whiners," says Redd Volkaert, former Merle Haggard sideman and twangster extraordinaire, "they're used to playing a certain way with their hand always in the one spot on their [other make of guitar]. They're used to one thing. And on a Telecaster, if you play up by the neck it's a completely different sound; play in the middle it changes completely again; back by the bridge it's bitey and gnarly. You use that kind of like you would use an effect, you know, for what you need on the song and all of that. So in that way it's a lot more versatile. You take one of the [other make of guitars], I don't care where you hit 'em, they all sound the same, and you pass it to the next guy, it's going to sound the same when he plays it. Where a Telecaster, I think, is a lot more versatile depending on who plays it, and how they play."

Solo artists and former Commander Cody guitarist Bill Kirchen concurs. "The Tele always strikes me as the bicycle of electric guitars: it's the most efficient way to get from point A to point B. And it's also the most bang-for-the-buck sound per pound, the least amount of material, almost, to get all that you need in an electric guitar. It always strikes me when I pick it up—and over 99 percent of my career has been on a Tele—and whenever I pick up a rock 'n' roll guitar, something with big fat frets, low action, and a big fat tone with a lot of distortion maybe, you know, it's almost too easy to play. I certainly don't want to denigrate the whole genre of rock guitar, because there are plenty of great players, but it almost seems to me like you have to wrestle with the Tele, you've got to work to get the sound out of it. And . . . there's a particular culture of hot-licks Tele playing that I think has been dictated, to a certain extent, just by the simplicity of the guitar."

From a tonal perspective, much of the Telecaster's mystique clearly has to do with its purity, clarity, and harmonic complexity, which are joint products of the ingredients that go into it—its design, the wood used to construct it, and the hardware and electronic components mounted to it. As such, many Tele fanatics will tell you that this guitar is the ultimate electric for playing clean. It drives the amp in a way that gives you the full resonant and overtone-laden potential of the guitar itself, and yet segues into optimum harmonic saturation when pushed into overdrive. With that in mind, let's break down some of the crucial components that contribute to this magic.

ELEMENTS OF THE TELECASTER DESIGN

Aspects of the Telecaster's basic design have, naturally, been covered throughout the course of this book, but it's worth summing them up here. By "design," I mean the on-paper template, specifications that are largely intangible rather than the material ingredients, but which nevertheless contributes to the guitar's sound and function. While they don't have the romance of a well-aged tonewood or a vintage pickup, these intangibles form a considerable part of the cornerstone of the Telecaster's tone.

The Solid "Slab" Body

This ingredient might seem a "given" since it forms the major part of the premise for putting the Telecaster on its pedestal as "first production solid-body electric," but its contribution to the tonal formula can't be ignored. Aside from the sonic properties of the common tonewoods used in Telecaster bodies, which will be discussed in their own right further along, the sheer method of construction of a guitar with a slab-styled body made from one or two pieces of the same wood, with minimal use of glue and lack of adornments, lends its own tonal characteristics to the instrument. It is difficult to quantify such factors, but suffice it to say that such a design allows a relatively unencumbered vibration of the wood itself, and since there is only one wood involved, it presents the pure characteristics of that wood. The end result is heard in the Telecaster's clarity and tonal purity, which is emphasized by other elements of the design, but is certainly anchored here.

Also, while some players will talk of a Tele as "lacking sustain," they are often actually hearing the single-coil pickups and the fact that these guitars are predominantly used for "cleaner" musical styles (though Teles have certainly made plenty of great rock music, too). Often, comparing both types unplugged, a good Telecaster will sustain longer than almost any popular set-neck, humbucker-loaded guitar you might compare it to.

(continued on page 146)

1952 Telecaster.
Fretted Americana

Custom Shop 60th Anniversary Broadcaster.
Fender Musical Instruments Corporation

Chrissie Hynde

Chrissie Hynde has wielded numerous Telecasters, but her blue model with a mirror pickguard has long been a signature of the Pretenders. *Ebet Roberts/Redferns/ Getty Images*

After struggling through her efforts to kick-start a career amidst London's punk scene of the late '70s, Chrissie Hynde emerged in the early '80s, Telecaster in hand, to offer some of the most infectiously tuneful creations of the early post-punk years. Born in Akron, Ohio, in 1951, Hynde was the archetypal high-school outsider and consummate music fan, irresistibly drawn to the excitement she perceived in the rock music world and, inevitably, her own part in the midst of it all.

While attending college at Kent State University in Ohio, Hynde briefly formed a band with Mark Mothersbaugh, later of Devo, then packed up and headed east to London, where the real action seemed to be in the early '70s. Even before forming the Pretenders, Hynde was involved in musical projects—often precursors to other punk and underground bands that would later emerge—with Mick Jones (the Clash), Jon Moss (Culture Club), Steve Strange, members of the Damned, Tony James (Generation X), and future Sex Pistols manager Malcolm McLaren. Dave Hill, the owner of London indie label Real Records, took Hynde under his wing in 1978 and helped her form a band. Bassist Pete Farndon was first into the fray, followed by guitarist James Honeyman-Scott and drummer Martin Chambers—and the Pretenders were born.

Early in 1979, the band logged an early hit with a cover of the Kinks' "Stop Your Sobbing." The eponymous debut album released later that year received wide critical acclaim and reasonable commercial success, and issued hit singles in "Brass in Pocket" and

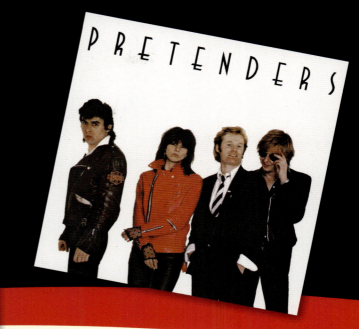

"Kid," as well as several other standout tracks. In the early '80s *Pretenders II* was another strong showing, with solid singles in "Talk of the Town" and "Message of Love," but it failed to catch fire like the debut album had nearly two years before. Adding to the strains of "the difficult second album," interpersonal issues within the band, exacerbated by Farndon's drug abuse, took a toll on the band. Farndon was fired on June 14, 1982—purportedly a crushing blow for the bassist—but more significantly, guitarist Honeyman-Scott was found dead of heart failure just two days later, following an apparent cocaine overdose. Less than a year later, drugs claimed Farndon's life, too.

Although such a twofold tragedy would be enough to destroy most bands, the Pretenders got back to the grindstone pretty quickly. Hynde and Chambers were joined by Rockpile guitarist Billy Bremner and Big Country bassist Tony Butler to record the hit single "Back on the Chain Gang," released in November of 1982. A song that pairs an upbeat arrangement to the melancholy tale about getting back to work after the death of Honeyman-Scott, it appeared on the band's next album, 1984's *Learning to Crawl*, alongside another hit dedicated to the former Pretender guitarist, the haunting ballad "2000 Miles." In the years that followed, the Pretenders continued to enjoy steady success, and Hynde also turned her hand to several guest appearances and side projects.

From the start, Hynde's own guitar duties were primarily to cover the rhythm, while Honeyman-Scott laid down tasty hooks and solos that displayed surprising maturity and a keen melodic sense for his young years (he was just twenty-five at the time of his death). Even so, Hynde's blue Telecaster mirror pickguard has long been a signature of the band, both sonically and visually. Not that the instrument has been entirely sheltered from lead duties: Honeyman-Scott borrowed Hynde's Tele to record the catchy intro riff and solo to the song "Kid," and can be seen playing a white-guard early '60s Telecaster with rosewood fingerboard (still with its original blonde finish and white pickguard) in photos shot in the studio from about that time. Later, Hynde also took gold and silver sparkle Telecasters on the road, as well as a more originally equipped early '60s Tele.

The 25½-Inch Scale Length

Guitar-maker Ralph Novak, in his lecture to the 1995 convention of the Guild of American Luthiers, stated that, of all factors that affect a guitar's tone, "scale length comes first because the harmonic content of the final tone produced by the instrument begins with the string. Factors such as structure and materials can only act as 'filters' to tone; they can't add anything, they only modify input. Therefore, if the harmonic structure is not present in the string tone, it won't exist in the final tone." Scale length is, therefore, a cornerstone of design for any thoughtful maker, and one of the first decisions to be settled when conceiving the voice of an instrument. The fact that Leo Fender settled on the 25½-inch scale for the Telecaster (and the Stratocaster and Jazzmaster that would follow) seems, in fact, to have been a happy accident, but the choice served to emphasize many of the other sonic characteristics that he was hoping to achieve with this guitar.

Put simply, the longer the "speaking length" of any guitar's strings (that is, its scale length, the distance between bridge saddle and nut slot), the more distance there is between the strings' harmonic points. The result is that relatively longer scale lengths have a greater presence of sonic qualities often described as "shimmer" or "sparkle" or "chime." Leo copied the scale length of a Gretsch archtop guitar when designing the guitar that would become the Telecaster, but it turns out that the 25½-inch scale length accentuates the qualities he was looking for more than if he'd chosen to model the guitar after a 24¾-inch Gibson.

It so happens that Fender's narrow single-coil pickups, his bridge configuration, and the bolt-on maple neck all further accentuate harmonic clarity and high-end presence, so the total package really is working together toward Fender's desired tonal ends. But, as Novak put it, "if the harmonic structure is not present in the string tone, it won't exist in the final tone."

The slightly longer Fender scale length also increases the string tension, making the strings feel a bit firmer to the fingertips. This is particularly true on the Telecaster, which lacks the Stratocaster's spring-loaded vibrato bridge and the somewhat forgiving feel that this component brings with it, particularly when a player is bending strings. The relative tautness of the Telecaster's strings is perhaps one other ingredient that has endeared it to country pickers, who can find shorter-scale guitars, or Stratocasters, a little too "floppy" when they dig in.

The 7¼-inch fingerboard radius on vintage Fender guitars (the curve at which the top of the fingerboard is milled) also contributes greatly to the guitar's playing feel, and to some extent has always dictated how it was approached. Smaller than the radius used on any other popular model of guitar, this tight circle results in more curve to the surface of the fingerboard, and in one sense, a neck that can feel extremely natural and comfortable in the hand, for basic open chords played in the lower positions in particular. The rounder the radius, though, the harder it can be to bend strings on the fingerboard, or to do so without "choking out," a phenomenon whereby the curvature of the fingerboard mutes a bent string and causes it to die out prematurely.

1952 Telecaster. *Fretted Americana*

(continued from page 142)

Obviously, plenty of players do bend strings successfully on the Tele, and the extremes of the "faux-steel bend" are a big part of country guitar playing in general. But the 7¼-inch fingerboard radius (compared to a flatter twelve inches on Gibsons, for example) might, in part, force Tele players into the more staccato, rapid-fire playing style that epitomizes hot country picking. "They don't have a tremendous amount of sustain," says Bill Kirchen, "so let's throw a few more notes in there! You get into the culture of hot licks, and of course there's hot licks playing on all kinds of guitars, but there's a particular culture of hot-licks Tele playing that I think has been dictated, to a certain extent, just by the design of the guitar."

The Bolt-Neck Construction

While the neck itself, the wood screws, and the mounting plate that hold it in place are all certainly "tangible" components, it is probably best to consider the so-called "bolt neck" in theory for its contribution to the Telecaster's voice, regardless of the wood and hardware that comprise it. Leo Fender adopted the bolt-on neck—which was at first derided by some traditionalists in the early 1950s—for its ease of construction and ease of repair, but this element of the Telecaster design brings a specific component to the guitar's tone, too.

A well-cut and tightly fitted screwed-on neck joint (as the Telecaster is, with wood screws rather than actual "bolts") can easily be as tight, and even tighter, than a glued neck joint, in terms of neck-wood-on-pocket-wood pressure. However tight such a joint might be, though, the neck and body woods remain the slightest bit decoupled, thanks to the inevitable presence of air gaps—microscopic though they may be—between the two surfaces, due to natural inconsistencies in wood grain, dimples, or irregularities in the finish, and so on. In reality, most vintage Fender neck pockets and neck heels are not cut particularly tightly in the first place anyway, and these joints are often not as tight as those on guitars made by many skilled contemporary luthiers. In any case, even if it has the potential to be tighter, the bolt-on neck is not as seamless a joint as

Neck plate of a 1954 Telecaster. *Guitar courtesy of Elderly Instruments, photo Dave Matchette*

a well-executed glued-on neck (or "set neck"), which has glue forming a bond between neck heel and body pocket, and this leads to noticeable changes in tone and response.

As heard in a traditional Telecaster, some sonic characteristics of the bolt-on neck joint include a certain percussive "snap" and "spank" in the tone, a more clearly defined sense of pick attack in the note, and an increase in that bright, shimmery characteristic that I can only think to define as "jangle" or "chime." While a glued neck joint contributes to an increased sense of warmth and depth on many set-neck guitars—simply put, more "hair" around the note—and a corresponding blurring of the attack and decay, a Telecaster often exhibits a distinctive "pop" in the pick or finger attack that is heard as if layered atop the body of the note, a sonic entity that is separate from the sound that tails off into the decay of that note. A big part of this comes to us courtesy of the bolt-on neck joint.

(continued on page 154)

1968 Telecaster. *Doug Youland/Willie's American Guitars*

Jim Campilongo

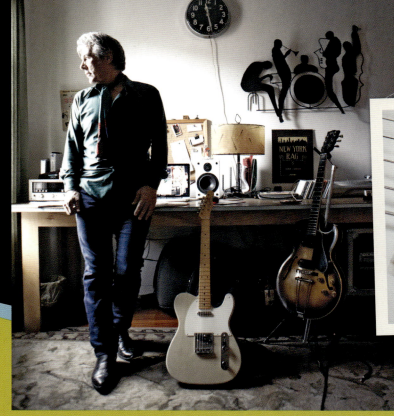

Jim Campilongo and his trusty 1959 Telecaster with top-loader bridge. *JR Delia*

Top-loader bridge without the side bolsters. *Fender Musical Instruments Corporation*

Although he originally hailed from the opposite coast and was born in the year that the senior Tele-wrangler began his professional career (1958), Jim Campilongo is often considered an heir apparent to the late Roy Buchanan, in musical spirit and unbridled eclecticism, as well as for sheer chops. Ask the San Francisco–born Campilongo what first inspired him (without postulating this rather flattering theory up front), and it's interesting to hear that there might be some sense to the notion. "Roy Buchanan. Absolutely," is the unequivocal reply. "I had listened to quite a bit of guitar even before I played guitar. Probably the first guitar line I really went bananas over was the 45 RPM version of [The Beatles'] 'Revolution.' It's like a 'Johnny B. Goode' kind of thing, but super distorted. I just went nuts over that, which obviously isn't a Tele, but when I heard Roy Buchanan—and I think I was twelve and I hadn't played yet—the sound just called my name. I think a lot of people share that."

Soon, however, Campilongo was indeed playing the guitar himself, and with a passion. Studying with noted Bay Area guitarist and teacher Bunnie Gregoire, he was schooled in everything from jazz to pop to folk, and began playing out in local clubs in his late teens. In the mid-'90s he gigged and recorded with the 10 Gallon Cats, but departed that outfit in 1998 to more fully embrace the full breadth of his own eclecticism, first expressed in the solo album *Table for One*. All the while, Campilongo had been teaching guitar to local students to make ends meet, and, having already embraced the Telecaster, one such lesson afforded him the opportunity to acquire another. "I taught this guy for like three years, and it got kind of tough—he was struggling," says Campilongo. "Anyways, he was a guitar collector, and one day he brought over this Telecaster. I had a Tele already . . . but I got his and put it on my chest, and all of a sudden it was like some flaws in my technical ability were eliminated. It was like I could play way more effortlessly and more dynamically, and if that's called 'falling in love with a guitar,' I guess that's what happened." Noting his

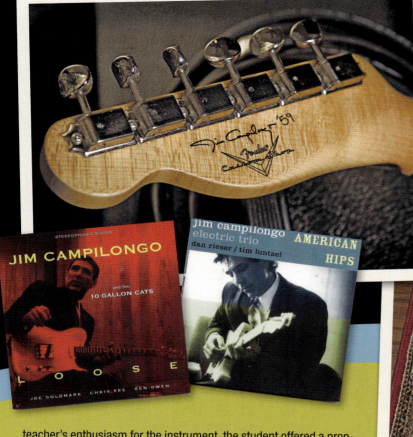

Custom Shop Jim Campilongo Signature Telecaster.
Fender Musical Instruments Corporation

teacher's enthusiasm for the instrument, the student offered a proposition: "He said, 'You know, if I ever learn guitar, I'll give you that Telecaster.' So I'm like, 'This figures!'"

As fortune would have it, though, the student who struggled on guitar one day brought in a Fender Precision Bass, asked his teacher to show him a few walking lines on the four-string instead, and picked it up with surprising ease. The bargain long forgotten by Campilongo, the newly christened bassist showed up one day with the Telecaster of his dreams and handed it over. "About eight months after I got it somebody tells me, 'Wow, that's a top loader!'" the guitarist recalls. "And he says, 'Top-loaders don't sound as good.' I told him, 'Really, but I love this guitar,' and I also really liked that it was a great writing desk, you could just turn it over and write on the back because there are no holes back there." For the following eighteen years, this blonde 1959 white-'guard "top-loader" Telecaster with maple neck was the tool behind Campilongo's blistering performances, both live and on record.

Some six years into his ownership of the instrument, a shorted bridge pickup would be re-wound, and over the following years several re-frets and considerable playing wear would usher it toward the inevitable retirement. "Basically, that guitar has been played to death. There are huge holes and crevices on the neck—it's really scalloped. . . . There are certain notes that you literally can't bend out of." Having segued through a T-style replacement by custom builder Chihoe Hahn, Campilongo now plays the Fender Custom Shop Jim Campilongo Signature Telecaster, a blonde top-loader like his beloved '59, crafted to the precise specs of the vintage original, without the divots and extreme playing wear.

In 2002 Campilongo took his bag east to New York City and became a fixture on that scene. In addition to recording and touring the United States and Europe, his own group, the Jim Campilongo Electric Trio (with Stephan Crump and Tony Mason), maintained a Monday night residency at the Living Room in NYC for several years. Campilongo also performed and recorded with the side project he set up in 2003, the Little Willies, a band that also featured Norah Jones, Dan Rieser, Lee Alexander, and Richard Julian. In demand as a session guitarist and sideman, Campilongo has also gigged and recorded with J.J. Cale, Norah Jones, Martha Wainwright, Gillian Welch, Teddy Thompson, Cake, Bright Eyes, and several others.

Marty Stuart

Marty Stuart slings the '52 Esquire that once belonged to Mick Ronson. Jason Moore/*ZUMA Press Inc./Alamy*

Like a handful of other Telecaster stars, Marty Stuart began his musical career as a child prodigy, and on an entirely different instrument, segueing smoothly to Tele-mastery the way so many country and bluegrass players have done over the years. Stuart was born in Philadelphia, Mississippi, in 1958 and took up mandolin and guitar at an early age. Displaying a prodigious talent, Stuart was playing professionally by his pre-adolescent years. Stuart landed a recording date with Lester Flatt at the age of thirteen, and was on the road with the legendary bluegrass guitarist soon after. From Flatt's band, Stuart worked as a hired sideman with Vassar Clements, Doc Watson, Johnny Cash, and others, before stretching out as a solo artist in his own right. Since the release of his self-titled debut solo album in 1986, and a notable string of country hits in the early '90s, Stuart has won five Grammy Awards and several other accolades.

A self-described "hillbilly rocker," Stuart has the chops of a top-tier hot-Tele player, but adds a certain grit and swagger to his playing. In aid of that tone, he has been a Telecaster player right from the start, and his guitar collection includes examples with some powerful pedigree to help him along.

In 1980, Stuart visited Susie White, the wife of late Byrds guitarist Clarence White, to ostensibly purchase another guitar that she was selling. After asking about White's original B-Bender guitar, Susie allowed him to play it, then offered it up for sale. Much to his own surprise, Stuart departed with one of country-rock's most storied instruments, and he has frequently recorded and toured with it ever since. "I've never considered it my guitar, really. It's his," Stuart told Rusty Russell for *Vintage Guitar* magazine in 2004, "and now it kind of has a life of its own. The spring gets dry and squeaks, so I spray WD-40 on it now and then, but I've never cleaned it. All the dirt inside and behind the strings is the original dirt. We call it 'Clarence.'"

Another Stuart favorite is a 1952 Esquire that once belonged to Mick Ronson, and two original Paisley Telecasters from the late '60s also adorn his collection. When we say "collection," though, we're not talking glass cases and climate-controlled vaults. As Stuart told *Guitar Player*, "They're still working guitars. I play every single guitar I have. They have to earn their keep." No doubt Leo Fender—and Clarence White, and Mick Ronson—would want it that way.

Bill Frisell

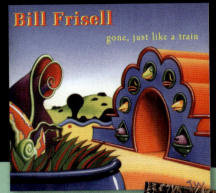

While the Telecaster may seem rather basic for a versatile performer like Bill Frisell, the guitarist cites its simplicity as its chief virtue. Here, he performs at the Cheltenham Jazz Festival in Cheltenham, England, in May 2008. *Steve Thorne/Redferns/Getty Images*

*T*he *New Yorker* once noted, "Bill Frisell plays the guitar like Miles Davis played the trumpet; in the hands of such radical thinkers, their instruments simply become different animals." It's hard to beat that for a definition of the otherwise indefinable style of this elusive Tele-meister. Often categorized as a jazzer, Frisell has offered stirring support to rocking artists such as Elvis Costello, David Sylvian, Ginger Baker, and Lucinda Williams. Of course, he has also logged his time with jazz greats, including his work with Jim Hall, Dave Holland, Elvin Jones, and the occasional trio made up of Ron Carter and Paul Motian. Frisell has played other guitars, but the Tele has returned time and again as his go-to.

Frisell's first significant break in the NYC jazz scene came when young jazz-guitar star Pat Metheny recommended Bill to fill in for a session that he couldn't make. The gig resulted in Paul Motian's *Psalms* album for EMC Records, and landed Frisell a steady job as a house guitarist of sorts for the prominent jazz label. In 1982, Frisell recorded his first outing as a solo artist in his own right, again for EMC, and since that time—he has never looked back.

He has owned and played several standout Telecasters throughout his career—including original examples from 1966 and 1974, as well as a Fender Custom Shop Relic Telecaster—but he doesn't seem particular about vintage specs or high-end models. "Actually, my main Tele is a Mexican one," Frisell told *Fender News* in 2011. "It was like $500, and it's great! That's what I've been playing for the last few months. One time I tried to figure out how many Fender guitars I've had in my life, and it was kind of horrifying!" And if the Telecaster seems a rather basic instrument for such a versatile and eclectic player, Frisell's arguments for its merits destroy such thinking. "They're so simple, and everything just works. . . . I can get from where it can almost sound like an acoustic guitar, or it can sound like a big, fat hollow-body guitar. Or it can have a 'stereotypical' Tele sound. People associate them with that 'twangy' thing, but they have this amazing clear low end. Just the range of what can happen with them is so extreme, without having eight-hundred pick-ups on it. . . . If something breaks on it, you can almost fix it with a pocket knife."

Vince Gill

Vince Gill performs in concert in Hollywood, Florida, in 2007. *Michael Bush/Alamy*

A consummate Tele-wrangler, Vince Gill is a player with an immense talent that is often too easy to overlook, given the ease and nonchalance with which he wields the blinding licks that have stopped other guitar greats in their tracks. An accomplished vocalist and songwriter, Gill is a truly gifted instrumentalist in his own right, rather than a mere "frontman," and therefore, he presents the entire package rather than just the "face" on the hits.

Gill was born in 1957 in Norman, Oklahoma, where he was encouraged from a young age to pursue his talent by a lawyer father who was also a part-time musician. Gill initially moved east to Louisville,

Since early in his career, Vince Gill's main instrument has been a '53 black guard that he bought in 1980 near Oklahoma City. *Rusty Russell*

Kentucky, to join the band Bluegrass Alliance. He was picked up by Ricky Skaggs for the band Boon Creek, then finally made the trek west to join ace fiddler Byron Berline's band Sundance.

Shortly after, Gill made the most notable leap of his early career, and was picked up as the new lead singer and guitarist for the band Pure Prairie League in 1979, with whom he recorded the crossover hit "Let Me Love You Tonight" a year later. After leaving Pure Prairie League in 1981, Gill did a stint with Rodney Crowell's band, the Cherry Bombs, before settling in Nashville to pursue a solo career.

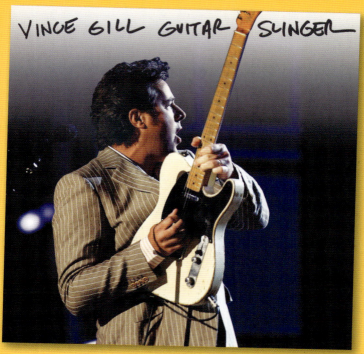

Since signing to MCA in 1983 Gill has enjoyed steady and ever-ascending success. He has earned twenty-one Grammy Awards and eighteen CMA Awards, and in 2007 he was inducted into the Country Music Hall of Fame. He has also been constantly in demand as a collaborator and session artist, performing with Mark Knopfler, Dolly Parton, Reba McEntire, Patty Loveless, Emmylou Harris, Rosanne Cash, Joe Bonamassa, and several others. For all the hits as a "traditional" Nashville artist, though (and there have been plenty—Gill has landed more than forty songs on *Billboard*'s Hot Country Songs chart, and sold more than 26 million albums), as his career progresses, the Tele slinger seems to want more and more to return to his roots as an instrumentalist. He told *Vintage*

Guitar magazine's John Heidt in 2011, "The older I get, the more I want to play . . . most people, at first glance, perceive me as a country Tele player, but there's a whole lot more influences than that in my playing and I think it's starting to come out." Gill's versatility as a guitarist was perhaps best displayed in his several appearances on the bill for Eric Clapton's Crossroads Festival, where he took the stage with artists like Albert Lee, Keb' Mo', James Burton, and Clapton himself. The guitars-first stance is also heavily in evidence on his 2011 studio album, *Guitar Slinger*.

Since early in his career, Gill's main instrument has been a 1953 black-guard Telecaster. Another notable Tele in the impressive Gill collection is a 1950 Broadcaster, which he played on the Grammy-winning duet "Cluster Pluck" with Brad Paisley, from the latter's album *Play*. These Teles, and other Gill favorites, were saved from the floods that severely damaged several instruments in his collection when his Nashville storage facility flooded in 2010. Fortunately, the guitarist's most-played instruments were still in the tour van when the disaster struck.

(continued from page 147)

The bold swamp ash grain visible through the finish of a 1954 Esquire. *Fretted Americana*

BASIC INGREDIENTS

Every single component of this guitar plays a part in shaping its tone, so let's examine the common body and neck woods, hardware, and electronics to see how they contribute to the glorious tone machine that is the Telecaster.

Body Woods

Although a few early Esquires were made with pine bodies, and some Fender reissues and boutique Tele-clone makers have turned again to that wood, ash really is the classic wood of the 1950s Telecaster. "Swamp ash," as it is known in its more desirable form, is harvested from the lower portions of ash trees grown in the wetlands of the southern United States, and it is very different from harder, denser northern ash. A good, well-aged piece of swamp ash will even exhibit different resonant characteristics, and usually be significantly lighter, than timber cut from the upper portions of the very same wetlands ash tree.

The tonal magic of a good piece of swamp ash is largely attributable to the porosity of the wood, itself attributable to the conditions in which it grows. Timber below or near the surface of a swamp or wetland absorbs greater quantities of water than higher parts of the tree, which causes the pores to swell. As the wood dries, these pores empty of water, leaving myriad tiny air pockets—and therefore, a relatively low density—in a wood that is nevertheless strong and workable.

"Generally speaking," says Chris Fleming, a master builder with the Fender Custom Shop, "ash can have a warm, round sound, with a bit of a focused cut to it. It can also be, depending on the guitar, a bit shrill, a bit snarly. But the best Teles sound wonderful; they're round sounding, they're rich, they're very loud, and they cut through a band very well." Dennis Fano, a builder best known for his Alt de Facto range that blends vintage Fender and Gibson specs and looks, adds, "Swamp ash is typically very 'alive' and has a brighter tone than mahogany or alder."

*1956 Esquire.
Fretted Americana*

It is clear from Leo Fender's goals in developing the Telecaster, however, that he was nearly as concerned with cost, supply, and ease of manufacture and repair as he was with pure tone. Although he would have valued the fact that swamp ash bodies produced a sound that contributed toward his aims for the guitar, this timber's tonal properties might not have been paramount among his reasons for selecting it. "Being a very frugal and production-minded guy," says Fleming, "he looked for woods that he could get cheaply and sustainably. At that time ash was a good candidate."

Sustainability of supplies was one of the major reasons Fender moved to the second most significant Telecaster body wood on many guitars made nearly a decade after the model's introduction. In the late 1950s good ash became more difficult to get. Older, well-dried stocks were being used up, and newer timber was often proving denser and heavier. Fender continued to use ash on most blonde Teles and Esquires and the early sunburst Custom models of the late '50s, but from the early '60s until the early '70s, most custom-color and sunburst Teles

and Esquires were made with alder, the primary wood used for Stratocasters from the latter part of the mid-'50s onward. This division of wood types according to guitar finish points out one motivating force in the lumber shed: Fender liked the way that ash's broad, attractive grain looked beneath a transparent blonde finish, whereas the fine, less dramatic grain exhibited by most alder was less appealing to the eye.

It also begs a question regarding "classic" Fender tonewoods: if swamp ash is considered the archetypal Telecaster body wood, why didn't the company—adept at promotion even in that innocent age—brag about its use in the guitars? As much as vintage aficionados rave about a great piece of swamp ash, there's no mention of body-wood species at all in Fender promotional literature from the '50s and early '60s. To the best of this author's knowledge, in fact, the first mention of body woods appears in the post-CBS Fender advertisements for the "Groovy Naturals" Thinline models, noting that they are available either in ash or mahogany.

Regarding the move to alder, and any considerations at early Fender of the tonewoods used for body construction, Chris Fleming speculates: "I think it was more important to have a steady source of acceptable-quality wood to put into their products, and one of the main reasons that they went to alder was that it was probably cheaper and more readily available." Even so, alder does have slightly different sonic characteristics than swamp ash, and tends to have a strong, clear, full-bodied, and well-balanced sound, often with muscular lower-mids, firm lows, and sweet highs. In many ways it might be considered a more "open" sounding wood than swamp ash, one capable of producing a guitar with a more versatile and better balanced tonal palette, although it has never quite been considered "the classic Tele tonewood."

Several smaller contemporary Tele-style guitar makers are producing guitars with bodies made of pine, or "sugar pine" as it is often called, and Fender has also produced reissues of the early prototypes in pine. Originally done in homage to the first Esquires made by Fender during the development of the model, this is now seen as a viable alternative, and another variable beneath the broad umbrella of Telecaster tonal options.

(continued on page 158)

D. Boon

D. Boon and his Telecaster Custom onstage at Swisher Gym, Jacksonville University, November 23, 1985. The Minutemen were touring in support of R.E.M. Boon died one month later in a van accident. *Margaret Griffis (margaretgriffis.com)*

Formed in San Pedro, California, in 1980, the Minutemen were one of the more original bands on the West Coast punk scene. Hardcore in attitude, they nevertheless eschewed the usual hardcore power-chord grind for a style that was equally fast, yet bouncy and wiry, more rhythmic than noise-driven. While each member of the trio offered a distinctive musical take on his role in the band—from Mike Watt's busy, lolloping bass lines to George Hurley's incessant, pounding drums—D. Boon's playing arguably stood out most of all. Simultaneously funky and frenetic, sounding remotely like Steve Cropper sitting in with Iggy Pop after downing one too many triple espressos, his guitar work offered a unique and compelling accompaniment to quirky American tales sketched out within the Minutemen's songs.

D. was born Dennes Boon in 1958 to an ex-Navy father and a family that lived on the outskirts of San Pedro, California. He met his future bandmate Watt when he jumped on him from a tree during a game of army when the pair were thirteen years old. Together with Hurley, they formed the band the Reactionaries in 1978, which segued into the Minutemen in 1980. The band's first glimpse of the "big time" came with an opening slot for Black Flag later in 1980, followed by a seven-inch vinyl EP, *Paranoid Time*, produced by Black Flag leader Greg Ginn, who was also the head of punk stable

SST Records. Over the next five years, the Minutemen undertook a grueling tour schedule and recorded four studio albums and several EPs, the best-known of the long-players being 1984's *Double Nickels on the Dime.*

Boon's bright, strident tone was most often produced by a brown, early '70s Telecaster Custom with a Wide Range humbucker in the neck position, a standard single-coil pickup in the bridge, and a maple fingerboard. He supplemented this guitar with a black Japanese Telecaster with two single coils, and later, another brown '70s Tele Custom with rosewood fingerboard. His amp of choice was a Fender Twin Reverb, though he also occasionally used a Bandmaster head and cab. In either case, he plugged straight in, using a single, long cable.

The Minutemen played their final show in Charlotte, North Carolina, on December 13, 1985. On December 22, during a road trip to Arizona, Boon was sleeping off a fever in the back of the van when his girlfriend fell asleep behind the wheel and veered off I-10 into a roadside ditch. He was thrown from the van, suffered a broken neck, and died instantly. Mike Watt—who formed the band Firehose in 1986 with Hurley and Minuteman fan Ed Crawford— has owned Boon's iconic Telecaster Custom ever since his friend's death. The guitar was used by Nels Cline (now of Wilco) on the song "The Boilerman" on Watt's 1997 solo album *Contemplating the Engine Room*, and has been played by Watt himself on some studio projects. In 2005, Rocket Fuel Films released the documentary *We Jam Econo—The Story of the Minutemen*, which features original live performance footage as well as more than fifty interviews with players on the early '80s hardcore scene.

(continued from page 155)

Pine bodies tend to be lighter than all but the lightest swamp ash, which appeals to many players, and—although the wood's rough-construction-grade origins might imply otherwise—they offer sonic enhancements that plenty enjoy, too. Pine Tele bodies tend to contribute a certain openness overall, with sweet highs and round, if not entirely firm, lows. They sound a little different from either swamp ash or alder, but however you slice it, they still keep a Tele a Tele. Bill Kirchen, who has largely retired his beat-up '50s Telecaster, can be counted among the notable pine-bodied Tele players working today. "I'm playing pretty much exclusively an all-pine, no-truss-rod Rick Kelly Tele-style guitar," says Kirchen. "I don't think it's true, but in my mind, the neck is made from a banister that Bob Dylan slid down at the Chelsea Hotel."

Neck Woods

Its body style makes a Telecaster easy to recognize, even from across a dimly lit concert hall, but the most distinctive characteristic of the guitar's construction is arguably its bolt-on maple neck. This entire configuration figured highly in Leo Fender's list of "easy to manufacture, easy to repair," options, and we have already discussed the characteristics of the screwed-on joint itself, but the wood from which these necks were made is another significant ingredient in the Tele formula.

Maple is a hard, dense wood, and it contributes characteristics of brightness and clarity to the overall sound of the instrument. Even beyond their tonal characteristics, maple necks offer elements of response and performance that blend with their sonic contribution, enhancing a Telecaster in a way that encompasses both the sound and "feel" of the guitar as an instrument. The immediacy of maple's response helps to give the guitars a perceived "snap" and "quack"—these are other characteristics that contribute to the classic twang tone.

As it happens, the maple neck also partners extremely well with an ash body to achieve clarity and articulation. While we might think of these as characteristics of the classic electric country guitar sound, and they certainly are, they also give the Telecaster plenty of cutting power amid more distorted tones. Listen to two

classic Telecaster outings through cranked tube amps, Jimmy Page's solo on "Stairway to Heaven" and Bruce Springsteen's solo on "Candy's Room." You hear a thickness and meatiness with an aggressive low-end growl that could, on one hand, almost fool you into thinking Les Paul or SG, except for the presence of a distinctive, eviscerating clarity that neither of those Gibsons can achieve without a struggle. Even the popular Stratocaster, while plenty bright and snappy, has a certain stabbing, glassy bite within its overdriven tone that pegs it as the single-coil Fender that it is. The Telecaster, on the other hand, is capable of a depth that can make it a real fooler in many circumstances.

Adding a rosewood fingerboard to an otherwise all-maple neck, as Telecasters featured almost exclusively from mid-1959 until the mid-'60s, does add some warmth, roundness, and smoothness to the guitar's overall tone. These enhancements, however, are typically less pronounced than they are often thought to be—a contribution, many experienced makers will tell you, of perhaps 5 to 10 percent or so of the overall tone. As with any ingredient, though, the picture isn't entirely black and white. "Using different materials for the rosewood," says Fender's Chris Fleming, "Indian rosewood as opposed to Brazilian rosewood—or what we use a lot of now, which is Madagascan rosewood—makes a lot of difference in itself. My favorite rosewood to use on a Fender is Indian. Most [rosewood used by Fender] was Brazilian up until the early '60s, and then it switched to mostly Indian because in the mid-1960s Brazilian began becoming a problem. But Brazilian, in my opinion, is a bit too bright. Once again, though, it depends on the actual piece. Brazilian can be very dense and ringing, which is nice in some combinations. . . . I'm not wild about Brazilian on maple, although other guys will tell you I'm crazy."

As discussed in History of the Telecaster, it is highly possible that Fender changed to rosewood for reasons other than tone. Having been happy to be the rebel at the time of the solidbody's introduction, Fender was perhaps trying a slightly classier presentation by the late '50s. The use of a rosewood fingerboard on the Jazzmaster in 1958 seemed de rigueur for a guitar aimed at the jazz crowd, while it also fit the direction of the Custom Telecaster, putting it in more traditional territory.

(continued from page 166)

G.E. Smith

G.E. Smith Signature Telecaster.
*Fender Musical Instruments
Corporation*

The archetypal "child prodigy" with a rock 'n' roll twist, George Edward Smith was born to play the guitar. He took it up at the age of four, and by the age of eleven he was playing a Fender Telecaster made in his birth year, 1952, and making a decent income playing with musicians far older than he. From this point on, schooling, for Smith, would be a mere footnote. Throughout his teens Smith played in local bars, at high school dances, and in Poconos resorts near his Pennsylvania hometown before "graduating" to near-instant success as an in-demand sideman. He would perhaps become best known for his long run as leader of the house band on NBC's *Saturday Night Live*, and Smith brought a Tele on stage with him for at least one number during every show in his ten-year run.

After a stint with the Scratch Band, a fixture on the East Coast club scene in the mid-'70s, Smith was first picked up for Dan Hartman's band (his initial Hartman gigs being a "lip-synch" tour of Europe following Hartman's 1977 hit "Instant Replay"). Then in 1979 he joined the band for *SNL* star Gilda Radner's *Gilda Live on Broadway*. The move would prove significant both for personal and professional reasons: not only would Smith make New York City his adopted home, but he and Radner also became romantically involved and married in 1980. Shortly before that time, however, Smith landed a gig that would catapult him into the rock stratosphere. Hired as lead guitarist with Hall and Oates in 1979, he toured the world with the band for the better part of six years and loaned his finely honed chops to major hits like "Kiss on My List," "Private Eyes," and "Maneater." When the dust settled in the mid-'80s, the guitarist was ready to put down roots in NYC even though the heavy roadwork had long ago put a strain on his marriage. He and Gilda Radner divorced in 1982.

In 1985 Smith was tapped to lead the house band for *SNL* and remained in that position for ten years, backing an array of stars. For a large chunk of that stretch, Smith also took up duties as lead guitarist with Bob Dylan, hitting the road with the iconic folk-rocker who had been one of his first musical heroes. Post-1995, the guitarist continued to pursue a solo career that had begun with the 1982 album *In the World*, while collaborating and touring with several other prominent artists. Through it all, he constantly returned to his Telecaster. In 2007, Fender honored his commitment to the instrument by issuing the Artist Series G.E. Smith Telecaster, which is distinctive for its "chopped" bridge plate and a bridge pickup that is screwed directly into the wood at the bottom of the route—a Smith modification—as well as carrying custom black-oval fingerboard markers. Of his lifelong love affair with his first 1952 Telecaster, Smith told Fender.com, "It has absolutely shaped my life into the person I am now. . . . I rode that Tele all over the world."

Brent Mason

The country scene was already thick with hot Tele players from Nashville to LA and back again by the time Brent Mason was born in Van Wert, Ohio, in 1959. By the time he had reached early adulthood, however, Mason would virtually define the role of Tele-wielding session ace and add an entirely new dimension and diversity to the "hot licks" ethos that defines so many players of Fender's seminal slab-bodied electric. Mason won a Grammy for Best Country Instrumental Performance, was Nashville Music Awards Guitarist of the Year for 1995, was Country Music Association Musician of the Year two years running, in 1997 and '98, and was named the Academy of Country Music's Guitarist of the Year a whopping fourteen times, including nine awards in a row from 1993 to 2001.

Through all the accolades, it can sometimes be easy to forget the heart and soul beneath it all: The simple truth is, Brent Mason is a stunningly gifted guitarist, and his playing moves people in ways that makes them want to have him on their records, too. As such, in addition to catching the blinding licks and melodic sensibilities on his own two solo outings—1997's *Hot Wired* and 2006's *Smokin' Section*—he is in evidence on recordings by a veritable who's who of country stars, including Willie Nelson,

Shania Twain, Brooks & Dunn, George Strait, Merle Haggard, Clint Black, Tanya Tucker, Toby Keith, Trisha Yearwood, Reba McEntire, Dolly Parton, George Jones, Randy Travis, Tim McGraw, and many, many others. Mason's evocative licks can also be heard in the instrumental cues of the soundtrack to the TV show *Friends*, as well as on soundtracks for movies such as *Bridget Jones's Diary*, *Ferris Bueller's Day Off*, *Home Alone*, *The Horse Whisperer*, *A Few Good Men*, *Something to Talk About*, and many, many more.

Mason was first turned on to the wonders of the guitar by his father's copy of Jerry Reed's *Nashville Underground* album, and his interest in country pickin' was further fueled by the playing of Roy Nichols and other Tele stars. But he cites a broad collection of influences, from Larry Carlton to George Benson to Lenny Breau and Pat Martino, and this diversity comes through in his own playing. Mason headed south to Nashville from Ohio at the age of twenty-one and immediately set about trying to find his feet in Music City. Where thousands of others have failed, young Brent found steady and substantial success fairly early on. A regular gig at the famed local showcase the Stagecoach Lounge brought Mason in front of the eyes and ears of artists such as Chet Atkins and George Benson, and by 1985 he was in the studio with both of these legendary guitar stars. From that point onward, Mason's status as a first-call Nashville session player—truly *the* first-call Nashville session player—was secured.

For many years Mason's main guitar was a 1968 Fender Telecaster, which he had modified with a mini-humbucker in the neck position, an added Seymour Duncan stacked Stratocaster pickup in the middle position, and a Seymour Duncan Telecaster pickup in the bridge position (a versatile configuration that is now often referred to as a "Nashville Telecaster," though often with a standard T-style single-coil pickup in the neck position). In 2003, Valley Arts Guitars of California released a Brent Mason Signature model, based on this '68 Telecaster, which Mason has often played since that time.

Duke Levine

Duke Levine picks his '53 Telecaster.

Although he has toured widely, Duke Levine is known as a fixture on a music scene less associated with hardcore twang than it is with either acoustic folk music or alternative rock. Born in Worcester, Massachusetts, in 1961, Levine has called Boston home for many years, and for the past twenty or so of those, has been known as Bean Town's first-call Tele ace. Like many Tele diehards, Levine wasn't necessarily born to the plank, but played a range of other guitars before being inexorably drawn to this addictive instrument. "The first Tele I ever got I still have," he told the author in 2011. "I was playing a Strat at the time. . . I guess I just kind of wanted one, and I found one in a local shop, the '63 Tele that I still play sometimes. It was really nothing special, only the body and neck were original. . . . I was playing both guitars for a while, and I just gravitated more and more toward playing the Tele all the time."

While Levine's core style encompasses the blend of country, blues, jazz, and rock 'n' roll that seems to be definitive for so many hot-licks Telecaster slingers, the demands of session work and live performance require him to turn his hand to a little bit of just about anything, whether it's taking the stage with Bono, Yo-Yo Ma, and the Boston Pops; cutting scores for films like *The Opposite of Sex* and *Lone Star*; or recording or touring with anyone from Aimee Mann to John Gorka to Bill Morrissey to Mary Chapin Carpenter to

Slaid Cleaves. Regardless, the Telecaster remains his go-to guitar. "A good Tele can be so huge and thick that people often don't even think it sounds like a Tele, it's got so much body to it. A Tele can do a Les Paul impersonation much more easily than a Les Paul can do a Tele impersonation."

While his changed-up '63 is certainly a "good Tele," Levine acquired a truly great Telecaster in the late '90s, a 1953 black-guard Telecaster that would be many a picker's dream guitar. He found it courtesy of his brother Buzzy Levine, the proprietor of Lark Street Music in Tea Neck, New Jersey. "I wasn't even looking for one, because even then they were outrageously expensive," Levine relates, "but Buzzy had gotten it in and I happened to be in his store one day. He said, 'Oh, you should play this guitar!' 'Cos I had never even really played one. . . . I played this '53 Telecaster—it hardly had any frets left on it, and I don't even think the ones that were there were original—and I was like, 'Wow, I've never heard a Telecaster that sounded like that!' It was just eye-opening."

As much as he can tear it up when called to do so, the guitarist says he has been getting back to the purity and simplicity heard in the work of many of the formative country and Western Swing players. "I always loved the honky-tonk stuff, especially the Bakersfield stuff, Merle [Haggard] and Buck [Owens], and it's kind of where I was coming from when I started to get into playing more country guitar. Lately, though, I've been listening to steel players more than just Tele players," Levine says. "Lately I've been digging just going back and listening to old Ralph Mooney and Tom Brumley and all that stuff, and really they all kind of played simpler back then anyway. . . . I think the 'chops' thing has almost gotten out of control. I mean, obviously Gatton and Buchanan were at the beginning of when it all got supercharged, but in the '60s it was often so simple and beautiful—it's easy to hear what they were doing, and there are plenty of beautiful, simple ideas you can grasp on to." Bean Towner or not, the Bakersfield boys would be proud.

Frank Black (a.k.a.) Black Francis

Frank Black used a range of Telecasters to help forge the loud/quiet/loud aesthetic, both with the Pixies and as a solo artist. Here, he performs with the Pixies at the Avalon in Boston in December 2004. *Evan Richman/The Boston Globe via Getty Images*

As the former (and occasionally reunited) leader of indie-rockers the Pixies, Frank Black has rarely played it straight—whether we're talking chord changes, song arrangements, or personal identity. Born Charles Michael Kittridge Thompson IV in Boston, Massachusetts, in 1965, the guitarist was raised in California and other parts west as first his father, then stepfather, relocated for work. Still known as Charles upon his return to Massachusetts during his senior year in high school and his enrollment at the University of Massachusetts, Amherst, a year later, Thompson's roommate in the second semester of his freshman year was Joey Santiago, who shared his interest in punk rock and guitar. Upon graduating from UMASS in 1986, the pair decided to form a band: an ad in the Boston press for bandmates with "Hüsker Dü and Peter, Paul, and Mary influences" yielded bassist and backing vocalist Kim Deal, who brought in Dave Lovering on drums. Santiago stabbed his finger at random into a dictionary to give the outfit a name, Thompson selected the stage name Black Francis, and the Pixies were born.

Through five critically acclaimed Pixies studio albums—from the 1987 debut *Come on Pilgrim* to the 1991 swan song *Trompe le Monde*—Black made the Fender Telecaster his weapon of choice. While he played a range of models, from reissue-styled Teles to more contemporary designs, Black's main guitar in the Pixies was often a Fender Contemporary Telecaster, or one of several, that he purchased in the late '80s. Made in Japan in the mid-'80s, this model had two humbucking pickups (one humbucker and two single coils optional) and a Floyd Rose–style vibrato unit, which Black largely ignored. Beginning in the late '80s, he gradually but steadily modified his contemporary Teles to be somewhat more traditional. He removed the arms from the vibrato units but still used them at times in his playing, slipping his fingers under the bridge plate to lift it and send the string flat, or depressing the entire thing backward with his palm to raise their pitch.

Upon going solo in the early '90s, Black changed his name again from Black Francis to Frank Black. The contemporary Telecaster stayed with him, but later he also played original 1968

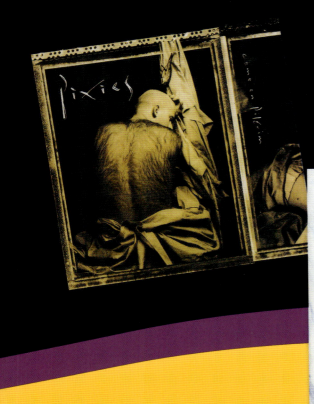

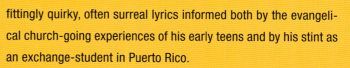

and '70 Telecasters, which were purportedly among the haul when a trailer containing all of the gear for his band, the Catholics, was stolen from a parking lot near the Philadelphia Airport in 2001. He also used Fender's Mexican-made Roadworn Telecaster, a pre-aged vintage-style guitar.

The Pixies' sound might widely be thought of as "heavy"—in places, at least, given the loud/quiet/loud ethos that they helped to coin, and which bands like Nirvana carried into the end zone after their demise—but, while Santiago's Les Paul-into-Marshalls rig certainly provided some characteristic wail to the arrangements, Black's Telecaster tone was more often a big, bold kerrang rather than a stereotypical rock crunch. In truth, the band's sound as a whole was inseparably defined by both players: Black's chunky, driving rhythm work, and Santiago's screaming, often dissonant leads and fills. And, of course, the nature of the songwriting itself contributed largely to the Pixies' distinctive sound. As the main songwriter, Black was—and remains—fond of unconventional chord changes that somehow sound natural in context, while continually piquing the listener's interest. These are dressed with

fittingly quirky, often surreal lyrics informed both by the evangelical church-going experiences of his early teens and by his stint as an exchange-student in Puerto Rico.

Even so, Black doesn't consider his work—with the Pixies or after—to be particularly far out of the mainstream, for all his acclaim as a trendsetter. "I was only ever trying to write pop songs," he told the author in 1993, upon the release of his eponymous debut solo album. "Somehow, things always just came out that way." In 2009 he told *Flavorwire*, "I take to heart what Iggy Pop says, 'It's all disco.' And, to a certain extent, it is. When you think about how classical music, over the decades and centuries, has changed . . . when you think about how much rock and roll has changed in fifty years. . . . But from another perspective, things haven't changed that much. We're talking about a backbeat. We're talking about a three-minute pop song. Verses and choruses. There's a lot more similarity in all these so-called genres than there are differences, I think." If, as Black asserts, the music hasn't changed much, why should that plank-bodied electric guitar upon which so many players chose to make it change either?

Jonny Greenwood and Thom Yorke

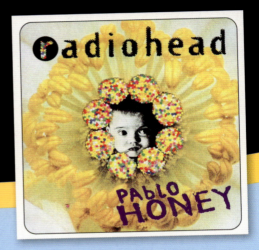

Jonny Greenwood often plays one of a couple of Telecaster Plus models outfitted with active Lace-Sensor pickups—a single unit at the neck and two at the bridge wired as a humbucker—and a contemporary six-saddle bridge. *Paul Bergen/ Redferns/Getty Images*

Although the band's breakthrough 1992 hit "Creep" might have pegged them as just another loud-quiet-loud alt-rock outfit in the footsteps of the Pixies and Nirvana, Radiohead has forged a reputation as one of the more creative and independent-minded bands working in popular music in the past couple of decades. And while the band's sound certainly leans on an artistic use of effects pedals, in addition to the sheer originality of their playing, guitarists Jonny Greenwood and Thom Yorke accomplish most of their avant-garde antics on a range of Fender Telecasters. Alongside them, partner-in-crime Ed O'Brien—although he often plays Rickenbackers, Stratocasters, and a Gibson ES-330 and ES-335—has also turned to a pair of Teles over the years.

The band that would become Radiohead was formed in 1985 by a group of pals at the Abingdon School, a private boy's school in Oxfordshire, England, who called themselves

On a Friday after their habitual rehearsal day. Eventual lead guitarist Jonny Greenwood, younger brother of bassist Colin Greenwood, initially tagged along on harmonica, then keyboards, before finding his niche as a six-string noise monger. The five (including Phil Selway on drums) kept the unit together through university and gained attention from the British record industry as their live performances ramped up shortly after. Upon signing to EMI in 1991, the band changed its name to Radiohead, at the label's request, and released its first EP, *Drill*, the following year. Although this release garnered little attention, the single "Creep" that followed it proved a slow-grower that would eventually be a massive hit, and the band's debut full-length album, *Pablo Honey*, released the year after that, firmly established their status as an indie band worth watching. In the few years following this early semi-success, however, Radiohead evolved into the band that most fans know it to be today.

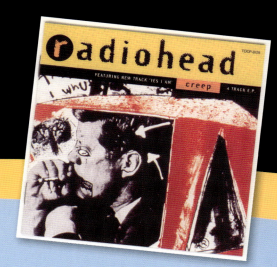

Disenchanted with the commerciality of the industry, Radiohead honed its sound. What eventually emerged on *The Bends* in 1995, and virtually every Radiohead release since, was a collage of dense soundscapes built of trenchant lyrics, soaring melodies, and atmospheric and even experimental instrumentation, all dressed in the guise of "traditional" guitar rock.

Perhaps the more extreme sonic sculptor of the band, Greenwood often plays one of a couple of Fender Telecaster Plus models, offerings from the late '80s and early '90s that never really caught fire with the playing public at large, and are therefore unlikely "star guitars" in the grand scheme of things. They have active Lace-Sensor pickups, which are both low-noise and high-output, with a single unit at the neck and two at the bridge wired as a humbucker (with coil-splitting capabilities), and a contemporary six-saddle bridge, as well as several modifications on Greenwood's own guitars. The

Telecaster Plus was never designed for the vintage purist, but scream, wail, throb, roar, and moan it will, especially when rammed through the Marshall Shred Master distortion pedal, ProCo Rat, Boss SD-1 Super Distortion, a DigiTech WH-1 Whammy, a DIY tremolo pedal, a DOD Envelope Filter, an Electro-Harmonix Small Stone phase shifter, a Roland Space Echo, Mutronics Mutator, and other pedals that Greenwood turns to for his aural hijinks.

Thom Yorke has long been fond of 1970s Telecaster Deluxes and Customs, as well as other customized Teles and a Fender Jazzmaster. Lead vocal duties, however, keep him from indulging in the same kind of sonic mayhem as Greenwood and O'Brien, and he typically just runs through a pair of ProCo Rat distortion pedals and a Boss DD3 Digital Delay for a little echo. A far, far cry from Luther Perkins's low-string twang on a '50s Esquire, Radiohead's sound—for all the electronic assistance—is still rooted in the purity and simplicity of the Telecaster, and perhaps inspired by the down-to-earth workingman's tool that this guitar was designed to be in the first place.

(continued from page 158)

Neck and Headstock Hardware and Appointments

With no binding, no headstock overlay, and only simple dot inlays in the fingerboard, there isn't much else to speak of in regards to the simple Telecaster neck, although the nut, string retainer, and tuners still deserve a mention.

Leo Fender used a bone nut from the start of the production, and this component is one of the guitar's few nods to tradition. Bone is known for its resonance and sustain-enhancing properties, and makes an excellent neck-end termination point for the strings' speaking length. As an organic material, it isn't as consistent from one blank to the other as contemporary synthetic nut blanks made from Micarta or Corian might be. The guitar-maker can encounter tiny air bubbles in this finely porous material that will lead to minor irregularities, and, therefore, slight changes in performance from one nut to the other. On the whole, though, it is a tone-enhancing component nevertheless, does its job very well, and can even be impressively long-lasting.

First up beyond the nut is the string retainer, which changed both in type and position through the course of the early to mid-'50s. From the introduction of the Esquire and Broadcaster in 1950 until 1955, the guitars had a single round metal string retainer with slots in the underside, attached to the headstock by a single screw and positioned just south of the G-string tuner post. For ease of manufacture, Fender necks are created without the back-angled headstocks that many others use to create adequate string pressure in the nut slots. Necks are carved so that the headstock sits on a slightly lower plane than the fingerboard, so the break angle from the nut down to the first few tuner posts is entirely adequate, but the B and high-E strings in particular (the only unwound strings when the guitar was introduced) have to make a much longer journey to their tuner posts. The retainer can be pulled down on the B and E strings slightly to produce adequate pressure in the nut slots and help prevent a droning ring from the dead lengths of these strings between nut and tuner posts.

Apparently it didn't provide quite enough pressure, though; after 1955 the retainer position was moved closer to the nut, to approximately adjacent the A-string tuner post, at which time

1968 Telecaster. *Doug Youland, Willie's American Guitars*

it was also changed to a thin, bent-metal "butterfly" clip. The change of retainer position also necessitated a change of position for the Fender and model logos, which were positioned to the nut side of the retainer pre-'55, and beyond the retainer after. With this single string retainer in place, helping to tension the two thinner strings on the guitar, the move to a thinner unwound G later in the '60s often left that string ringing between nut and tuner in an undesirable manner that can sometimes be heard through the pickup. To combat this, many players wind the G string further down the tuner post (that is, put more wraps around the post when stringing up) to increase the pressure from nut slot to tuner. Many later Telecaster models from the early '70s onward carried two "butterfly" retainer clips to achieve the same result.

The asymmetrical, six-in-line headstock design is another visual characteristic of the Telecaster, and of all classic Fender guitars. As discussed in History of the Telecaster, it has performance benefits in addition to creating a distinctive style for the model. Fender's headstock design enables a straight line for each string from nut slot to tuner post, and, therefore, resists the tuning instabilities that can occur when strings stick or hitch in nut slots from which they must break at angles out toward their respective tuners on wider headstocks, such as those used by Gibson, Gretsch, Epiphone, Rickenbacker, and many others. Simple, elegant, and stylish, the characteristic Fender headstock is also therefore extremely functional.

The Kluson tuners loaded onto pre-CBS Telecasters are another part of their classic vibe, and many players and makers will tell you that they have a slightly different "sound" than the heavier replacements by Schaller or Grover that some players added to their guitars, but this ingredient is rather minimal from the sonic perspective. The design of these tuners' back covers changed very slightly over the years, namely in how the brand name was stamped into these gear covers, from a single-line "Kluson Deluxe" to no line (no brand stamp), back to single line, and finally double line—with "Kluson" and "Deluxe" stamped on opposing edges of the cover—by the mid-1960s. In 1967 the Kluson tuners were dropped in favor of Schaller tuners that were made in West Germany to Fender's own design and stamped with the new, thicker "F" of the Fender logo.

Bridge Assembly

Of all the hardware components mounted to the guitar, the bridge truly makes a Tele what it is. Build a guitar that is otherwise like a Telecaster, but give it a different bridge and tail-piece—a Gibson-style tune-o-matic or wraparound bridge, for example—and its tone and response will be altered out of the realm of Teledom.

The Telecaster's bridge and bridge-mounted pickup really should be examined as an integral unit, although the pickup's own make-up and electronic specifications will be explored in their own right in the section that follows. Regardless, in addition to the construction of the bridge and the pickup as independent, stand-alone components, their union in the marriage of ingredients that make up this guitar as a whole has an effect on the tone that takes them beyond the contribution of either as an individual. In fact, ask either a hard-core Telecaster player or a maker of original or reproduction Tele-style guitars, and they will be hard-pressed to discuss either the bridge or bridge pickup entirely independently of one another.

"I think, as a rule," says Redd Volkaert, "just the Telecaster system of the bridge pan and the bridge pickup, that combination makes for a really barky cutting-through-the-band-mix, kind of a high-mid sparkly sort of sound, that a Strat doesn't give with the pickup hangin' off the pickguard, danglin' in a hole, suspended. Part of a Strat's sound too, I think, is the springs in the back hole of the one with the tremolo, the harmonics and the noise and the little rattley clangy midrange thing you get out of that chamber, that adds to the sound of a Stratocaster. As the bridge-plate pan of a Telecaster does. A lot of 'em, when you turn the amp up really loud, you can tap on the bridge pan with your fingernails and you can hear where all the midrange comes from. It goes "doot, doot, doot" [imitates microphonic honk], you know, that really dorky kind of sound. But when you're playing that adds to the really hollow kind of jangliness that only that bridge pickup combination on the Telecaster can give."

Pickup maker Jason Lollar is happy to dissect this component in a little more detail: "The bottom plate of the pickup being metal makes a very subtle difference, but that bridge, that's where you get a 15 to 20 percent boost in volume, midrange, and bass. You take that plate away and just use a Strat bridge, or put a Telecaster bridge pickup on a Strat, and it doesn't sound like a Tele."

Mike Eldred, director of marketing for Fender's Custom Shop, concurs with the importance of the entire Tele bridge/pickup unit. "There are so many variables on that pickup, and they all add up," Eldred says. "With the plate on the bottom, and with the whole thing screwed into the bridge plate, you have put some major variables in there. But with a Strat pickup, it's mounted on a plastic pickguard; if I change that plastic and I use phenolic or nitrocellulose or vinyl, it's not going to change that pickup much. But man, you take a Telecaster pickup with that plate that's already on the bottom of it, and now you have machine screws that screw into that through a bridge plate, and now say I go punch that bridge plate out of nickel silver, or I punch it out of brass . . . it's a totally different sound, completely different."

The way in which the base plate is mounted to the guitar affects the sound in a degree that is, perhaps, as significant as the way in which the pickup is mounted into the plate. Attached by four screws drilled through holes near the back edge only, between the saddles and the string holes, the plate thus remains "semi-floating," and therefore prone to micro-phonics that leak into the pickup through its mounting bolts while also enhancing the acoustic ring of the strings. Given that the bridge-saddle adjustment screws make direct contact with this plate and transfer the strings' vibrational energy directly into it, we can think of it almost as a small, steel banjo head, or the volume-enhancing aluminum cone of a resonator guitar, and as such it adds a little extra ring into the pickup and the sound of the guitar as a whole (the source of Volkaert's "doot, doot, doot").

The Tele bridge was derived from Fender's lap-steel guitar bridges, which themselves were devised from two perspectives: first, as a means of providing a solid body-end anchor point for the strings, and second, as a means of mounting the pickup. We tend to think of the traditional Telecaster bridge as being the integral unit of the stamped-steel bridge plate and three brass or steel saddles, but viewed from the perspective of Fender's original intentions for it, we might more accurately see it as a stamped-steel pickup-mounting plate, upon which the three bridge saddles conveniently rest. However you tackle them, though, these components work together to create a substantial part of that hallowed Tele magic.

Atop the punched-out steel base plate rest three bridge saddles that handle two strings each in their duty of determining the body-end termination of the strings' speaking length. One classic ingredient of early '50s Broadcasters, Esquires, and Telecasters is the brass bridge saddles that were replaced by steel late in 1954 (although many of the earlier pre-production guitars were also made with steel saddles, albeit of a slightly larger diameter than those brought back in the mid-'50s). Brass saddles are generally rather warm and rich sounding, with good sustain and plenty of bite. The smooth steel saddles of late 1954 to '58 are often considered to be a bit sharper sounding, perhaps more archetypal "twang," while the threaded saddles that replaced these in mid-'58 arguably brought a little more "zing" to the Tele tone.

In addition to their tonal contribution, the three-saddle configuration has major implications for string height and intonation adjustment. As difficult as it might be to believe today, at the time of this bridge's introduction in 1950, these were perhaps the most easily adjustable saddles available on a production guitar. The height of each individual string can easily be adjusted by raising or lowering the saddle at the grub screw at each of its outer ends, while a "best compromise" intonation for each of two strings can be set by the intonation bolt that runs from the center of each saddle to the back lip of the base plate.

From 1954 onward, by standards set by both Gibson's tune-o-matic bridge and Fender's own Stratocaster bridge, the Tele's intonation adjustment would perhaps seem rather crude, but most players find it's still "good enough for rock 'n' roll" regardless—or find ways of improving upon it. One common old fix was to bend the adjustment bolt to angle the saddle and put each of its ends (and hence each of the two string break points) at a slightly different position. A better engineered, and perhaps more obvious, solution came in the form of the six-saddle bridge that Fender introduced to the Custom Telecaster in the mid-'70s and offered as a replacement part, which many players added to their three-saddle Teles. Splitting the saddle duties from three to six produced an arrangement with more moving parts, less mass to the saddles, and a little less solidity overall, and many players swear that a six-saddle bridge just doesn't sound the same as a traditional three-saddle version. Several parts manufacturers today offer vintage-style saddle sets with adjustment-bolt holes that are drilled at a calculated angle, to yield more precise intonation for individual strings without resorting to the old "bend it with the pliers" technique.

(continued on page 172)

Bridge assembly and pickup on a 1968 Telecaster in a rare Teal Green custom color. *Doug Youland, Willie's American Guitars*

Graham Coxon

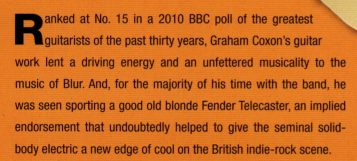

Graham Coxon Signature Telecaster, released 2011. *Fender Musical Instruments Corporation*

Ranked at No. 15 in a 2010 BBC poll of the greatest guitarists of the past thirty years, Graham Coxon's guitar work lent a driving energy and an unfettered musicality to the music of Blur. And, for the majority of his time with the band, he was seen sporting a good old blonde Fender Telecaster, an implied endorsement that undoubtedly helped to give the seminal solid-body electric a new edge of cool on the British indie-rock scene.

Formed in London in 1989, Blur was one of the dual epicenters of the U.K.'s Brit-pop scene in the early '90s—alongside sometime rivals Oasis—and scored big with a succession of hit albums, including 1994's *Parklife*. By the mid-'90s, the band was about as big as it gets for British indie-rock, until 1997's *Blur* and its single "Song 2" with its infectious "woo-hoo" chorus took them to new heights around the world. The follow-up, 1999's *13*, was a dense, often somewhat rambling (if engagingly so) affair in which Coxon indulged the greater breadth of his musical imagination. The album also signaled the early crumbling of Blur as an entity, with individual members, Coxon among them, undertaking solo projects during the extended break that followed the album's promotional tour.

In 2002 Coxon left the band officially, but other than the sporadic reunions from 2009 onward, he seems never really to have returned to the fold after seeking treatment for alcoholism in 2001. Though he had already made three well-received solo albums during his time with Blur, his status as an artist in his own right grew considerably following his departure from the band. One album after another, including 2006's epic double-live set *Burnt to Bitz: At the Astoria* and 2009's acoustic concept album *The Spinning Top*, reveal a guitarist and songwriter at the top of his creative game.

With a chameleon-like style that is difficult to pin down, Coxon's guitar playing has been vociferously praised by fellow musicians Jonny Greenwood of Radiohead, Noel Gallagher of Oasis, and bandmate Damon Albarn of Blur, and has clearly inspired a new generation of Tele players. He hops nimbly from jangly pop to driving crunch-rock, from adventurous and folk-tinged chord shapes to noise-art and atmospherics, and all the while sounds simply like Graham Coxon. He has owned and played several Telecasters, but his main squeeze was most often a '50s reissue model in Butterscotch Blonde from the late '80s. Fender's Graham Coxon Telecaster of 2011 was, however, a late-'60s remake with rosewood fingerboard, tortoise-shell pickguard, and a humbucking pickup in the neck position.

John 5

John 5 is known for modified Telecasters that have inspired two Custom Shop numbers, including this one with a stacked humbucker at the bridge, Fender's Twisted Telecaster at the neck, and a Bigsby-licensed tailpiece. *Robert Knight Archive/Redferns/Getty Images*

John 5 Signature Telecaster. *Fender Musical Instruments Corporation*

Taking the Telecaster 180 degrees from its straight-on country roots, John 5 was originally inspired to play the guitar at the age of seven while watching Buck Owens play his Fender on the TV show *Hee Haw*. While he is now known for some of the most blistering rock shred ever performed on a Tele, he can still burn up the fretboard with country-style picking. Born John Lowery in Grosse Pointe, Michigan, in 1971, John 5 was another teen prodigy who used his Tele to make a good living even before he was old enough to legally patronize the establishments in which he earned his pay. John 5 headed west to LA upon turning eighteen and quickly established himself as a session ace and sideman.

Prior to earning his first jump to fame in 1998 as the guitarist with Marilyn Manson—who converted John Lowery to John 5—the young gun recorded and performed with Lita Ford, k.d. lang, Rob Halford, and David Lee Roth, and played extensively on TV and movie soundtracks with producer Bob Marlette. The Manson gig, however, launched him into the spotlight and gave John 5 a larger-than-life persona of a successful industrial-metal artist. In 2004, John 5 left Marilyn Manson and recorded his first solo album, *Vertigo*, then formed the band Loser. A year later, he signed on as guitarist for Rob Zombie, a gig he retains at the time of writing.

While he can shred right alongside the best rock players working today, John 5's playing is still, perhaps, distinguished most by his incorporation of the kind of country playing that first turned him on to the guitar. "I love Jimmy Bryant and I love Albert Lee," John 5 told *MusicRadar* in 2001. "Roy Clark. Chet Atkins. I love those pickers. That's a whole other world. It's shredding; it's fast; it's tough to do. I like a challenge."

Although he has occasionally picked up a "plain old Telecaster," John 5 is particularly known for the modified guitars that have inspired his signature models. Two Fender Custom Shop J5 Telecasters have been issued, with a high-output bridge humbucker and single-coil neck, and two single coils respectively, the latter with Bigsby vibrato tailpiece. The Squier J5 Telecaster doubles the humbucker content, putting them in both positions, while the J5 Triple Tele Deluxe revives the Strat-style vibrato bridge of the '70s Telecaster Deluxe, but with three Wide Range humbuckers.

(continued from page 169)

It's worth remembering that Leo Fender really didn't design the Telecaster bridge to be seen, so he can be excused for the rather industrial look of this component when left uncovered. As witnessed in early promotional literature, the unit was to have exhibited a minimalist elegance, appearing only as a shapely chrome cover from which the strings emerged on their journey from the unseen bridge saddles. Designed both as a cover and a right-hand rest for picking, this detachable part was rarely left in place by the guitarist, who usually found that playing without them offered more versatility. Without the cover, a player could easily dampen or mute strings by resting the edge of the palm against the front of the saddles, producing bold, bright tones when picking right above the pickup or close to the saddles, and so forth. The "ashtray," as its alternative use inevitably dubbed it, was nevertheless a part of the original conception of the Telecaster, and remained in production until 1983.

Any discussion of a guitar's bridge must include consideration of the tailpiece that partners it. Some designs, such as Gibson's simple "wraparound" bridge or Fender's Stratocaster bridge, are integral, in that the string anchor points and bridge saddles all occur as part of the same unit. Others require entirely separate anchoring hardware, as do Gibson's tune-o-matic bridge with "trapeze" or "stopbar" tailpiece, or Fender's own Jazzmaster, Jaguar, and Mustang vibratos with their separate rocking bridges. Other than those on the "top loader" guitars of late 1958 to late '59, the bridges used on classic Esquires and Telecasters aren't really either/or, but something rather different. They include no tailpiece as such, the strings instead anchoring in steel ferules set into the back of the guitar, from which they pass through six individual holes drilled through the body and on through six holes in the base plate behind the saddles.

If a guitar maker's goal with this hardware was to achieve a solid body-end anchor point for the strings, well, it doesn't get much more solid than Fender's strings-through-body design. The ferrules, which are like small steel cups, provide an immovable seating for the strings' ball-ends, and, therefore, aid tuning stability in their resistance to movement, particularly when compared to the old trapeze tailpieces that most other electric guitars carried in the late '40s to early '50s. Perhaps more significant, though, is this design's enhancement to resonance and sustain. The through-body stringing works in partnership with the base plate and bridge saddles to create a solid string anchor, a severe break angle over the saddles, and therefore, optimum downward pressure of strings upon saddles, all resulting in a clear, ringing, piano-like tone. Telecasters are sometimes thought of as guitars that "don't have a lot of sustain," but this misconception usually has more to do with their single-coil pickups, and the fact

Neck pickup on a 1956 Telecaster. *Guitar courtesy of Elderly Instruments, photo Dave Matchette*

that they are more often (if not always) played through cleaner amps that don't generate much sustain-inducing feedback. Pick up a good Tele with solid hardware and a tight neck joint, and, entirely unplugged, pick that open low-E string and check how long it rings. Put your ear to the body edge, and it might surprise you how long the note sustains.

Pickups

Any electric guitar's pickups form an enormous part of its character, but the Telecaster's two pickups are arguably more intimately entwined with the guitar's voice and character than most. And unlike several other pickup types—Fender's own Stratocaster, Jaguar, or Jazzmaster pickups; Gibson's humbucker or P-90; Gretsch's Filter'Tron or DeArmond 200—the Telecaster pickup set comprises two distinctly different units. They are both narrow single-coil pickups, with individual magnetic pole pieces slotted within the coil, but beyond that they are dissimilar. Both of the pickups that Fender would use on the Telecaster had evolved from units used on the young company's steel guitars, and had already proved themselves in that capacity.

Other than a few early variables that will be acknowledged below, the classic Telecaster bridge pickup is made with approximately 9,200 turns of 42-gauge plain-enamel-coated wire wound in a relatively narrow coil around six individual Alnico V rod magnets that constitute its pole pieces. Winding machines were hand-operated, rather than automated, so the number of turns of wire on any pre-CBS pickup—and earlier units in particular—could vary greatly. The final DC resistance of most bridge pickups fell within the 6.8k ohms to 7.8k ohms range, although some particularly overwound vintage pickups soared to well above this. The pickup has no "bobbin" as such, in the way that a Gibson-style humbucker or P-90 does, but instead it has a pair of fiber top and bottom plates that hold the magnets in place and provide protection for the coil wire, which is wound directly around the magnets after a thin layer of insulating tape is wrapped around them. Finally, a copper-plated tin base plate is attached to the bottom of the pickup, through which the three mounting bolts inserted through holes in the bridge's base plate are threaded.

All in all, it is a fairly simple and efficient construction, and it produces a tone that stabs straight at the heart of what Leo Fender was hoping to achieve. The narrow coil enhances a narrow magnetic field—think of it as a "string-sensing window"—that keeps the signal tight and focused, which works toward both firm lows and pronounced highs. Using magnetic pole pieces within the coil also helps to emphasize clarity and articulation.

Fender's design meant that the pole pieces on the Tele pickup were nonadjustable, although the pickup's overall height could be raised and lowered by the three mounting screws: two behind, and one in front. For the first five years of production, the pole pieces were loaded flush to the top of the pickup's top plate. After late 1955, longer segments were used for the D and G pole pieces, bringing these closer to their strings to compensate for the lower output of these thinner wound strings. At the time, a wound G string was still common, meaning this one was often the weakest of the six, all else being equal. When unwound G strings came into use in the late '60s (or earlier if you were James Burton and put banjo strings on your guitar for easy bending), the G was suddenly the thickest of the plain strings, and could really boom out through that high pole piece.

The outward design of the Telecaster pickup might seem very much like that of the Stratocaster pickup that would follow it four years later, other than in the way it is mounted into the bridge, which, as we have already acknowledged, also plays its part in shaping the guitar's tone. There are, however, several subtle differences that make it very different from the Strat pickup, and any experienced player will tell you that the magic often lies in those subtle differences. "They are so different," agrees Fender's Mike Eldred. "The bridge pickup on a Telecaster sounds like no other bridge pickup. You just look at the construction of that pickup: the bobbin is squatter, there's a larger area to put more wire on that thing, and then you add that plate on the bottom. There are so many variables on that pickup, and they all add up."

Pickup maker Lindy Fralin, who is known for his vintage-style Tele and Stat pickups, as well as a range of other types, has put plenty of thought into the role of the plate attached to the underside of the Telecaster bridge pickup, and even offers them on his Strat-style replacement pickups. He emphasizes, in fact, that there really is no such thing as "a Telecaster pickup" independent of its bridge—that the base plate, bridge plate, and the pickup itself all work together to do what they do so well. "You've got a piece of steel under the pickup, and a piece of steel around the pickup. Both of those focus the magnetic field in a positive way, to get the most output out of that coil. So they really seem louder than the same number of turns on a Strat pickup."

Given that the body size and density and the neck woods and construction are all really very similar between a '50s Telecaster and an ash-bodied, maple-necked Stratocaster, the pickup and bridge assembly are clearly two of the main reasons for their considerable difference in tone. Thick, meaty, and muscular, yet still clear and twangy, the archetypal Tele bridge-pickup tone simply can't be reproduced on a standard Stratocaster's bridge pickup—a state of affairs that has sent thousands of Strat players in search of tweaks to correct that disparity, once they have experienced that thick Tele goodness.

By the same token, however, many players will tell you that the Strat's hallowed neck-pickup tone simply can't be reproduced on a Telecaster's neck pickup, although a great Tele neck pickup can sound outstanding in its own right.

The neck pickup is different from the Tele bridge pickup in several subtle but significant ways. Most notable of these are its smaller size, and the metal cover that conceals its pole pieces. The poles are similar Alnico rod magnets, but the smaller coil is able to hold less wire than its partner at the bridge position. Both neck and bridge pickups were originally wound with 43-gauge wire— this being one of the above-mentioned differences in the very early Esquire/Broadcaster bridge pickups, along with the zinc (rather than tin, then steel) base plate beneath it. When bridge pickup windings changed to 42-gauge wire very early in the life of the guitar, the neck pickup continued to be wound with 43-gauge stock. The thinner the wire, the more you can pack onto the coil, and this finer gauge gives Telecaster neck pickups an average resistance reading somewhere around 7.5k ohms or a little higher, which often gives the impression, on paper, that they are "hotter" than their counterparts in the bridge. Since any such specs aren't comparing like for like, however, they don't present an accurate account of what we can expect from these different

pickups in terms of tone. A greater number of turns of slightly thicker wire gives the bridge pickup a fatter, meatier tone with slightly greater output (in most instances, at least), though its positioning means it is still brighter than the neck pickup, which tends to sound a little weaker thanks to its smaller coil size.

The neck pickup doesn't benefit from the bridge pickup's very interactive mounting arrangement either, but rather than being suspended from a plastic pickguard like the Strat pickup, it is mounted into the wood of the body, which in turn adds some depth and woodiness to its tone. While some players have been frustrated by the underwhelming tone from the Tele neck pickup, as compared to the roaring, twanging beast of a bridge pickup (or many Strat neck pickups), the better ones can sound outstanding: warm, woody, thick, and rich. "If you looked up the definition of *electric guitar*," says guitarist Jim Campilongo, "the neck position would be that. Like, it just sounds like an acoustic guitar that's amplified. It's really beautifully organic."

The bridge pickups mounted into single-pickup pre-CBS Esquires are often ascribed some sonic magic by players, although there's nothing to suggest that these pickups were any different from those mounted into the Telecasters that came off the line at the same time, and they were most likely taken from batches wound side by side without regard to whether they were "Telecaster" or "Esquire" pickups. Other very real differences between the Telecaster and Esquire, however, might indeed give the latter more perceived tonal girth in the bridge position.

First, although Esquires were made with Telecaster bodies and include a neck-position pickup route that simply was never filled, the absence of that pickup—and its magnets, in particular—meant that the strings were allowed to ring more freely near the maximum point of their vibrational arc, without the magnets imposing their slight drag upon them. Many players will tell you that an Esquire rings more loudly as a result, and that the extra energy is taken into the pickup and transmitted on to the amplifier.

Second, the Esquire's different wiring configuration includes a rear-pointing switch position that bypasses the tone control in routing the volume control's output to the jack, and that results in a slightly bolder signal than anything present on a Telecaster,

1968 Telecaster. *Doug Youland, Willie's American Guitars*

all else being equal. Although they lack the added options that a neck pickup brings (and most players consider the forward-pointing switch position's preset "bassy" sound nearly useless), good Esquires can be powerful performers, and surprisingly versatile despite their simplicity.

It's notable that most other significant guitar makers sought to progress from single-coil to humbucker in their quest for the achievement of the "ideal," whereas Fender's single-coil tone set a benchmark that really didn't need to be bettered. The Wide Range Humbucking Pickup developed by Seth Lover for Fender in 1970 was never really a replacement for the Tele's single-coil pickups. It provided a means of competing with Gibson, and of offering an alternative for rock, blues, and jazz players who were adding humbuckers to existing Telecasters, in the neck position in particular, but who were never really in the majority of Tele players either. Regardless, few players or manufacturers would attempt to better the tone achieved by a good vintage Telecaster bridge pickup, only to reproduce it. It is worth noting here, though, that in developing the Wide Range Humbucker, Lover used magnetized pole pieces made from cunife rod magnets (an alloy of copper, nickel, and iron), which are soft enough to be threaded. His design thus maintained the Fender pickup standard for "magnet within coil" rather than using steel pole pieces within the coil, with a magnet beneath, as used in his legendary humbucker design for Gibson.

Controls and Switching

The wiring and associated controls and switching employed in the Telecaster's simple electronics layout chiefly determine how the existing pickup tones can be routed, but also play a part in shaping those tones. It could even be argued that elements of the original Telecaster wiring schemes—both that used briefly from 1950 to '52 and the revision used from '53 to '67—imposed further (arguably undesirable) sonic elements upon the guitar, while inhibiting certain otherwise existing, and desirable, tonal options. With this in mind, the Telecaster presents a rare case in which a common modification from the original design might be considered a "standard" of sorts, or at least deserves to be addressed in this examination of the guitar's tonal capabilities.

(continued on page 178)

Brad Paisley

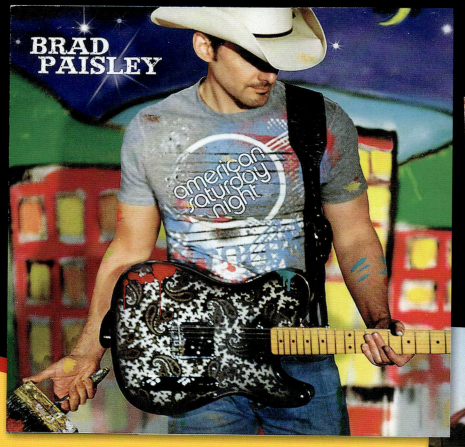

It might seem a little "obvious," but if you're born with the name Brad Paisley perhaps you really have little choice. While the majority of iconic Telecasters, and those the country pickers tend to lust after most, are pre-CBS models, this hot gun of the current Nashville is bound by fate to wield a model that was not introduced until well into the CBS years. Regarded for many years by plenty of traditional players as looking rather like some marketing man's rendition of a hippie acid trip, the Paisley Tele was first given some respectability by James Burton and has recently been raised to new heights by Brad Paisley, acknowledged savior of traditional country Tele picking. He has used an original '68 Paisley Red Telecaster that's older than he is on all of his significant recordings and most live tours (where it is supplemented by four Tele reproductions made by luthier Bill Crook).

However, the original Paisley Teles were by no means post-CBS dogs. While pre-CBS Fender guitars still remain most prized, the Paisley Tele is one of a handful of CBS-era models that have attained collectible status over the years, thanks in part to its limited production numbers. Although "Paisley Red" by name, the effects of the paisley stick-on graphics on the top of the guitar, as well as the aging of the finish, give it a much lighter look, and it's often referred to as a "Pink Paisley" model. Brad Paisley says it's more than just the eye-catching looks that make these instruments desirable, though. "I feel the maple-capped neck is one of the factors that makes those such good instruments," he told *Vintage Guitar* magazine's Ward Meeker in 2005. "Also, some of the lightest guitars Fender ever made were from the late '60s. A lot of people think of early '50s Teles as being these really light, perfect guitars."

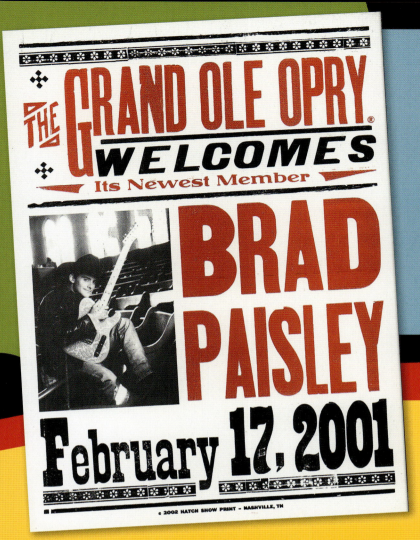

© 2002 HATCH SHOW PRINT - NASHVILLE, TN

"People were always saying I should be playing a Paisley Tele, but I just thought they were ugly. And then it evolved. I was always into James Burton—he was one of my heroes—so I went and found one at a guitar show and that's the main one I have now. I had a bender put in it, fell in love with it, and it's my main guitar."

—Brad Paisley

But they were very inconsistent. Most of them had a magic all their own, but some of them weren't as light as late '60s Telecasters. Those two factors—a great piece of wood and a great neck . . . and quality control hadn't yet gone downhill in the late '60s."

Paisley was born in 1972 in Wheeling, West Virginia, and raised in the small town of Glen Dale, in staunch bluegrass and country music territory. Paisley's grandfather gave him a Danelectro electric at the age of eight and taught him to play. Soon he was performing at church, school functions, and local events, and, while still in his early teens, he was invited by radio station WWVA to appear on the long-running *Jamboree USA*. The success of that guest spot led to an invitation to be a permanent fixture on the show, and for the next eight years Paisley opened for national country stars such as Ricky Skaggs, George Jones, Steve Wariner, The Judds, and many others. After two years of study at the nearby West Liberty College, Paisley transferred to Nashville's prestigious Belmont University as a music business major.

Soon after graduation, Paisley signed on as a songwriter with EMI Publishing and was picked up as an artist by Arista records not long after that. Since the release of his debut album, 1999's *Who Needs Pictures*, he has accrued twenty-one No. 1 country radio hits and won three Grammy Awards, fourteen Country Music Association Awards, and another fifteen Academy of Country Music Awards, all attesting to his success as a vocalist and songwriter, as well as his skills as a guitarist.

Paisley is often credited with bringing authentic Tele twang back to Nashville in an era when over-polished, rack-processed tones threatened to take over Guitar Town. For archetypal examples of the Brad Paisley—and Paisley Telecaster—tone, listen to tunes such as "The World" or "Alcohol" from *Time Well Wasted*, or "Throttleneck," an instrumental track from *5th Gear* that won him his first Grammy Award. Paisley is the first to acknowledge that it takes more than a good guitar to create a hit sound, though, and he gives his amps credit for a big part of the winning formula. Long enamored of a 1962 Vox AC30, which he still often uses in the studio, Paisley is also a fan of several Dr. Z models, often playing a Stingray (prototype of the production model Stang Ray), a Z-Wreck, and others. Paisley also uses amps by Trainwreck and Tony Bruno, usually running through several together both live and in the studio.

(continued from page 175)

Rather bizarrely, Fender's original selections for the three-way switch in the Broadcaster's control section shunned the obvious choices of neck, middle, and bridge pickup with a tone control in circuit for all of them. Perhaps it was just a bid to be too clever, or a notion that they needed to make this guitar at least approximate the sound of a big, boomy archtop for players who might expect that. Whatever the thinking, two-pickup guitars made in the first two years of production were wired to offer the following (from frontward to rearward switch positions respectively):

1. Neck pickup with a low-frequency emphasis created by a small network of one capacitor and one resistor, no tone control

2. Neck pickup straight to volume control, no tone control

3. Both pickups together with "tone" control actually wired as a blend control to add the neck pickup as desired

Oddly, with the above configuration, having created the greatest twang machine the music world had ever seen, Fender gave the Broadcaster, and the Nocaster, and early Telecaster that

Custom Shop 60th Anniversary Nocaster.
Fender Musical Instruments Corporation

followed it, no means of instantly switching to that now-legendary bridge pickup, other than by keeping the blend control wound down to zero.

The revised wiring scheme of late 1952 did little better, and arguably worse. It added a conventional tone control that was now in-circuit in two switch positions, but dropped the both-pickups setting—arguably a greater loss than it was a gain. Switch settings now looked like this:

1. Neck pickup with low-frequency emphasis and no tone control (similar to the previous number one setting, although now employing only a capacitor)

2. Neck pickup with conventional tone control

3. Bridge pickup with conventional tone control

Crazy, right? It's little surprise that so many players modified their Telecasters to the more conventional neck/both/bridge switching, with the tone control in-circuit for all settings. What is surprising, though, is that plenty of players didn't—as well as the fact that Fender itself didn't change the post-'53 wiring until 1967.

The pickups' signals also pass through the volume potentiometer, so it's clear that this component will affect the guitar's tone, too. A volume pot works by determining the balance of how much of the signal introduced at its input is passed along to either of its two remaining terminals. As used in the Telecaster, and most electric guitars, the second terminal goes to the output jack, the third to ground. With the pot turned fully clockwise, the entire signal flows to the output jack, but as you rotate it counter-clockwise, an increasingly greater proportion is tapped off to ground, decreasing the signal at the output. In addition to this purely functional behavior, however, pots of different values also lead the resultant tone to sound different. Roughly speaking, the higher the potentiometer's value, the more high-frequency content it retains in the signal, although its taper will be more dramatic.

Fender originally used a 250k-ohm potentiometer for the volume control, which retained plenty of highs in the signal

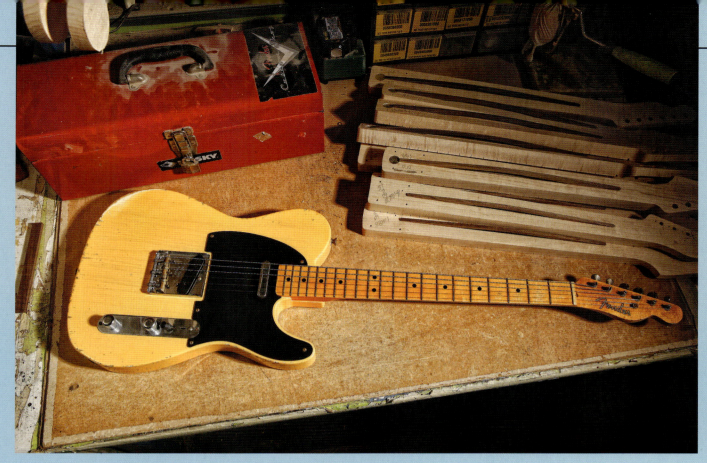

Custom Shop 60th Anniversary Broadcaster. *Fender Musical Instruments Corporation*

(these are bright pickups, after all, with more than enough treble for most tastes) and offered a smooth taper (or "roll-off") as the volume was decreased. In the late '60s, starting a year or two after the switch wiring was changed to the more conventional selections, Fender introduced a 1M-ohm potentiometer to the Telecaster, which impeded the guitar's highs even less than the former 250k pot (which, again, offered little noticeable impedance anyway). To this, a small .001uF disc cap was wired between terminals one and two (the input and output), to retain high-end presence as the pot was turned down. The overall result was some extremely bright Telecasters, guitars on which players looking for more classic meaty twang and snarl were more likely to jump to the tone controls to roll off some highs.

A 250k tone pot has always been used on traditional Telecasters, connected to the grounded terminal of the volume pot via a .05uF capacitor (often actually a .047uF cap, the closest value available from many manufacturers), as well as directly to the volume pot's input terminal. The signal doesn't "pass through" the tone pot as such, but this control performs its function by bleeding off high frequencies according to the rotation of the pot, at a frequency shelf determined by the tone capacitor.

The heavily knurled chromed knobs atop these controls are a familiar part of the Telecaster's look and feel. Other than the tall, flat knobs of the first Esquires and Broadcasters, these evolved from the more rounded-domed brass knobs of the pre-'57 Nocasters and Teles to the taller, flatter-topped steel knobs of the post-'57 guitars, though even within those periods a surprising variety of subtle variations is evident. Whatever type it carries, these distinctive pieces of hardware don't affect the tone of the instrument, but a Tele just wouldn't feel like a Tele without that rough metal knob to wrap your little finger around.

Beyond these components, little can be said to have a significant effect on the sound of the Telecaster. Purists do like to see the correct switch tip, strap buttons, pickguards, and even the correct pickguard mounting screws on their vintage guitars, or purportedly accurate reproductions thereof, but these can't lay claim to much sonic virtuosity one way or the other.

PART III

THE STRATOCASTER

THE SUBLIMELY SEXY AND SUPERBLY VERSATILE STRATOCASTER, released in 1954, was a quantum leap from the bare-bones Esquire and Broadcaster that had come out four years before (the guitar soon and forever after known as the Telecaster). Even if you are first and foremost a Telecaster fan, you can't deny that the Stratocaster took the electric guitar into an entirely different plane of existence design-wise. Compared to the Telecaster, even today, the Stratocaster appears a bold departure in the form; at the time, it must have looked like a music machine from another planet. Or at least from another generation—one capable of putting the frights into the knife-creased slacks of the generation that came before.

With the Stratocaster, Leo Fender finally left behind any semblance of what our common conception of "guitar" had been just a half dozen years before, other than in the six strings and E-A-D-G-B-E tuning. From out of the slab-bodied, two-pickup, hardtail twanger had grown an extremely versatile performance machine with the looks to match its revolutionary sonic capabilities. In light of its humble origins, the Stratocaster is all the more impressive, coming not from a large, established maker with several decades of success in the industry, but from one self-driven man with a hat full of great ideas, a few maverick helpers, and a willingness to thoughtfully examine the true needs of musicians of the day.

1954 Stratocaster. *Chicago Music Exchange (www.chicagomusicexchange.com)*

HISTORY OF THE STRATOCASTER

IN THE EARLY 1950S, WITH THE TELECASTER doing relatively well in its first years, Fender was earning a broader following. After the Tele's debut in 1950, Leo logged another major first in 1951 with the release of the Precision Bass. The Fender amplifier line was growing apace, and another classic of the steel-guitar lineup was launched in the form of the Stringmaster in 1952. To gain even more customers, Fender needed a somewhat different and more versatile addition to the lineup. The development of a new and even more radical second Fender solidbody six-string was a team effort, bringing in a new design talent, a Tele endorsee who seemed to never have been entirely happy with the design, and ultimately winning over a major name who outright rejected the slab-bodied single-cut. Just exactly when it all happened, though, and precisely who was at the drawing table (or was holding the pen, at least), seem to be points of debate that will never be entirely settled.

1954 Stratocaster. *Chicago Music Exchange, www.chicagomusicexchange.com*

Even if you don't know his name, or know it only from other books on Fender history that you might have read, you will have heard at least one example of Freddie Tavares's steel-guitar playing on countless occasions, in the form of the iconic lap-steel glissando that opens the theme to vintage *Loony Tunes* cartoons. Tavares was a far more skilled and accomplished player than this novelty example might imply, though, and he had a background that would seem primed to be bent to the will of a growing Fender company. He was born on the Hawaiian island of Maui in 1913, one of twelve children born to Portuguese immigrant Antone Tavares and his wife, Julia Akana, who was of Hawaiian, Chinese, English, and Tahitian-Samoan descent. He took up the guitar at the age of twelve when his older brother left his own instrument behind upon heading to law school, and in 1934, at the age of twenty-one, he joined Harry Owens and the Royal Hawaiians, the famed house band at the Royal Hawaiian Hotel in Waikiki. The Royal Hawaiians, with Tavares on the steel, frequently toured the United States over the course of several years and recorded numerous sides and movie soundtracks in Hollywood in the process. Tavares, his wife, and two young sons eventually settled for good in the Los Angeles area, where he dedicated himself mainly to session and radio work—avoiding extensive touring to remain home with the family—and performed on recordings by the Andrews Sisters, Deanna Durbin, Dean Martin, Bing Crosby, Sons of the Pioneers, Spike Jones and the City Slickers, and even Elvis Presley.

In addition to his playing achievements, Tavares had taught himself electronics and other mechanical crafts and had built his own steel guitars and amplifiers. While playing at LA's Cowtown Club with the Ozark Mountain Boys in 1953, Tavares was introduced to Leo Fender by fellow steel guitarist Noel Boggs. Legend has it (as detailed in a story by Shannon Wianecki in *Hanahou* magazine, September 2012) that Tavares pointed out several faults in Fender's amps—in answer to which Leo Fender pulled out a screwdriver, removed the back panel from Tavares's own homemade amp, checked the work inside the chassis, and then offered him a job in the Fender development lab on the spot.

Most credible accounts of the development of the Stratocaster indicate that Tavares's job was tasked with concocting the body shape and general design of the new guitar, which was but a basic concept in Leo's mind at the time of Freddie's arrival at the Pomona Street factory in spring 1953. In his book *The Fender Stratocaster* (Hal Leonard, 1994), A.R. Duchossoir quotes Tavares as saying, "The first real project that I had was to put the Stratocaster on [the] drawing board. It was about April or May 1953 and Leo said, 'We need a new guitar,' and I said, 'How far apart are the strings at the nut, how far [at] the bridge?' I got those parameters and I said, 'What's the scale?' Then I knew where the strings are and we started from there."

Leo Fender was himself quoted as saying that he was already working on elements of the Stratocaster's design in 1951 and 1952, and it seems some players—Bill Carson among them—were asking for a new and more deluxe solid-body electric, and particularly one with a built-in vibrato unit, perhaps as early as this. No clear records exist, however, of drawings or prototypes or dated accounts of Stratocaster R&D going on as early as this, and, while Leo wasn't afraid to take his time and get things right, most new models were moving more quickly from prototype to production by this time than the ponderous three years that Leo's account implies. Ultimately, as with some other things, it might be that Mr. Fender's memory was a little hazy by the time he stated such things in interviews.

It seems we are unlikely to ever know precisely who concocted exactly what detail and when, other than that there was input to a greater or lesser extent from each of several individuals, including Fender employees Tavares and George Fullerton, performers Bill Carson and Rex Galleon, Fender sales director Don Randall, and of course Leo Fender himself. A look at what is known of the development of different aspects of the Stratocaster, however, even if the credit given—or claimed—is sometimes apocryphal, should bring us closer to an understanding of what a groundbreaking undertaking it was in its day.

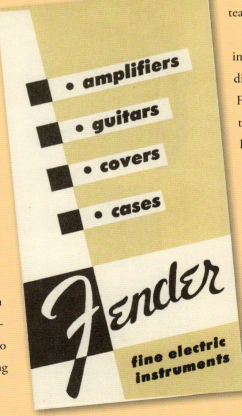

THE SALESMAN DRIVES A REVOLUTION

While we bicker and argue over who designed the Stratocaster, it can often be too easy to ignore the role played by the man at Fender who very likely asked for this new model in the first place and was in a position to see it fit into the new and growing market. Don Randall, Leo Fender's partner in the Fender Sales arm of the business and the head of the team responsible for getting Fender guitars and amplifiers into the stores, was the single biggest hub for receiving consumer feedback from dealers and players and directing it to where it would do some good. As such, he was adept at translating that into features that Leo and the design team could use to make the products more saleable. Randall had input on several features of Fender guitars over the years, details that would either appeal to players, thus making the instruments easier for RTEC reps to sell to dealers, or that might prevent warranty nightmares that would cost the company money. Adjustable bridge saddles, adjustable pickups, multiple pickups and switching, and stylistic elements involving body and headstock shapes might all seem the purview of the guitars' designers, but as often as not these were concocted at the direct urging of Randall and his sales team.

In addition to his influence on designs in the lab, Don Randall had an even more direct impact on the public perception of Fender products that were floated onto the guitar market. Randall named the Broadcaster due to the vast popularity of radio, the dominant form of media at the time of the guitar's release. In a genius stroke of foresight, he renamed it the Telecaster in spring 1951 after the Gretsch company objected to the first model name's similarity to its "Broadkaster" drum kit. Randall, a licensed pilot, would also be the man to take the next major Fender guitar into the stratosphere in 1954 with an appropriately thrusting name.

THE TEAM PUTS THE PIECES TOGETHER

The easiest way to see how much the new Stratocaster brought to the table might be to start with the Telecaster as a template—which is certainly how the Fender team, and the players and sales reps who influenced them, would have perceived the venture—and examine what was changed or added to the formula. The neck, of course, remained virtually the same, other than gaining a larger headstock shape, purportedly at Don Randall's request, to more proudly display the Fender logo. The body was still crafted from solid swamp ash, and the pickups were still of a thin single-coil design, employing individual Alnico rod-magnet pole pieces with a coil wound around them. Other than these, though, virtually every detail of the new guitar was entirely different.

Radical new elements in the Stratocaster design included the following:

- a more comfortable body shape, with contours where it met the player's ribcage and right forearm
- a broader sonic range, courtesy of three individual pickups
- a more ergonomic control layout, along with a recessed jack for accidental pull-out safety
- a built-in vibrato unit
- not least of all, superbly stylish new looks

Added together, the result was arguably the most comfortable-feeling and versatile-performing guitar on the market at the time, anywhere, and this just four years after Fender had entered the Spanish-electric guitar market in the first place. The impressive thing is that none of these ingredients, so ubiquitous today that we largely take them for granted, came about merely by whim or chance. All were enacted for one good reason or another, and they coalesced toward a spectacular whole from sometimes disparate points of origin.

Guitarist Bill Carson seems to have been looking for changes to the Telecaster design from the start, or at least from the time he made Leo Fender's acquaintance around mid-1951. Carson has

This 1955 nontremelo Stratocaster belongs to ZZ Top's Billy F Gibbons. *David Perry* said in several interviews that he often suggested Fender build a guitar with a built-in vibrato. He is also frequently credited with coming up with the ideas to contour the Stratocaster's body. As Carson told A.R. Duchossoir in 1988 in interviews for *The Fender Stratocaster*, "The thing I didn't like about the Telecaster was the discomfort of it, because I was doing a lot of studio work at the time on the West Coast and sitting down its square edges really dug into my rib." That said, Leo Fender himself has also been quoted as saying, in interviews with Duchossoir and elsewhere, that the contouring notion came from local guitarist Rex Galleon before it was suggested by Carson. Either way, it's likely that multiple recommendations from respected performers helped the idea to achieve a sort of critical mass with Leo and resulted in the two bandsaw swipes for the tummy and forearm contours that produce the extremely comfortable feel of the Stratocaster body as we know it today.

As for the development of what might arguably have been the Stratocaster's most innovative advancement on the form, the built-in vibrato bridge, well, it seemed this one required quite a bit more effort. While Carson has also, via several sources, claimed responsibility for suggesting this one, the vibrato unit was unlikely to have been his idea alone, or even first. Leo knew not long after the Telecaster started gaining acceptance that he would need to build a guitar with a vibrato, to fend off competition from the guitar Paul Bigsby originally designed and built for picker Merle Travis, a solidbody that preceded the Esquire and Broadcaster's release. In addition, the Bigsby vibrato unit that soon showed up retro-fitted to Gibson and Gretsch guitars was gaining momentum. It is likely that Don Randall had urged the inclusion of this feature, as with so many other things, because it would have been a major feature upon which to sell the new guitar. Nevertheless, a player like Carson still helps us understand the appeal of this piece of hardware. "Steel guitar played a large part in country and western swing bands," he told A.R. Duchossoir. "When I was doing studio sessions with a foot control [volume pedal] that Leo made me, I could use a vibrato and do steel guitar things and I would sometimes get paid double for the session." For the musicians, it was all about the functional tool, and that was something Leo Fender had understood—and gotten right—from the start.

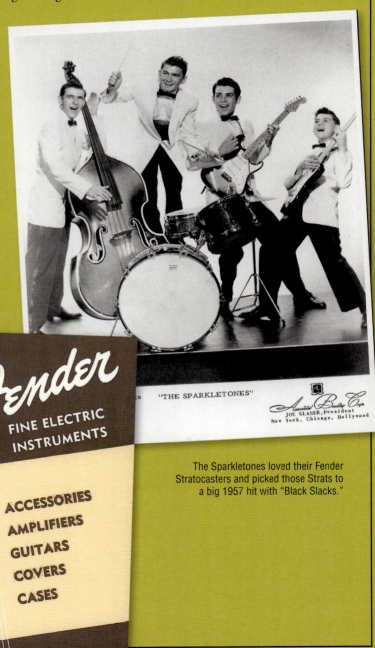

The Sparkletones loved their Fender Stratocasters and picked those Strats to a big 1957 hit with "Black Slacks."

While the concerned parties at Fender pretty much knew the new model would at least carry a vibrato, well before either the shape of the vibrato or the guitar itself were anything close to final conception, tackling that task would prove more time consuming than all other elements of the new design. According to George Fullerton, as quoted in an interview in Tom Wheeler's *The Stratocaster Chronicles*, "The vibrato was the new guitar's last piece. . . . We already had the body contouring, pickup design, third pickup . . . the new headstock shape, the tooling—everything except that vibrato had already been accepted."

NEW PICKUPS AND ELECTRONICS

Whereas Gibson largely used the same pickup design throughout the model range from the late 1940s to the mid-1950s, Fender went with three different pickups for its flagship Spanish-electric guitars in the space of just a few years. All might have shared some similarities in that they were relatively narrow single-coil pickups with individual rod magnet segments for pole pieces, but each was unique regardless. The Telecaster carried quite different pickups in its bridge and neck positions, with a wider, longer coil in the former than in the latter, and Leo had determined that something different still would be needed for the new model.

As discussed earlier, treble content—which aided brightness, clarity, and cutting power—was valued highly at the time, and Leo sought the same in his new pickup. In order to achieve an adequate blend of bite and body, Fender settled on 42 AWG copper wire wound in a narrow coil around six individual pole pieces cut from Alnico V rod magnets, all supported by thin fiber top and bottom plates. This was essentially the same construction used in the Telecaster's bridge pickup at the time, wound into a slightly narrower coil with a little less coil wire, although the earliest Broadcaster bridge pickups, and ongoing Telecaster neck pickups, used a finer 43 AWG wire. The result was a pickup with slightly less beef in the tone than that of the Tele's bridge pickup, for a bright, cutting sound in the bridge position, and a fat and warm, yet clear and articulate, tone in the neck position.

All Fender pickups were noted for their excellent string-to-string articulation, a feature enhanced by the individual pole pieces cut from actual magnets, and the Strat certainly retained this desirable characteristic. To further enhance the string-to-string balance, Fender also used magnets of staggered heights on the new Stratocaster pickups, with lower magnets on the louder strings for a comparable overall output across all six.

The inclusion of three of these new pickups on the new guitar would also prove a feature the sales team could brag about, and the trio sure looked impressive up against what was available in the day. Even if the three pickups didn't give the Stratocaster, with its three-way switch, any more tone selections than the Telecaster already possessed, the ones it did have were arguably already more usable (see Stratocaster Tone and Construction for further discussion of these points). The Stratocaster's switching and control complement didn't yet tap the full potential of the trio of pickups and their various combinations; it was more versatile than many guitars of its day. The use of a master volume control with direct routing of the bridge pickup from switch to volume, along with individual tone controls for the bridge and middle pickups, yielded a clear, crisp tone from each of the three switch positions (fulfilling that Fender objective yet again), where the Telecaster still retained a pre-set "bassy sound," with the neck pickup wired through a small capacitor network in the forward switch position, a tone that many players found virtually useless.

In addition to the wiring schematic beneath them, the positioning of the switch and controls themselves was arguably more ergonomic than that of any production electric guitar seen before. The Fender team very consciously placed the master volume control within easy access of the player's right-hand "pinky" finger for easy, on-the-fly volume swells, while the three-way switch was equally accessible for quick pickup changes. The result was a guitar that, from head to tail, would be deemed by many musicians to be more playable and sonically versatile than any to have come before it.

PROTOTYPING AND PERFECTING THE FENDER VIBRATO

Deciding you need a built-in vibrato on your new guitar and actually developing an original unit that functions well in every respect are two different things. The task proved one of the greatest undertakings of Fender's early years and was also the slowest

1956 Stratocaster. *Michael Dregni*

piece of the Stratocaster puzzle to come together. Note, too, that this unit was far more than just "a built-in vibrato." Rather than a separate piece of hardware that could be added behind whatever bridge existed—somewhat like the Kauffman Vib-Rola or Bigsby vibrato (or later, the Gibson's Maestro Vibrola or Burns Vibrato)—the final product was an entirely new design that encompassed both bridge and tailpiece in one unit. The eventual result would include several other major innovations, in addition to the vibrato effect of which it was capable, but it took some time and several iterations to get the "all-in-one-unit" part of the equation, as well as the several details within it, just right.

Again, we have to accept that memories and accurate chronologies might have grown a little hazy with time, but Tom Wheeler writes in *The Stratocaster Chronicles* that George Fullerton reported that Fender had already started putting one hundred Stratocasters through the line—and had completed one guitar—with the first "final" rendition of the bridge. Fender was making a major effort to get the guitar to the summer NAMM show in June 1953, but it was not to be. "I couldn't wait that morning to get the first one off the line," Fullerton told Wheeler. "I grabbed that one and tested it out, and it was terribly bad sounding. . . . I rushed to the lab, Leo and I looked at it, and we called Freddie over to look at it. That vibrato sounded like a tin can. We all agreed it wasn't going to work, so we shut down the line. It was a sad day. It was then that Leo went back to the drawing board."

This "first final" rendition of the important new component, while manufactured to be an all-in-one, drop-in unit, included a tailpiece that was separate to the bridge and moved with the player's depression of the vibrato bar, along with roller saddles to help the strings return accurately to pitch. The main problem, it seemed, was that with so many moving parts, as well as some side-to-side movement in the saddles themselves, the unit lacked the mass and solidity needed to provide adequate sustain and to achieve a solid tone in the first place. Rather than continue to address details of the existing design to correct its faults, extending an effort that had already taken several months to get the vibrato to its current state, Leo, Freddie Tavares, and George Fullerton abandoned the thing altogether and started in on an entirely new approach.

As familiar as the final rendition of the Stratocaster vibrato unit is to us now, it's easy to overlook what a brilliant piece of design it is. In going back to the drawing board, Leo and his team stripped this thing down to what we can now see are the bare essentials for an all-in-one bridge and tailpiece with sensitive and accurate vibrato functions and individual and fully adjustable saddles. The saddles alone were revolutionary in their day and provided players with an unprecedented degree of fine-adjustment of intonation and playing action (Gibson's Tune-o-matic bridge, which also hit the market in 1954 on the Les Paul Custom, had individual saddles that were adjustable for intonation, but only global adjustment for bridge height via thumb-wheels at either end of the bridge). What really made Fender's new vibrato work right, however—and, more importantly, sound right—lay beneath its relatively simple surface components.

To compensate for the lack of body mass in the string anchoring of the vibrato bridge (a situation created by anchoring the strings to a moving part), Leo devised a steel inertia block that he mounted below the vibrato's base plate. The strings were loaded through holes drilled through the block and, as a result, were anchored with the mass needed for satisfactory tone and sustain. The inertia block also served as the connection point for the springs (up to five), which were anchored at their other end at a "spring claw" screwed into the body, at the far end of a channel routed into the guitar's back. The steel bridge base, with bent-steel saddles above and inertia block below, had knife-edge fulcrum points in its six mounting holes, which anchored against hardened steel screws to minimize friction while in motion. The end result was a unit that moved fluidly and returned to pitch well but still provided a solid strings-to-body anchor, with a good, ringing tone and impressive sustain.

It might have put the development of the new model as a whole back by a good six months or so, but the new vibrato really was a wonder of engineering. The lack of "dead" string space between a tailpiece and the bridge saddles, and the fact that the strings didn't need to slide over the saddles to produce the unit's pitch fluctuation, meant far fewer tuning instabilities than experienced in some other vibrato units. In addition, the ingenious inertia block proved a wondrously simple solution to a problem that had threatened to sink the entire enterprise in the final hour.

Although Fender dubbed the new unit the "Synchronized Tremolo Action" when it released the Stratocaster and billed it as one of the new guitar's top features, it was, of course, a "vibrato" and not a "tremolo." Tremolo more accurately describes the modulation of volume, rather than frequency or pitch. A vibrato, on the other hand, modulates pitch, which is exactly what Fender's "Synchronized Tremolo" does. Conversely, Fender also usually referred to the genuine tremolo effect on many of its amplifiers as "vibrato," even though it did not fluctuate the pitch of the guitar signal in any way, but pulsated the volume. Fender repeated the misnomer on his patent application for the new "Tremolo Device for Stringed Instrument," filed August 30, 1954, and granted a little less than two years later.

PROTOTYPE TURNS TO PRODUCTION

For all the work that went into pulling together the Strat's revolutionary new ingredients—including having prototypes in the field for testing by mid-1953, and the ongoing development of new components—we have far fewer verifiable reports or photos of genuine Stratocaster prototypes than we do of Telecaster prototypes. In his book *Fender: The Sound Heard Round the World*, Fender historian Richard Smith published photos taken by Leo Fender of a supposed Stratocaster prototype from 1953. The photos showed a "breadboard" guitar of sorts, with a black fiber pickguard, knurled silver Telecaster-style knobs, and a back route wide enough to take only three springs rather than the standard five. Otherwise, there has always been a lot of gray area between "late prototype" and "early production," and it's possible that several genuine prototypes were either lost, or intentionally destroyed, once the Stratocaster proper was actually released.

1956 Stratocaster. *Michael Dregni*

Regardless, by early 1954 Fender's new guitar had found its ultimate form and was ready to hit the market. The final ingredients were a nifty new jack plate design—and a name. The former took shape as a recessed jack plate mounted conveniently on the top of the guitar, alongside the switches, which both prevented the usual blind fumbling around trying to insert the ¼-inch plug into the hole normally found on the lower edge of the body, and let the plug pull out cleanly if you accidentally stepped on your guitar cord, rather than bending the cord's plug end or, worse, ripping out a chunk of wood as you crowbarred the entire jack from the guitar.

The name came courtesy of Don Randall, head of Fender Sales, who was a licensed pilot and was known to fly his own plane to important meetings and sales opportunities. His coinage of "Stratocaster" fit perfectly with the times: it pitched the guitar beyond the present, into a soaring future that the day's musicians—and Cold War citizenry in general—were only beginning to imagine. Regarding the team effort of putting together this new model, and the several apocryphal tales related to it, Randall told Tom Wheeler, "A lot of these guys who claim credit for the Stratocaster didn't have a damn thing to do with it. I don't mean to put any of them down, but the salesmen and I, we were the ones who knew the business, knew the competition, and we knew what we needed." What they needed was a guitar that both walked the walk and talked the talk, an electric that both looked and sounded unlike anything that had come before and could be boldly promoted as such. In the new Stratocaster, they received all that and more.

Early-production Stratocasters started rolling through the Fender factory by spring 1954, and Randall's sales team, now an independent entity after the creation of Fender Sales in summer 1953, was hot to crow about it. One notice to Fender dealers sent in early spring 1954, "Announcing the new Fender Stratocaster," declared "shipments are expected to begin May 15." The same notice claimed, of the new Synchronized Tremolo, "This sectional bridge is a patented feature which no other guitar on the market today can duplicate. . . ." In fact, the actual patent application

Duane Allman's 1955 Stratocaster. *Will Ireland/ Total Guitar Magazine/Getty Images*

wouldn't be filed for some three months, and the patent wouldn't be granted until two years later.

Regardless, Fender widely proclaimed this built-in tremolo to be a "first," and the feature would be one of its major selling points, along with its "Comfort Contoured" body, three pickups, new tone controls and switching, and surface-mounted "plug receptacle." The first print ad to promote the new guitar, published in the May issue of *International Musician* magazine (on the shelves in April), touted all of these features, along with an illustration of the new Stratocaster above a sketch of protons whirling through their orbits around a stylized atom. Whoever penned the ad, it certainly bore Don Randall's signature.

Despite this optimism over shipping dates, the Stratocaster didn't ramp-up to full production until later that summer. The first hundred or so guitars were numbered 0100 to 0207 on the back of their spring-cavity covers (at a time when Telecasters' serial numbers were stamped into their bridge plates). From around late fall 1954, both the Telecaster and Stratocaster had their serial numbers stamped into the plates that reinforced the screws attaching neck to body. The guitar's initial retail price was set at $249.50 with Synchronized Tremolo (the Telecaster was $189.50 at the time), or $229.50 for the "hardtail" version without vibrato, plus $39.95 for the hardshell case covered in "grain hair seal simulated covering," according to early Fender sales literature.

Some historians like to refer to Stratocasters produced prior to September or October as "pre-production models," although since Fender Sales had already announced the availability of a production model in May of that year, it seems sensible to think of the earliest guitars from spring 1954 onward simply as Stratocasters with rare early specs. Other than a handful of early guitars produced with anodized aluminum pickguards, the main differences were the somewhat smaller knobs made from slightly pearloid-looking white plastic found on the earliest Stratocasters, followed by a more brittle plastic, often referred to as Bakelite, that was used for knobs, pickup covers, and pickguard for a brief period. The wear that the pickup covers underwent in particular, it would seem, from constant abrasion from the player's pick or finger-nails, led to the use of a more durable plastic for these components by early 1955.

STANDARD EARLY APPOINTMENTS

Alongside these relatively superficial cosmetic details of the early run of Stratocasters, which nevertheless excite collectors to no end, the early specs and appointments of the model are probably even more significant from the perspective of performance. Some of these details will be discussed at greater length in Stratocaster Tone and Construction, but these basics essentially defined the original Fender Stratocaster of 1954 and the first few years that followed.

Swamp-Ash Body

The Stratocaster debuted with a body made from solid swamp ash, still the wood used for the Telecaster at the time, with forearm and ribcage contours—the latter in particular—that might seem extremely deep to those more familiar with later examples of the breed, making it a very comfortable guitar to play. In 1956 the wood of choice shifted to alder, although ash was still used beneath the blonde finish on most so-called "Mary Kaye" Stratocasters, and on some other custom-order examples.

All-Maple Neck

A solid maple neck with the truss rod inserted into a channel in the back (with tell-tale walnut "skunk stripe" and headstock "teardrop") was used from the guitar's debut until around mid-1959. While these appeared outwardly similar throughout the era, the profile (back shape) changed significantly over the years, giving quite a different playing feel to Stratocasters from different points within the decade. The early necks had a beefy, rounded shape, but by 1955 a chunky V-neck, or "boat-neck" shape arrived, which thinned out somewhat through the course of 1956 and 1957. During 1958, necks became more rounded and C shaped,

2012 Custom Shop 1956 Ash Desert Sand Heavy Relic Stratocaster. *Fender Musical Instruments Corporation*

though less chunky than the original 1954 necks, and began to slim out even more going into 1959 and 1960.

Six-in-Line Headstock

Fender had already used a six-in-line headstock for the Telecaster, but the shape introduced on the Stratocaster has become even more iconic and a universal symbol of the brand. It is frequently pointed out that the solid-body guitar built in the mid-1940s by Paul Bigsby, initially for artist Merle Travis and then others, had a similar headstock long before the Strat, and even before the Broadcaster and Esquire, but Leo declared his own reasons for using the all-on-one-side design: "That's a very old idea that has been around for thousands of years. The Croatians, near Poland, have several instruments with tuning pegs located on one side of the guitar and they invented this years ago," he told *Guitar Player* magazine in 1971. And the reason to use such a design in 1954? Putting the tuners all on one side of the headstock allows a straight line from nut slot to tuner post, thus reducing hitching in the nut slots and resultant tuning instabilities.

Vibrato Bridge and Kluson Tuners

The most revolutionary element of the Stratocaster's hardware set, its Synchronized Tremolo, has already been covered in some detail. It was such a comprehensive component that the guitar didn't carry much else in the hardware department other than its Kluson tuners. The guitar also had a round string guide at the front of the headstock between the B and high-E strings that increased the tension of these in the nut slots on their long journeys to the tuner posts.

Single-Coil Pickups

The three narrow single-coil pickups that Leo and his team had developed for the prototype guitars at least a year before the Stratocaster's official production began, and which were intended as a major selling point of the new model, remained the standard at the guitar's release. Well known to players today as the ubiquitous "Stratocaster pickup," these had six individual pole pieces cut from Alnico V rod magnets to somewhat different lengths for staggered heights to balance out variances in string output. They were originally wound with an average of 8,500 or so turns of 42 AWG Formvar-coated wire.

Master Volume, Two Tones, Three-Way Switch

Although it has become another "standard" of sorts, the Stratocaster's complement of a single volume control, individual tone controls for the neck and middle pickups, and a three-way selector switch defined an impressive control setup when the guitar was released in 1954 and was another of its saleable features. Fender didn't change the main specifications of this configuration for a full twenty-three years—a five-way switch finally arriving as standard in 1977—although some players did modify it to suit their own particular playing needs. Quite early on, several guitarists would find use for the funky sounding in-between switch settings that blended the bridge-middle and middle-neck pickups by balancing the three-way switch between positions; others would find the second tone control more useful on the bright bridge pickup than on the warm neck pickup, and rewire accordingly.

Sunburst Finish

Although custom colors were more prevalent on the Strat than on the Tele, with a handful of notable examples early on, then several more later in the decade, the only truly "standard" finish available on the Stratocaster for twenty-five years was sunburst. This was a two-tone sunburst, running from dark edges to a golden-amber center, from the guitar's arrival in 1954 until mid-1958, when a three-tone sunburst included a red middle band between them. This red finish faded prematurely on many early examples, making many vintage Strats from 1958 to 1960 appear two-tone regardless, until a stronger, fade-resistant red tint came into use at Fender.

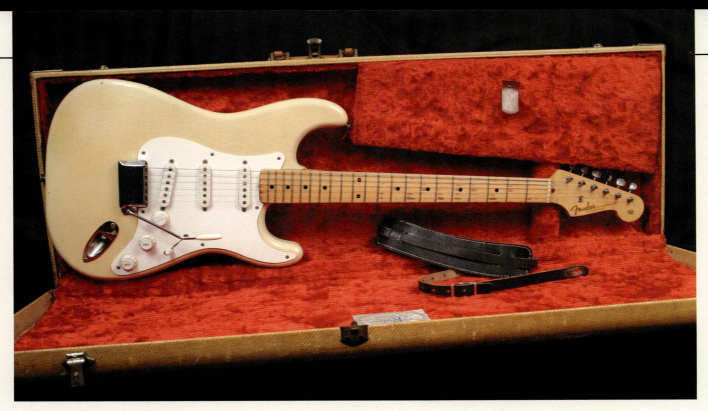

1956 Blonde Stratocaster. *Rumble Seat Music*

THE STRATOCASTER: LAUNCHED INTO THE STRATOSPHERE

Added together, these simple—yet, revolutionary—ingredients paint the picture of the instrument that hit an unsuspecting music world in mid-1954 and ascended steadily toward its soon dizzying heights. It is impossible to comprehend today, with countless Strat-a-likes available in the form of everything from sub-$100 imports to $10,000 luthier-grade recreations, just how new the Stratocaster must have appeared in 1954 and what its impact must have been, both in look and in tone. This was a world that needed the Fender Stratocaster, but until it actually came along, there was nothing remotely like it, either in the music world or in pop culture in general.

The economy and the culture were booming in the post–World War II, early–Cold War era of the early 1950s, yet by 1954 so many of the revolutionary cultural and commercial developments that would be commonplace by the end of the decade had yet to make their impact. Just imagine this world for a moment: The U.S. Navy commissions its first nuclear submarine. Hydrogen bomb tests are in full swing on Bikini Atoll in the Pacific Ocean. The first organ transplants are carried out in hospitals in Boston

and Paris. *Brown v. Board of Education* makes segregation in U.S. public schools illegal. British athlete Roger Bannister runs the first under-four-minute mile. NBC's *The Tonight Show* first airs, with host Steve Allen. Marlon Brando stars in two major hit movies, *On the Waterfront* and *The Wild Ones*. America's first jet airliner, the Boeing 707, takes its maiden flight. Swanson sells its first TV dinner. The term "rock 'n' roll" is only beginning to enter the lexicon, thanks in part to the release of the movie *Blackboard Jungle*, featuring "Rock Around the Clock" by Bill Haley and the Comets and the start of Elvis Presley's recording career. Amid it all, here comes the Fender Stratocaster: startling, radical, stylish, and entirely awe-inspiring, even in this fast-paced, future-now context.

For all its potential and invention, however, the Stratocaster didn't set the guitar world ablaze overnight. After all, this was a conservative crowd (for that matter, guitarists' tastes, en masse, still run to the conservative today), and Fender was still struggling uphill for acceptance amid the traditional names of the industry. Keep in mind, too, that even large, traditional makers often had their more adventurous efforts shot down by a wary buying public. Not only did Gibson's radical Flying V and Explorer guitars fail to find any significant market, even in the rock 'n' roll hotbed of the late 1950s, but another of the three undeniable solidbody classics, the Les Paul, sold so poorly in its final years, 1958–60, that it was dropped from the catalog and didn't reappear for years.

Fender had to work to establish the Stratocaster's place in the guitarists' lexicon. Several of Leo's Western Swing test-bed buddies and their pals took up the cause with some gusto, and the Stratocaster, in its infancy, gained acceptance rather more steadily than had the Telecaster before it. Often, too, the early adopters seemed to have been won over by the glamour of a custom finish—always a badge of honor on the country scene, to some extent—even when no custom-colored Strats were yet officially available.

Bill Carson was clearly delighted with the release of the new model he had given input on and was one of the first artists seen in print ads for the new product, proudly cradling his own early custom-color Cimarron Red Stratocaster (which often looked merely black in the monochrome photos). Eldon Shamblin, guitarist for Bob Wills and His Texas Playboys, had virtually denied the entire premise of the Telecaster when it was first presented to him, but he was an enthusiastic recipient of a gold-finished Stratocaster, a guitar that seems to have been either a late prototype or a very early production model, and probably something from that gray area in between.

Soon after, the Stratocaster sidestepped successfully into rock 'n' roll. Two of Gene Vincent's guitarists (we might call them "Cliff Gallup stand-ins"), Howard Reed and Johnny Meeks, both played Stratocasters—and custom-color examples at that, Black and Blonde models, respectively. But the Strat really landed in the hands of its first pop-idol frontman when Buddy Holly took up a late 1954 or early 1955 model at the start of his career and continued to play one until his death in 1959. He went through four or five guitars in his short career. His first was stolen from a tour bus in Michigan in

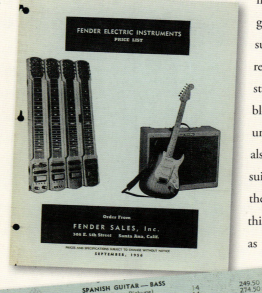

1956 Fender price list.

1955, and his second, a new '57 Stratocaster, was stolen from the band's station wagon during a restaurant stop in St. Louis in April 1958; but the similar look of these, all in standard sunburst finish, helped to establish the model nationwide through his many TV and concert appearances. By the late 1950s, about half a decade since its introduction, the Stratocaster was going strong and getting stronger in virtually all genres of popular music. Even so, it provides some perspective on the times to consider that few people today can name more than half a dozen prominent artists who were regularly using a Stratocaster by the end of the decade—and to consider, in that light, what a classic it already was and what a legend it was on its way to becoming.

WOODS EVOLVE: ASH TO ALDER, MAPLE TO ROSEWOOD

The Stratocaster's specs didn't change as much over its first few years of production as did those of the Telecaster. We have already mentioned the change in plastics that occurred over the course of the early production models of 1954. The next significant change of spec came with the uptake of alder as a primary body wood in 1956, with ash remaining in use mainly in Blonde custom-colored Strats. Leo Fender was always concerned with consistency and basic quality, and alder appeared a suitable substitute for the more highly figured swamp ash, which was getting more difficult to obtain in adequate supplies. While ash's broad grain was still readily apparent under the Telecaster's standard blonde finish, and that of the few blonde Strats, alder looked perfectly good under a sunburst or opaque finish and was also easier to obtain in adequate supplies of suitably light timber. The change did alter the Stratocaster's core tone somewhat, but this was a sonic shift rather than a decline, as alder itself has many desirable sonic properties (as discussed in more detail in Stratocaster Tone and Construction).

(continued on page 217)

Bill Carson

Country guitarist Bill Carson was one of Leo Fender's favorite pickers and guitar testers. Here, Carson holds his 1954 Cimmaron Red Stratocaster with gold anodized pickguard.

The name "Bill Carson" might be best known by Fender fans today for its frequent appearance in the written history of the development of the Stratocaster, but Carson was a true journeyman musician of the electric guitar and a significant name on the scene at the time. He undoubtedly played a significant role in bringing the Stratocaster into being, but he also deserves recognition for his musical career.

Carson was born in Meridian, Oklahoma, in 1926 and was raised in Amarillo, Texas. He eventually followed the road to California that had lured so many "Okies" and Midwesterners to

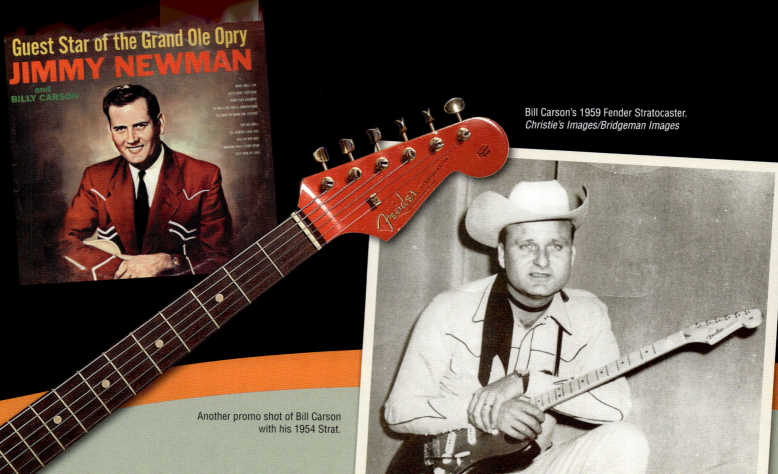

Guest Star of the Grand Ole Opry
JIMMY NEWMAN
and
BILLY CARSON

Bill Carson's 1959 Fender Stratocaster.
Christie's Images/Bridgeman Images

Another promo shot of Bill Carson with his 1954 Strat.

the land of milk and honey—which was, in his case, the land of Western Swing. Shortly after his arrival in Los Angeles, Carson established himself as a reliable A-list sideman with a string of major acts on the scene, including Spade Cooley, Hank Thompson, Lefty Frizzell, Wade Ray, and others. At the time, the lap steel player was often the star of the guitar world, since that instrument had been a success to amplify before the solid-body Spanish guitar came along. As such, Carson's playing style and sound were closely aligned to the clean, fluid, gliss-heavy approach of the steel players, and he often found work copping steel-style parts on guitar to double his session fees. Back in the day, though, even that kind of work was barely enough to keep a musician afloat, and Carson, like so many others, needed a solid "day job" to help sustain his playing. He found it as a byproduct of his quest for a better instrument and forged a forty-year career as a result.

As legendary as the Fender of the early 1950s might seem to guitar fans today, it was part of what was then a pretty small world. Carson was fond of telling the story of how he visited the Fullerton factory in 1951 in search of a Telecaster and an amp to go with it and was greeted by Leo Fender himself. The relationship that ensued found Carson not only a Fender player, but soon a field-tester of guitars in development and an actual Fender employee. Carson first worked on the assembly line while maintaining his career as a gigging and recording guitarist, then dialed back his musical career in 1957 to move up the ladder at Fender, first as a production supervisor, then head of artist relations, and eventually sales manager. Bill Carson's name has been established in Fender lore, however, largely for his contributions to the design and development of the Stratocaster in 1953 and 1954. Among the major new features that he is likely to have influenced—in part, at least, if not wholly—were the inclusion of a vibrato unit (Carson liked to use it, in conjunction with a volume pedal, to fake pedal-steel sounds) and the comfort-contoured body. Bill Carson worked at Fender well into his seventies, before passing away in 2006 at the age of eighty.

Eldon Shamblin

Bob Wills and His Texas Playboys, circa 1950, with Eldon Shamblin cradling his grand Gibson ES-5 archtop in the days before he switched to his Stratocaster. *Michael Ochs Archives/Getty Images*

Eldon Shamblin's 1954 Gold Stratocaster, serial number 0569. *Ronny Proler (Anonymous Texas Collector); Photo by Dirk Bakker, Artbook*

Leo Fender was a country music fan through and through, so it's little surprise that one of the first Stratocasters presented to an artist was given to a country picker. And considering that Bob Wills and His Texas Playboys were about the hottest country band going circa 1954, it's also no surprise that Leo gave the guitar to Wills's hot player, Eldon Shamblin.

Whether he was picking his original Gibson archtop or the futuristic Strat, Shamblin became hugely influential in Western Swing, country, and jazz. He helped create Wills's sound, arranged many of his most famous songs, such as the band's trademark tunes "San Antonio Rose" and "Faded Love," and even managed the big band for a time. Fellow Texas Playboy Joe Ferguson crowned Shamblin "The Chord Wizard." Years later, *Rolling Stone* named him "the world's greatest rhythm guitar player." Merle Haggard, with whom Shamblin played in later years, wrote in his 1981 autobiography *Sing Me Back Home*, "Eldon's guitar work is so great that he can just stop everybody in their tracks."

Shamblin was born in Weatherford, Oklahoma, on April 24, 1916. He taught himself to play as a teenager, and in 1934, he got a job picking on a regular program with an Oklahoma City radio station. This exposure won him a seat with Dave Edwards's Alabama Boys, playing an upbeat hybrid of country and jazz that became known as "Western Swing." The band performed on KVOO radio station in Tulsa, where a cigar-chewing, hooting-and-hollering fiddler named Bob Wills was also building his reputation. "I was the first one out of the Alabama Boys to join the Wills band," Shamblin remembered, "but they all gradually joined."

Wills's Texas Playboys was soon staffed by the best Western Swing players anywhere. The band prolifically toured and recorded, building Wills's reputation as the King of Western Swing. Shamblin cowrote a number of the band's classics, including "Twin Guitar Special" with steel-guitar maestro Leon McAuliffe.

The 1954 Strat that Leo Fender presented to Shamblin was painted metallic gold, perhaps following the style of Gibson's Les Paul goldtop. Serial number 0569 wore a neck dated June 1954. But beyond the golden finish, the guitar was pretty much stock, not even having gold-plated hardware. Shamblin remembered, "It was pretty beaten up when I got it; must have been some demonstrator." Shamblin added many miles and many a show to its history, using the golden guitar the rest of his life.

—Michael Dregni

Pee Wee Crayton

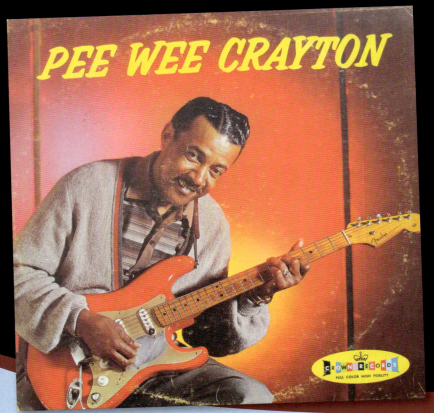

Crayton's 1960 Crown LP featured his custom-color Strat front and center.

2009 Custom Shop 1958 Candy Apple Red Stratocaster with gold-anodized pickguard, inspired by Pee Wee Crayton's guitar. *Fender Musical Instruments Corporation*

Swinging bluesman Pee Wee Crayton's 1955 recording of "The Telephone Is Ringing" on Vee-Jay 214 just may be the premiere recording of a Stratocaster. Whether it was indeed the first or not—we may never know—the song showcased a tone like no other record before. Crayton played his big bends and bluesy pentatonic riffs, punctuated by shimmering ninth chords, with a unique, biting sound. The tone was unlike that of T-Bone Walker's archtop Gibson ES-5, with its woody, out-of-phase-pickup voice, or Clarence "Gatemouth" Brown's snarling Fender Esquire. It was a sound all its own.

Connie Curtis Crayton was Texas-born and influenced primarily by Texan guitar slingers, such as Walker and jazzman Charlie Christian. He began by emulating T-Bone, playing his jazz-inflected blues licks on a big archtop Gibson before he was given a Stratocaster and a tweed Twin amp by the factory, likely in 1954. No one seems to remember the circumstances behind the present—how, where, or when Leo Fender or anyone else from the factory met Crayton. In fact, as Leo was a staunch country music fan, his giving such an early and special Strat to a bluesman seems odd in retrospect.

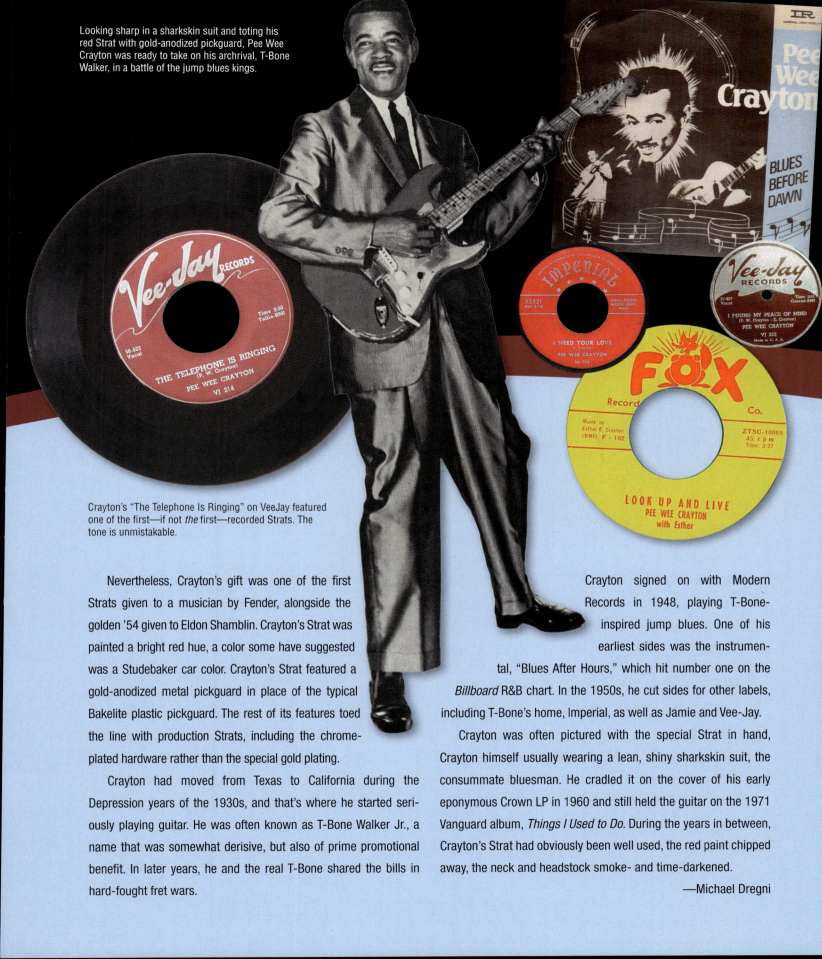

Looking sharp in a sharkskin suit and toting his red Strat with gold-anodized pickguard, Pee Wee Crayton was ready to take on his archrival, T-Bone Walker, in a battle of the jump blues kings.

Crayton's "The Telephone Is Ringing" on VeeJay featured one of the first—if not *the* first—recorded Strats. The tone is unmistakable.

Nevertheless, Crayton's gift was one of the first Strats given to a musician by Fender, alongside the golden '54 given to Eldon Shamblin. Crayton's Strat was painted a bright red hue, a color some have suggested was a Studebaker car color. Crayton's Strat featured a gold-anodized metal pickguard in place of the typical Bakelite plastic pickguard. The rest of its features toed the line with production Strats, including the chrome-plated hardware rather than the special gold plating.

Crayton had moved from Texas to California during the Depression years of the 1930s, and that's where he started seriously playing guitar. He was often known as T-Bone Walker Jr., a name that was somewhat derisive, but also of prime promotional benefit. In later years, he and the real T-Bone shared the bills in hard-fought fret wars.

Crayton signed on with Modern Records in 1948, playing T-Bone-inspired jump blues. One of his earliest sides was the instrumental, "Blues After Hours," which hit number one on the *Billboard* R&B chart. In the 1950s, he cut sides for other labels, including T-Bone's home, Imperial, as well as Jamie and Vee-Jay.

Crayton was often pictured with the special Strat in hand, Crayton himself usually wearing a lean, shiny sharkskin suit, the consummate bluesman. He cradled it on the cover of his early eponymous Crown LP in 1960 and still held the guitar on the 1971 Vanguard album, *Things I Used to Do*. During the years in between, Crayton's Strat had obviously been well used, the red paint chipped away, the neck and headstock smoke- and time-darkened.

—Michael Dregni

Mary Kaye

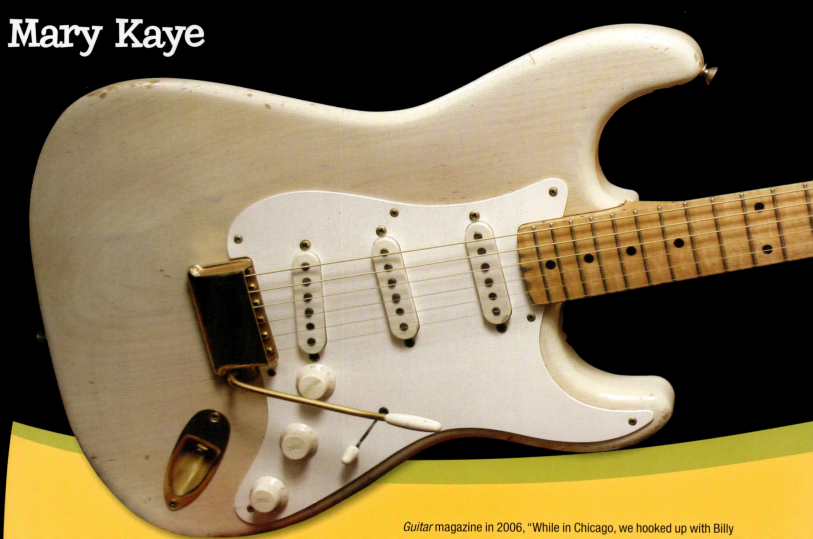

Mary Kaye—the guitarist whose name became synonymous with the beautiful Blonde Stratocaster highlighted by golden hardware—never actually owned a Mary Kaye. Fender promised her the guitar she's holding in the catalog and promotional photos and played in the 1956 film *Cha-Cha-Cha Boom!*, but the guitar remained in Fender's hands. This wrong was finally righted in 2002 when Fender presented Kaye with a one-and-only Custom Shop Stratocaster christened the White Beauty and bearing serial number MK001.

For much of her career, Kaye was actually a D'Angelico player. Her full surname was Ka'aihue, which she also recorded and played under before switching to the stage name "Kaye." Her father was Hawai'ian royalty; her mother a Detroit socialite. From that background, Kaye became one of the first Las Vegas lounge acts.

Kaye began her professional career playing in her father's band, before starting the Mary Kaye Trio. As she told *Vintage*

Guitar magazine in 2006, "While in Chicago, we hooked up with Billy Burton, who became our manager. He brought us to the Frontier Hotel in Vegas. . . . While playing our first gig in the main show-room of the Frontier, we were asked to stay over after our four-week engagement had ended. Without a room to go to, I suggested a stage be built in the bar area and it could be called a 'lounge.' Jack Kozloff, the owner, and Eddie Fox, the general manager, had it constructed immediately. During its first week of operation, Frank Sinatra and friends dropped $120,000 on the tables during what became known as the 'dusk til dawn' hours. This impressed the other hotels to the point where they began to stay open twenty-four hours. . . . Hotels began hunting for entertainers to fill their newly constructed lounges. Not all entertainment worked, but smaller, tight-knit groups were working out better than the big bands of that time."

In Vegas, Kaye was introduced to Fender sales maestro Don Randall: "Around 1954, Don brought me a Fender guitar—not the Strat—to play onstage. Though I refused to play it, Don started bringing me Fender amps to use with my D'Angelicos. In '55, Fender

1957 Mary Kaye Stratocaster. *Rumble Seat Music*

"It was a small mom-and-pop shop, like a carpenter's factory, with the floor covered in the day's wood debris. It was what I had expected. I was greeted by Leo Fender himself; he was very nice."

—Mary Kaye on visiting the Fender factory, circa 1955

Mary Kaye holds the Mary Kaye—a Blonde Stratocaster with gold hardware that she was loaned by Fender for this photo shoot. Then she had to give the guitar back.

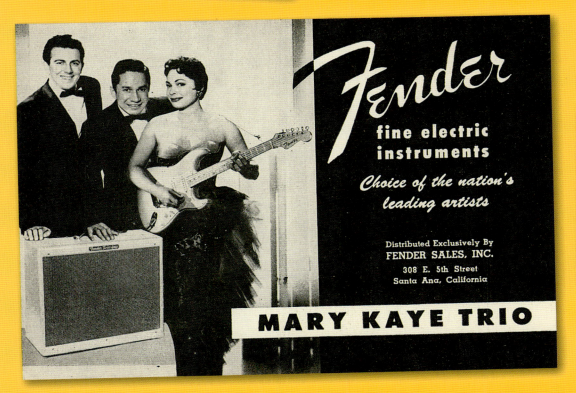

The photograph that launched a legend, appearing in Fender catalogs and ads in 1956–57.

Mary Kaye

"Cha-Cha-Cha BOOM!"
A CLOVER PRODUCTION · A COLUMBIA PICTURE

Copyright 1956 Columbia Pictures Corp. Country of Origin U.S.A.   Property of National Screen Service Corp. Licensed for display only in connection with the exhibition of this picture at your theatre. Must be returned immediately thereafter.   56 \353

Mary Kaye played the original Mary Kaye Strat for a sequence in the 1956 film *Cha-Cha-Cha Boom!* but then had to hand it back to Fender, again.

delivered the Blonde Strat to me, prior to the Trio going onstage at the Frontier Hotel, for the famous publicity shot, taken backstage. [The guitar] was returned to Fender later that evening.

"Six months later, Billy, our manager, set up an arrangement with Fender to let me use the Blonde Stratocaster in a Columbia movie [*Cha-Cha-Cha Boom!*], and again it was returned to Fender."

Thanks to those publicity photos and movie appearance, the rare Blonde Stratocasters crowned by gold hardware have been referred to ever after as Mary Kayes. As Kaye herself said, "I remember Billy was upset that the guitar was returned to Fender after Leo Fender had promised it to me. We were too busy with the Trio's career to ever look back and correct the mistake." And Kaye was too busy picking her beloved D'Angelicos.

Although Kaye might not have gotten that original Mary Kaye Strat, Randall did keep her supplied with free Fender amps throughout her life.

—Michael Dregni

2006 Mary Kaye Tribute Stratocaster. *Fender Musical Instruments Corporation*

Ike Turner

Ike Turner plays his Strat with his Kings of Rhythm in 1956. In the back row, from left, Jackie Brenston, Raymond Hill, Eddie Jones, Fred Sample, and Billy Gayles. Front row, from left, Jesse Knight Jr., Turner, and Eugene Washington. *Gilles Petard Collection/Redferns/Getty Images*

With saxman Jackie Brenston singing, Turner's Kings of Rhythm recorded one of the first—if not the first—rock 'n' roll songs of all time, "Rocket 88," at Memphis's Sun Studios. The song was licensed to Chicago's Chess Records for release in April 1951.

CHESS RECORD CORP.

U-7316
N.M.P.C.
B.M.I.

Vocal
Jackie Brenston

ROCKET "88"
(Jackie Brenston)
JACKIE BRENSTON
and his
Delta Cats
1458
MANUFACTURED BY CHESS RECORD CORP. - CHICAGO, ILL.

The Soul of IKE & TINA *Turner*

Featuring All Their Hit Singles
A Fool In Love
I Idolize You
Letter From Tina
The Way You Love Me
I'm Jealous
You're My Baby
& others.

Ike Turner was not one of the Kings of Rhythm, as his longtime band was known. He was *the* king.

Rechristening the band "Jackie Brenston and His Delta Cats" for a session at the Memphis Sun Studios in 1951, he cut "Rocket 88," often tagged as one of the first rock 'n' roll songs. Ever. With Annie Mae Bullock—renamed for the stage as Tina Turner—he launched his Revue, shaking up the 1960s with a rafters-rattling blend of rock, R&B, and soul. Ike's career was often controversial, but throughout his life he made phenomenal music.

Ike was also one of the first—if not the first—bluesmen to take up the Strat. Photographs of the Kings of Rhythm dated

circa 1955–56 show Ike armed with an early sunburst Stratocaster.

From the early days of the Ike and Tina Turner Revue, Ike was toting the Strat that he made famous: a Sonic Blue guitar with rosewood fretboard that was believed to date from 1961. He played that guitar and other Strats for the rest of his career.

Ike was born in 1931 in the heart of the Mississippi Delta in the county-seat town of Clarksdale. He was hardened early in life when

With Tina Turner fronting the Kings of Rhythm and Ike Turner playing what became his trademark Sonic Blue Strat, R&B would never be the same again. Here, they perform in Dallas, Texas, in 1962. *Michael Ochs Archives/Getty Images*

he witnessed his Baptist minister father beaten and left for dead by a mob of white men. His mother remarried a violent alcoholic, who beat the young boy until Ike knocked him out with a piece of wood and ran away to Memphis. Ike began playing piano and guitar, forming the Kings of Rhythm in high school; he kept the name of the band throughout his career.

Along with playing across the South, Ike became a music scout. He brought B.B. King and Howlin' Wolf to the attention of Sam Phillips at Sun Records, who first recorded them and leased the sides to the Bihari brothers' Modern Records in Los Angeles. Ike himself recorded in the 1950s and 1960s for Modern, Chess, Flair, and Mississippi's local label, Trumpet. With the Revue, he graduated to larger labels, including Sue, Blue Thumb, and eventually, United Artists. Together, he and Tina won two Grammys and were nominated for three others.

Ike's personality came through in his guitar sound: a biting tone and a driving sense of rhythm that propelled his band. Like James Brown, he was domineering and demanding of his Kings of Rhythm, not settling for less than music perfection and thrilling showmanship.

Playing that Sonic Blue Strat, Ike would intermix chords, riffs, and bass lines, much like a piano player. As Ike's then-guitarist in the Kings of Rhythm, Seth Blumberg, detailed, "His life is the rhythm—that's why his band is called the Kings of Rhythm. . . . Ike's all about energy, and he says, 'I don't wanna hear that mama-papa two and four. It makes me tired. You got to lay it down, man. Don't step around it—you got to step in it.'"

—Michael Dregni

Buddy Guy

There's no better example of supercharged, hard-blowing, electric Chicago blues than Buddy Guy. His guitars of choice—and the amps he plays them through, for that matter—are staples of the bluesman's toolbox. As simple as these ingredients may be, they are capable of producing no end of firepower when used with attitude. Although Guy has occasionally strutted his stuff with Guild Starfire semi-acoustics, he is far and away best known for his use of Fender Stratocasters and has played plenty of examples of this legendary model throughout his career. For decades, Guy wielded vintage 1950s Strats with maple fingerboards, but in later years Fender issued not one but two Buddy Guy signature models.

The Fender Buddy Guy Standard Polka Dot Stratocaster expresses his desires in a modified Strat, as well as his flair for fashion and performance. The Polka Dot Stratocaster follows classic Strat lines, with an alder body and all-maple neck, vintage-style vibrato, five-way switch, and single-volume and dual-tone controls (for neck and middle pickup only), but its pickups gain a little extra poke courtesy of their ceramic magnets. The second of Guy's Fender signature models, the high-end Artist Series Buddy Guy Stratocaster, changes the alder body for ash, the ceramic-magnet pickups for three Lace Sensor Golds, and adds a mid-boost to the guitar's electrics. Both aim to offer classic Strat playability and versatility, but to hit the amp harder than many bluesmen might seek to do.

Guy's amps deserve some consideration in their own right, as does the way in which he uses them. Throughout his early career,

The passing of the torch: Buddy Guy plays his guitar on stage in 1962, showing Eric Clapton the wonders of the Strat. Clapton's loyalties would soon shift to Fender, resulting in his playing Brownie and Blackie for the next several decades. *David Redfern/Redferns/Getty Images*

Buddy Guy

Buddy Guy's 1958 Stratocaster.
Rick Gould

Guy preferred a model that can lay claim to the tag "ulti-mate blues amp of all time": a late 1950s Fender Tweed 5F6-A Bassman. Purportedly, he played these 4x10-inch combos with all knobs wound up toward max, save the bass tone control, which he kept down low. Like most artists with his sort of longevity in the business, Guy has diversified his arse-nal over the years. In the late 1990s and early 2000s, Guy often played a Victoria 45410 (a hand-wired reproduction of a Bassman) and has lately endorsed the Buddy Guy Signature Series Amp from Chicago Blues Box, which is modeled specifically on Guy's own favorite '59 Bassman. Between guitar and amp, Guy has often favored a Crybaby wah pedal, a duty now performed by the Jim Dunlop Crybaby Buddy Guy Signature Wah—in black with white polka dots, naturally.

As with most guitar stars, though, it's not so much the ingredi-ents as the way the artist attacks them that accounts for the hot, stinging tone. And into his eighties and counting, Buddy Guy still hit those strings hard.

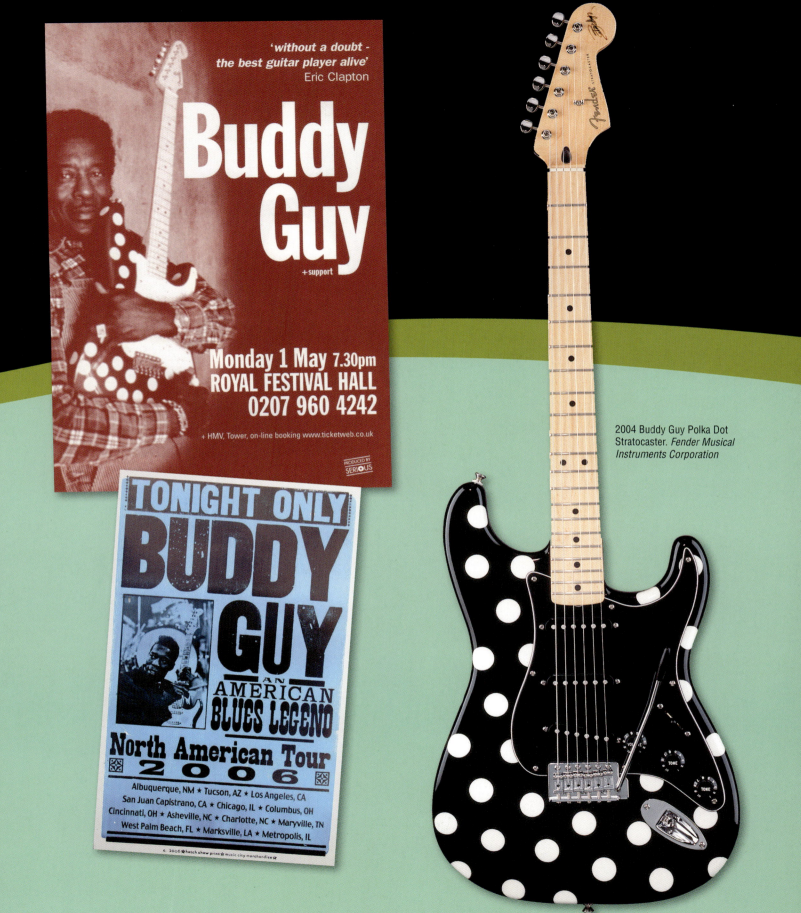

2004 Buddy Guy Polka Dot Stratocaster. *Fender Musical Instruments Corporation*

Buddy Holly picks his Strat on stage in March 1958. *Harry Hammond/V&A Images/Getty Images*

Beaming out from photos with his thick-rimmed glasses and the bright smile of a schoolboy on picture day, Buddy Holly might not appear like much of a rebel. But Holly was nothing less than a rock 'n' roll revolutionary, with a knack for innovation in just about everything he did. In an age when recording artists were still largely packaged by record company execs and backed by studio house bands and Tin Pan Alley songwriters, Buddy Holly and the Crickets established a template that would define

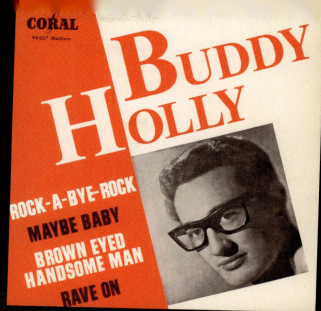

the genuine rock artist: they wrote their own songs, played their own recording dates, and—with the aid of an occasional sideman—took it all out on the road, too.

Holly's playing was likewise innovative, blending chunky rhythm and high-string lead work in a style that owed an equal tip of the hat to country, R&B, and rockabilly (and to his predecessor, Bo Diddley, among others). Amid all this avant-garde behavior, his guitar choice was radical, too: While other heroes on the burgeoning rock 'n' roll scene were playing Gretsches or big-bodied Gibson archtops, Holly—with a loan from his brother Larry—purchased a new Fender Stratocaster, a guitar that had been designed for country players and released onto the market just a year before. In doing so, Holly (born Charles Hardin Holley) also became the first household name in popular music to perform regularly on a Stratocaster.

Holly played his first Stratocaster, a late-1954 or early-1955 model, for about two years and used it to record his first hits, including "That'll Be the Day" and "Peggy Sue," before it was stolen from a tour bus in Michigan in the fall of 1957. The 1957 Stratocaster

that he acquired to replace it, however—purchased hurriedly in Detroit in time to make the show that evening—is possibly the most recognizable of all of the four or five Strats Holly owned. Another two-tone sunburst model with maple fingerboard, it appears in several popular photos of Holly performing in 1957 and 1958 and is notable for the wear that soon developed in the covers of the middle and neck pickups just below the high E string.

This iconic 1957 Stratocaster accompanied Holly on many of his most prominent performances of the time and certainly helped to establish Fender's modernistic new model as a standard of solid-body design. It was played on appearances on *The Ed Sullivan Show* and *The Arthur Murray Dance Party* and traveled to the U.K. with Holly for his historic British tour. In April 1958, Holly lost yet another Stratocaster when the 1957 instrument was stolen from the band's station wagon during a stop at a restaurant in St. Louis, Missouri. The star acquired two or three more Strats before his death in 1959, one of the last of which is on display at the Buddy Holly Center in his hometown of Lubbock, Texas.

1958 Fiesta Red Stratocaster.
Outline Press Ltd.

(continued from page 197)

Although it's less obvious at a glance, the Stratocaster's neck profile evolved rather steadily throughout the 1950s, too, parallel to that of the Telecaster. The chunky, rounded C shape of the early necks segued into a beefy V profile in 1955, which slimmed down through 1956 and 1957, then flattened into a slim, then slimmer, C shape as 1958 rolled into 1959 and 1960. From around mid-1959 to mid-1961 or so the Stratocaster's neck shape reflected a contemporary predilection for extremely thin necks, which were considered "fast" at the time. Interestingly, many Gibson electrics, notably the Les Paul and SG, were given similarly thin necks over roughly the same time period.

Alongside the change in neck profiles, the shape and depth of the Stratocaster body's ribcage and forearm contours evolved slightly. Earlier guitars tended to have a greater depth and a more prominent overall curve to these areas, whereas the contours flattened out slightly through the early 1960s and into the middle of the decade. Since these contours were both rough-cut and finished by hand—cut first on the bandsaw following a line of a prescribed angle, then sanded smooth—they always varied somewhat anyway, but their depth over time tended to follow a trajectory toward the more shallow.

As the end of the decade approached, a more noticeable change was visited on the neck of the Stratocaster. A new Fender model, the Jazzmaster, brought a rosewood fingerboard to the Fender stable when it was introduced at the 1958 summer NAMM show, proving a successful test subject for a change that would hit the Stratocaster and Telecaster midway through 1959. Several reasons might have been behind the change of fingerboard woods, and indeed the true motivation might have been a combination of several or all of them. It's likely that Fender felt the more traditional looking and feeling neck was a necessity on any guitar with pretensions toward jazz—the Jazzmaster's original target market—and with any hopes of appealing to the more traditional musicians who played it. It seems that many Fender dealers, however, and hence the reps at Fender Sales, had been inquiring about the availability of a rosewood 'board on the Tele and Strat for some time, and for reasons of their own. The darker neck would ally Fender guitars with more traditional

instruments, and therefore make for easier acceptance in corners that were still reticent to embrace the "plank." Simultaneously, it would do away with the detrimental image of the smudged, poorly wearing maple fingerboards that were showing up by this time, nearly ten years into the life of the Telecasters and five years after the Stratocaster's arrival. The rosewood fingerboards brought a new look to the Stratocaster, as well as other Fenders, and served as a dividing line between the guitars of the 1950s and those of the early 1960s.

For about the first two and a half years, these separate fingerboards were sawn with a flat underside and glued to a flat-neck face, a style that has since been dubbed the "slab board" for its thick, flat-bottomed appearance. Partway through 1962 Fender introduced the practice of radiusing the face of the maple neck as well as both sides of the fingerboard, which enabled the use of a thinner piece of rosewood and created what is now often referred to as a "laminated" or "round-lam" fingerboard. (By request from the mid-1960s, and as an official option from 1967, maple fingerboards would again be available, but until 1969 such necks were made much like the rosewood fingerboards, with a separately milled piece of maple glued to the face of the neck, a construction now known as a "maple cap" neck.)

Along with the rosewood fingerboard came off-white "clay" position-marker dots, which have come to represent another of the hallmarks of the pre-CBS Stratocaster. These were first inlaid in the same size and pattern as the black plastic dots that preceded them on maple fingerboards, namely with a wider spacing between the two twelfth-fret dots. In the latter half of 1963, the two twelfth-fret dots were moved slightly closer together. Another appointment change that accompanied the rosewood fingerboard was the new three-ply pickguard mounted with eleven screws, replacing the single-ply white plastic guard mounted with eight screws. Ostensibly white with a black center layer, the new guard was made from celluloid (a.k.a. nitrate) and had a slight greenish tint.

Add them together and these minor alterations in the formula—the rosewood fingerboard, clay dots, and "green guard"—are the obvious signs of guitars from the final era of the pre-CBS Stratocaster, which ran from around mid-1959 to mid-1964. (Although the clay dots and celluloid pickguard weren't replaced until early 1965, with pearloid and plastic respectively, a change of headstock decal to the new-styled "Fender" logo in late summer 1964 tends to mark the end of the pre-CBS era for many collectors.)

DETROIT-STYLE FLASH
COMES TO FULLERTON

Something that gets collectors even more hot and bothered than these several alterations of the late 1950s is the increased uptake of the custom color program at Fender. Custom colors were officially available from 1957, and as we have seen, several notable players had requested truly custom paint jobs right from the start of the Stratocaster's availability. But the changing musical and social styles of the late 1950s seemed to bring with them a greater demand for less-traditional guitar finishes, and the production of Stats in a range of custom colors increased considerably from the end of that decade and into the early and mid-'60s. Relatively few custom colors other than Blonde, Fiesta Red, and Shoreline Gold were seen before 1960, and even those are extremely rare (and therefore highly collectible).

The first actual chart of custom colors was produced in 1960 and included fourteen official paint options plus Blonde, each of which could be ordered through a Fender dealer at a 5 percent premium on the guitar's list price. It was money well spent if you hung onto the guitar for several decades: A custom color on a pre-CBS Stratocaster can today add as much as 50 percent to the value of the guitar, as compared to another Stratocaster in sunburst from the same year and in similar condition. Included on the official 1960 Custom Finishes chart were those listed below:

- Lake Placid Blue Metallic
- Daphne Blue
- Sonic Blue
- Shoreline Gold Metallic
- Olympic White
- Burgundy Mist Metallic
- Black
- Sherwood Green Metallic
- Foam Green

- Surf Green
- Inca Silver Metallic
- Fiesta Red
- Dakota Red
- Shell Pink

An additional option, not listed on the chart but mentioned in its caption, was the Tele-like Blonde finish, which was almost invariably applied over an ash body. In 1963, Shell Pink was dropped and Candy Apple Red Metallic added. Two years later, in 1965, Daphne Blue, Shoreline Gold Metallic, Burgundy Mist Metallic, Sherwood Green Metallic, Surf Green, and Inca Silver Metallic were also dropped, replaced by Blue

1962 Foam Green Stratocaster.
Rumble Seat Music

Ice Metallic, Firemist Gold Metallic, Charcoal Frost Metallic, Ocean Turquoise Metallic, Teal Green Metallic, and Firemist Silver Metallic. In what seemed quite a natural rock 'n' roll tie-in, most of these colors equated with paints used by one or another Detroit automaker from the late 1950s to the mid-1960s, and Fender's custom-colored guitars could see their twins in cars made by Pontiac, Chevrolet, Ford, Cadillac, Lincoln, Buick, Mercury, Oldsmobile, and Desoto.

Most custom colors were ordered by customers via local dealers, so guitars weren't always built from the ground up with that particular option in mind. As a result, many were finished in the standard sunburst before being shot with a custom-color coat and sent on their way, unbeknownst to their new owners. Over time, playing wear imposed on some custom-color Strats occasionally reveals a fresh undercoat of vibrant sunburst, even if the guitar is officially and entirely originally a "custom-color Stratocaster."

Meanwhile, the color of the standard sunburst finish was livened up in mid-1959, along with so many other changes. Roughly from the start, the standard procedure had been to spray the sanded body in a clear primer coat to seal and fill the grain (using a product called Fullerplast from 1963 onward), then dip it in a vat of yellow stain, then spray the edges in black lacquer to create the original two-tone sunburst look before hitting it with a lacquer clear-coat. In 1959 Fender added a red band between the black and the yellow stain visible toward the center of the guitar, but on many early examples this pigment faded severely over time and exposure to light, leaving guitars that looked much like they had only received two-tone finishes. From the early 1960s, though, Fender found a red that would better withstand exposure and survive the rigors of time, creating a more prominent three-tone sunburst (and one that, when sprayed a little too boldly toward the mid-1960s, rendered some gaudy "bull's-eye burst" guitars that were a little less appealing to collectors as a result).

(continued on page 226)

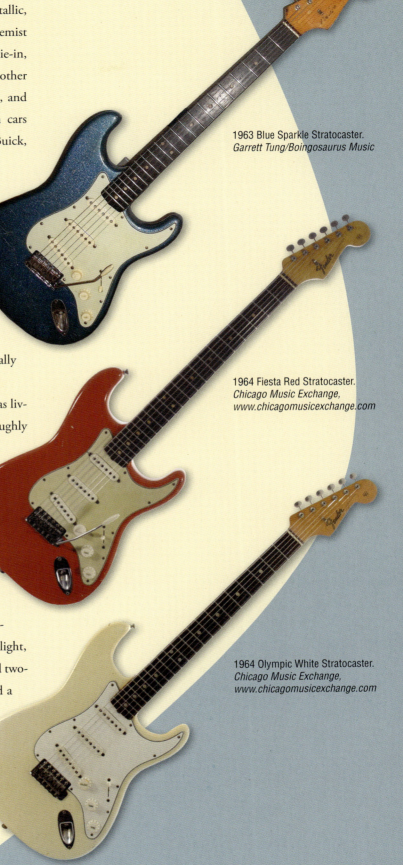

1963 Blue Sparkle Stratocaster.
Garrett Tung/Boingosaurus Music

1964 Fiesta Red Stratocaster.
*Chicago Music Exchange,
www.chicagomusicexchange.com*

1964 Olympic White Stratocaster.
*Chicago Music Exchange,
www.chicagomusicexchange.com*

Dick Dale

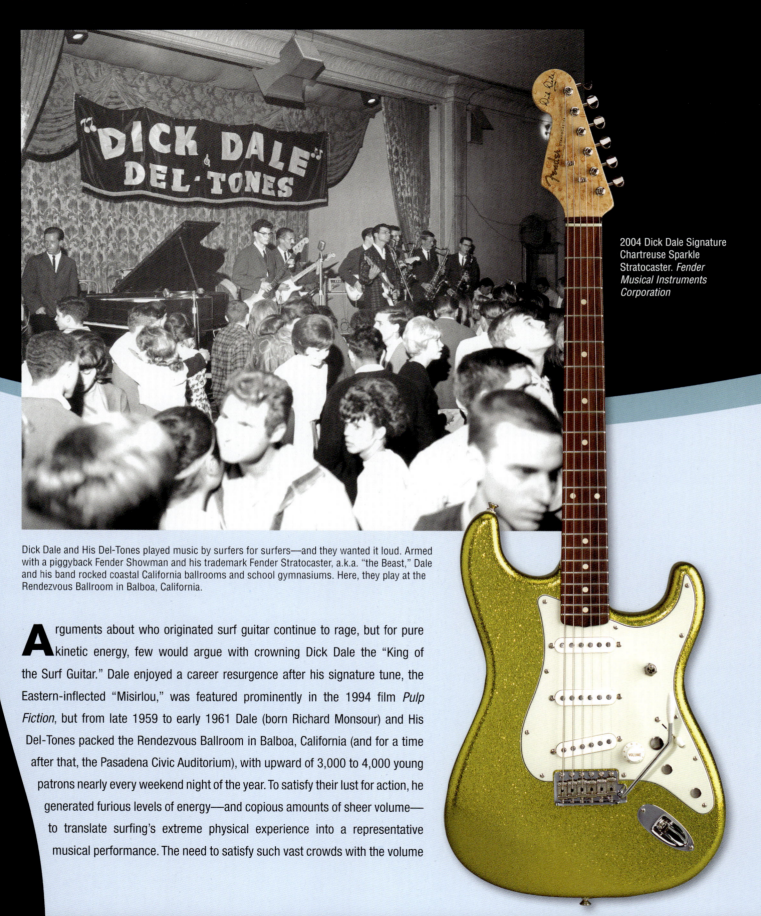

2004 Dick Dale Signature Chartreuse Sparkle Stratocaster. *Fender Musical Instruments Corporation*

Dick Dale and His Del-Tones played music by surfers for surfers—and they wanted it loud. Armed with a piggyback Fender Showman and his trademark Fender Stratocaster, a.k.a. "the Beast," Dale and his band rocked coastal California ballrooms and school gymnasiums. Here, they play at the Rendezvous Ballroom in Balboa, California.

Arguments about who originated surf guitar continue to rage, but for pure kinetic energy, few would argue with crowning Dick Dale the "King of the Surf Guitar." Dale enjoyed a career resurgence after his signature tune, the Eastern-inflected "Misirlou," was featured prominently in the 1994 film *Pulp Fiction*, but from late 1959 to early 1961 Dale (born Richard Monsour) and His Del-Tones packed the Rendezvous Ballroom in Balboa, California (and for a time after that, the Pasadena Civic Auditorium), with upward of 3,000 to 4,000 young patrons nearly every weekend night of the year. To satisfy their lust for action, he generated furious levels of energy—and copious amounts of sheer volume— to translate surfing's extreme physical experience into a representative musical performance. The need to satisfy such vast crowds with the volume

and power that the music demanded meant that he also became one of the first proponents of the entire rig, and arguably the first artist to front a truly arena-worthy backline.

Fender's Jazzmaster and Jaguar have come to be known as classic surf guitars, alongside the Mosrites that other artists, most notably the Ventures, also gravitated toward, but Dick Dale played a Stratocaster from the outset of his professional career and stuck with it for more than fifty years. Having started out as an aspiring country singer and guitarist, Dale was drawn to the Strat shortly before solidifying his stance as a surf guitarist. As a left-hander, he played the guitar strung "upside down," the way many lefties would approach the instrument upon flipping over a right-handed guitar. After initially being given a right-handed Stratocaster by Leo Fender in the late 1950s and told to "beat it to death," as Dale recalled, he moved over to left-handed Strats (most notably a chartreuse metal-flake example known as "The Beast"), but continued to string the guitar with the low E on the bottom.

Other than this quirk, Dale's use of a Strat for the bright, cutting tones of surf guitar really isn't all that unusual. The model is designed to excel in these tones just as much as the Jaguar and Jazzmaster. The bigger part of Dale's sonic revolution came in his amp of choice and his promotion of that super-wet, reverb-laden

sound, although it was not always thus. In order to broadcast his big sound to the big crowds he was drawing, Dale used his budding relationship with Leo Fender to acquire a suitable amp. Accounts of how much input the guitarist himself had on the development of the Showman amp vary greatly (with Dale's own recollections often putting him right there at the drawing board), but the powerful new Fender model, introduced in the new Blonde Tolex covering in 1960, was undoubtedly designed specifically to belt the young surfing guitarist's music to the masses.

As wet as the surf sound eventually became, however, Dale's first hit single, "Let's Go Trippin'," his entire first album, *Surfer's Choice*, and his legendary early Rendezvous Ballroom shows were all performed sans reverb. Once the Fender Reverb Unit hit the streets in early 1962, though, with prototypes having been road-tested by Dale, there was no turning back from the big splash.

The Ventures

The Ventures were all Fender—until they switched to Mosrites, of course. Don Wilson gets happy with his Stratocaster while Bob Bogle strums a Jazzmaster and Nokie Edwards holds his bass. *Michael Ochs Archives/Getty Images*

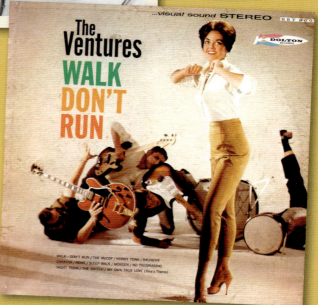

Don Wilson and Bob Bogle were Seattle masonry workers who played some guitar after hours just for fun. In 1958, they decided to put together a band, which they humbly named the Versatones before changing their moniker to the Ventures. Their guitar-driven instrumental tunes were almost instant radio-friendly hits, and even though neither Wilson nor Bogle surfed, their songs soon became a soundtrack to the surfer world, along with cuts by Dick Dale, the Surfaris, and others.

In 1960, they recorded a hopped-up version of "Walk Don't Run." The song had been penned by guitarist Johnny Smith and recorded by Chet Atkins, but it was the Ventures' version that became a

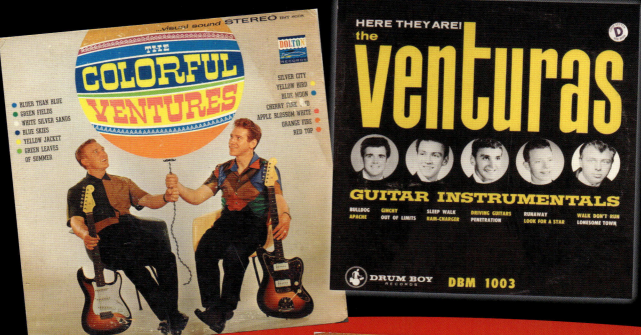

mammoth hit. Still, the group didn't really hit their stride until bassist Nokie Edwards moved over to guitar duties in 1962, with Bogle taking up the bass. They went on to sell more than 110 million albums and log a whopping thirty-seven albums on the *Billboard* charts. In a short time, they had become the world's biggest-selling guitar instrumental act.

Early on, the Ventures played Fender guitars, crafting their trebly, twangy sound with Stratocasters, Jazzmasters, and Precision Basses. On many of their album covers and singles picture sleeves, they were pictured proudly toting those Fender products, such as on *The Ventures*, *Bobby Vee Meets the Ventures*, and *The Colorful Ventures*. Their sound and their songs provided inspiration for many a youth yearning to learn guitar to save his paper-route money for a Strat.

Ironically, Fender never quite realized what a good thing it had in the Ventures. The company let a huge promotional opportunity slip through its corporate fingers and into the grasp of the minuscule guitar-making firm of Mosrite. Shortly after his move to guitar, Edwards borrowed an early Joe Maphis model from Mosrite founder Semie Moseley to test out in the studio, and he was hooked. Before the end of 1962, Edwards, Bogle, and Wilson began using prototypes of the Ventures model Mosrite guitars and basses, and the line was officially released in 1963. The band's name and popularity helped put Mosrite on the map.

Still, the earliest Ventures classics all boasted that Fender sound. The Ventures were often credited as "The Band That Launched a Thousand Bands," and their use of Strats and Jazzmasters launched many thousands of Fender fans.

—Michael Dregni

Hank Marvin

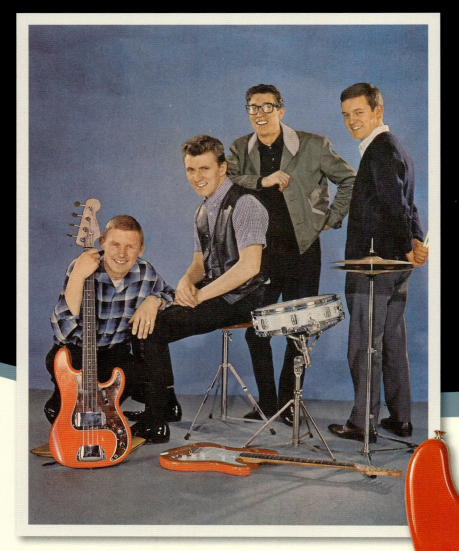

Hank Marvin and the Shadows, with one of Marvin's famous red Strats in the foreground.

Hank Marvin's 1959 Stratocaster with gold hardware, the first Strat imported directly into England. The guitar has since been restored. *Outline Press Ltd.*

Most of the early stars of the electric guitar were American musicians, an understandable phenomenon given rock 'n' roll's birth on the left side of the Atlantic and a U.K. ban on U.S. imports through much of the 1950s that deprived British musicians of American-made guitars. Shortly before this embargo was lifted in 1960, though, Hank Marvin received a guitar that became famous as the first Stratocaster owned by an English guitarist. It was brought into the country by singer Cliff Richard, whom Marvin backed in the Shadows.

Marvin was already on his way to stardom by this time, thanks to the Shadows' early instrumental hits, but with red Strat in hand the lanky, bespectacled guitarist forged a more recognizable

identity on both sides of the pond and went on to become one of the most influential early British rock 'n' rollers. With hits split nearly fifty-fifty between Shadows' instrumental releases and vocal numbers recorded as Cliff Richard and the Shadows, Marvin was at the forefront of sixty-nine British Top 40 chart singles, a number that includes a whopping twelve number one hits. The most seminal of these, the classic "Apache" among them, were laid down with his '59 Stratocaster.

Marvin's acquisition of said Strat involves a now-famous case of mistaken identity. A fan of James Burton's work with Ricky Nelson, Marvin discovered that Burton played a Fender, but he didn't know precisely what model. While perusing a catalog in 1959 with his front man Richards, Marvin spotted a red Stratocaster with gold-plated hardware. "I decided that had to be the model he played," Marvin told this writer in a 1994 interview for *Teletext*, "because it was the most expensive one, and I figured James Burton must play the top model." An upcoming trip that Richards was making to the United States afforded Marvin the chance to acquire a guitar just like the one in the catalog with which he had become besotted. Weeks later the singer returned with red Strat in hand. Marvin didn't discover until a short while later that James Burton actually played

a Telecaster, but by this time it didn't matter—the Strat was the guitar for him.

And what a fortuitous error it was. The Stratocaster's bright, well-defined sound, and its versatile vibrato system in particular, became a major part of Marvin's playing style. He used the vibrato bar on just about everything he played, applying it to subtle tremulous wiggles and deeper, emotive bends that evoked a rich, atmospheric tone through the tape echo unit he used between the guitar and Vox AC15 amplifier (later an AC30). All told, this setup established a sound that Pete Townshend, Mark Knopfler, and even Frank Zappa have acknowledged as a major influence.

Marvin's original '59 Stratocaster is now in the possession of Shadows bandmate Bruce Welch, although Hank has continued to play Strats—alongside the occasional Burns guitar—throughout his career.

(continued from page 219)

A PROLIFERATION OF PLAYERS

The Stratocaster's early acceptance among some of the more adventurous country players on the West Coast is fairly well documented, and we have already seen how it segued from there into the rock 'n' roll and rockabilly scenes. The Strat had yet to rock heavily, though—or as heavily as it would eventually be known for—nearly a full decade into its existence, although several blues players were perhaps giving it a serious workout. B.B. King did plenty of memorable work on a sunburst 1956 Stratocaster, and Buddy Guy laid down some even more aggressive licks on his own late-1950s model (performances that a sheepish Chess records generally failed to capture in the day, feeling Guy's aggressive live style needed to be tamed for the studio).

Perhaps unexpectedly, though, the most creative early use of the Stratocaster's versatile vibrato unit in a pop-music context arguably occurred on the other side of the pond. In 1959, Hank Marvin of the Shadows received what is widely considered to be the first Stratocaster brought into the United Kingdom. The

Fiesta Red Strat with gold hardware was brought to him by Cliff Richard (a singing star with whom the Shadows performed as backing band, in addition to logging several hits as an instrumental outfit), and quickly became a major part of Marvin's sound. Blending proto-surf and twangy pop stylings, Marvin's riffs were peppered with emotive vibrato bends and trills, and made a real feature of Leo's marvelous "Synchronized Tremolo."

Back in the United States, while Fender's Jazzmaster—and soon, Jaguar—would be more heavily associated with the surf scene, Dick Dale was laying down seminal surf riffs played by surfers, for surfers, on a gold 1959 Stratocaster dubbed "the Beast," given to him by Leo himself. Otherwise, in addition to thriving in the genres in which it was conceived, the Stratocaster was proliferating on the pop-rock scene in the early 1960s, but would prove a tool of even more adventurous artists a little later in the decade. Even so, Stratocaster sales declined slightly in the early mid-1960s, a fact likely attributable to the plethora of competition at the peak of the guitar boom, both from other makers and from other Fender models.

Bob Dylan's use of a Stratocaster in his infamous "gone electric" moment at the Newport Folk Festival in 1965 marked it as a rebel, but it was Jimi Hendrix who took that image over the top, sonically as much as visually, with his groundbreaking playing as a solo artist in 1967 and beyond. Where the heaviest players in rock so far had mostly rediscovered Gibson's discontinued Les Paul Standard with humbucking pickups, Hendrix showed what the Stratocaster's crystalline single-coil pickups could do when cranked to the max through a Marshall stack and tickled with some inventive whammy abuse. Up to this point, the Stratocaster had ascended rather steadily through the ranks of solid-body electric guitars in its thirteen years on the planet, but many would argue, and with just cause, that Hendrix's use of the guitar was what finally punched it through into the stratosphere.

Jimi Hendrix Plays Fender Stratocaster

Fender
MUSICAL INSTRUMENTS

CBS Musical Instruments
Columbia Broadcasting System, Inc.

FREE CATALOG/Write Fender Musical Instruments, Dept. BL-9, 1402 E. Chestnut, Santa Ana, Calif. 92702

THE STRAT SLIDES SOUTHWARD UNDER CBS

In a deal that had been pursued at least as early as mid-1964 and negotiated throughout the latter part of that year, Fender Musical Instruments was officially sold to Columbia Broadcasting System Inc. (CBS) on January 5, 1965. For most diehard Fender aficionados, CBS's acquisition of Fender serves as a turning point for the start of a noticeable decline—at first gradual, then more pronounced—in the quality of Fender guitars. As such, the term "pre-CBS" has come to stand as an identifier of the more valuable and collectible vintage Stratocasters (and other Fenders), with post-CBS indicating less desirable later examples. To be fair, though, the quality of the instruments certainly wasn't impacted the second the ink dried on the contract, or even for several years after. Fender, under CBS, continued to produce plenty of excellent Stratocasters for some time, although the days—or years—were numbered, and the change of owner pointed toward a future where the Strat would one day be but a shadow of its original self.

The thicker, more modern-looking Fender logo that had begun to appear on Stratocaster headstocks in late summer 1964 is often considered the first sign of the post-CBS guitars, even though the sale of Fender to CBS had not yet been completed, and the guitars themselves—other than the change of that thin, water-slide decal—were much the same as they had been earlier in the year, in a firmly pre-CBS era. The new logo, initially a bold gold logo within a thin black outline, was joined by a broader headstock shape at the end of 1965, which essentially bookended the era of the "transition Strat," which ran from late 1964 until that time. By then, as of the winter of 1965, the clay of the fingerboard position markers had been changed to pearloid dots, and the greenish celluloid pickguard was changed for a white three-ply guard made from actual plastic. (For some other minor changes in pickup construction see Stratocaster Tone and Construction.)

(continued on page 248)

Jimi Hendrix

Hendrix plays his Strat at Royal Albert Hall in London on February 24, 1969. *David Redfern/ Redferns/Getty Images*

The gear of all major guitar heroes attracts some attention, but the equipment used by Jimi Hendrix, and his Fender Stratocasters in particular, has drawn more intense analysis than most. Hendrix played several Strats during his short time at the top, and famously also used a Gibson Flying V and SG. His supposed preference for later-1960s CBS-spec Strats over early- to mid-1960s Strats remains a hotly debated issue. Certainly the last Stratocasters the world saw him playing were CBS-era models with large headstocks, modern logos, and maple fingerboards. Among these, the white Strat played at Woodstock in 1969 and the black Strat played at the Isle of Wight in 1970 are the instruments he was most photographed with.

In the early days, however, around the time of *Are You Experienced* and his inflammatory performance at the Monterey Pop Festival in 1967, Hendrix was usually seen playing one of a handful of pre-CBS or transition-era Stratocasters

The first Strat that Hendrix burned on stage. He set the 1965 Strat alight in March 1967 at Finsbury Park Astoria in London. *Andrew Cowie/Photoshot/Getty Images*

Jimi Hendrix's 1968 Olympic White Stratocaster.
Outline Press Ltd.

with small headstocks and "spaghetti" or transition logos. Hendrix played two Strats at Monterey: a black mid-1960s model with characteristic rosewood fingerboard and small headstock, and a guitar at the center of what is possibly the most legendary "Hendrix moment" of all—the Stratocaster that Hendrix doused in lighter fluid and lit on fire at the end of his performance of "Wild Thing," a transition-era '65 Strat, also with the early-style small headstock. Seen little before the Monterey appearance, it had recently been customized by Hendrix, who painted approximately half of the Fiesta Red body white and adorned it with floral graphics. Otherwise, the standard late-'65 Stratocaster carried a short-lived combination of features, including a fatter new-style gold logo with black outline on a small headstock and rosewood fingerboard with pearloid inlays. Another '65 Stratocaster, a sunburst model, was also played, burned, and smashed by Hendrix at the Finsbury Park Astoria.

Many Hendrix-philes believe Jimi preferred post-'65 guitars for tone-based reasons. One theory is that he found the extra wood in the larger post-CBS headstocks to increase sustain. Another holds that the slightly weaker single-coil pickups of the late-1960s Stratocasters added up to a bigger sound when injected through his 100-watt Marshall stacks.

Perhaps the best authority on these theories is the tech who worked with Hendrix and had hands-on experience with Jimi's guitars. British effects guru Roger Mayer not only built and modified many of the pedals that Hendrix used, but he also worked as an all-around righthand man and even helped select and set up many of the star's guitars. What does he have to say about the wide headstock/greater sustain theory? "No, Jimi wouldn't have considered that," Mayer told this writer. "All the guitars that we used were bought out of necessity; there weren't that many Stratocasters around [in London] in those days, and they were very expensive. Also, in the 1960s nobody paid much attention to whether pre-CBS Fenders were any better than CBS Fenders. They were all about the same. I can't see a slightly bigger headstock making any difference anyway."

Of course, the final word in all of this is that the Strats Hendrix played are iconic simply because he played them—and whatever Strat Jimi wailed on, it was sure to make a heavenly sound.

Jim Hendrix's 1968 Stratocaster.
Christie's/Bridgeman

Eric Clapton

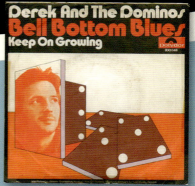

Eric Clapton plays Brownie with Derek and the Dominos in 1971.
Elliot Landy/Redferns/Getty Images

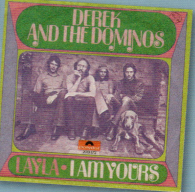

Throughout his career, Eric Clapton has been an arbiter of tone, and while he has moved through several makes and models of guitar over the past fifty years, he has been extremely devoted to each at certain periods and has inspired major guitar lust in the hearts of many at every stop along the road.

Before Clapton was able to get his hands on a Strat, he wielded a red early '60s Fender Telecaster with white pickguard and rosewood fingerboard that was a "band guitar" rather than Clapton's own, purchased by the Yardbirds' management as a group asset to be used by the band as a whole. He is shown here with the Tele in 1964. *Jeremy Fletcher/Redferns/Getty Images*

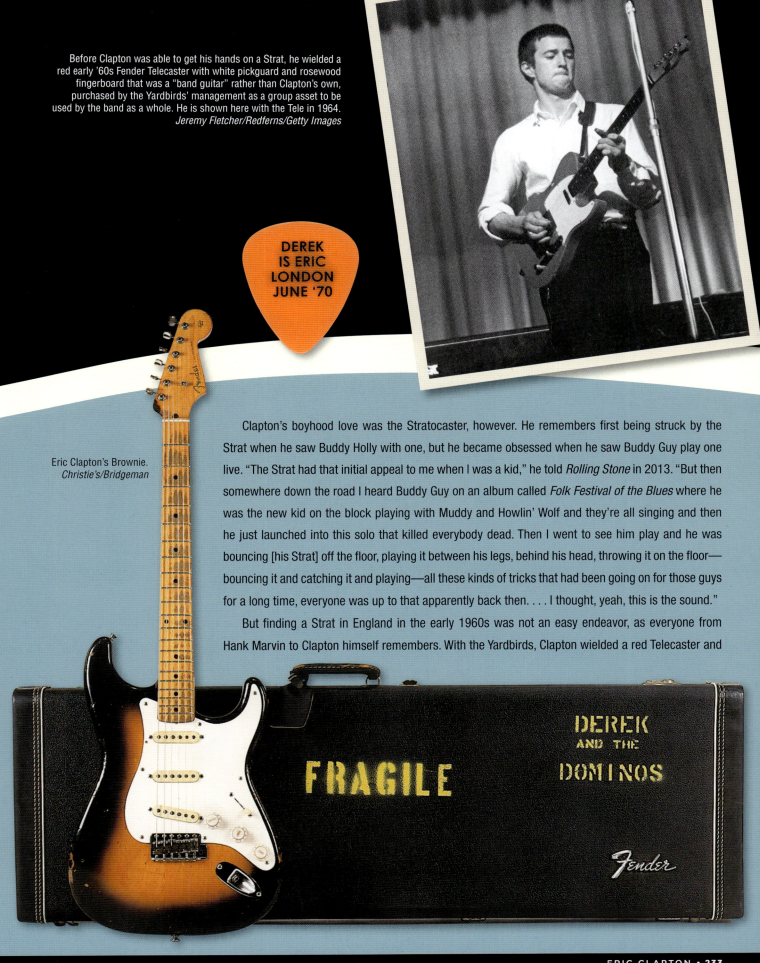

DEREK
IS ERIC
LONDON
JUNE '70

Eric Clapton's Brownie. *Christie's/Bridgeman*

FRAGILE

DEREK
AND THE
DOMINOS

Fender

Clapton's boyhood love was the Stratocaster, however. He remembers first being struck by the Strat when he saw Buddy Holly with one, but he became obsessed when he saw Buddy Guy play one live. "The Strat had that initial appeal to me when I was a kid," he told *Rolling Stone* in 2013. "But then somewhere down the road I heard Buddy Guy on an album called *Folk Festival of the Blues* where he was the new kid on the block playing with Muddy and Howlin' Wolf and they're all singing and then he just launched into this solo that killed everybody dead. Then I went to see him play and he was bouncing [his Strat] off the floor, playing it between his legs, behind his head, throwing it on the floor— bouncing it and catching it and playing—all these kinds of tricks that had been going on for those guys for a long time, everyone was up to that apparently back then. . . . I thought, yeah, this is the sound."

But finding a Strat in England in the early 1960s was not an easy endeavor, as everyone from Hank Marvin to Clapton himself remembers. With the Yardbirds, Clapton wielded a red Telecaster and

Eric Clapton

Clapton plays Blackie on stage in 1978.
Richard E. Aaron/Redferns/Getty Images

FRAGILE*ELECTRONICS

THE DUCK BROS

LONDON OL 486 8056

Eric Clapton's Blackie. *Getty Images*

Custom Shop Blackie replica. *Fender Musical Instruments Corporation*

a double-cutaway Gretsch Model 6120. He first established a must-have sound in the hearts and minds of other tone hounds when he took up a late-1950s sunburst Gibson Les Paul to record *John Mayall Blues Breakers with Eric Clapton*, otherwise known as "the Beano album," in 1966. Clapton's exemplary Les Paul, believed to be a late '59 or '60 model, served as the midwife that took blues into blues-rock when the star rammed it through a cranked Marshall 1962 combo (forever after known as a "Bluesbreaker") and warned the recording engineer that he intended to play loud. The result was one of the first widely chased guitar tones in the history of rock.

Eric Clapton

SLOWHAND
TOUR
1978

ERIC CLAPTON
SLOWHAND

Clapton himself, however, was forced to evolve somewhat, due to the theft of the Les Paul in the summer of 1966.

After that, Clapton gigged and recorded with a few borrowed Les Pauls but, unable to find one that he liked as much as his lost "Beano" guitar, eventually he settled in with a Gibson SG and an ES-335 for the majority of his work with Cream. The SG, a 1964 or 1965 model, became famous for the paint job given to it by the Dutch artists collectively known as The Fool, a name also given to the guitar itself. Todd Rundgren acquired the SG in 1974, and its bridge, tailpiece, and paint job were updated sometime after. Despite the SG's memorable appearance, the cherry-red 1964 ES-335 that Clapton used toward the end of the Cream era and early on with Delaney and Bonnie is arguably more memorable in a tonal sense in the ears of many fans. Purchased new by Clapton during his tenure with the Yardbirds (though it was more often seen in the hands of bandmate Chris Dreja at the

time), the red ES-335 has had the longest tenure of any of the artist's guitars to date and was surrendered in the 2004 Crossroads guitar auction, where it sold for $847,500.

The end of the 1960s signaled Clapton's movement, by and large, from Gibson to Fender. "Jimi was playing [a Strat] while I was still playing an SG. I didn't get to it then, but I got to it right away afterward," he explained. But still, finding the perfect Strat remained difficult.

"What I would always look for on a Strat was a maple neck that had been worn out," he remembered. "That was the thing: if it looked brand new [shakes his head]. . . . I just thought that if it had all those worn-out patches, it meant that it had been well favored."

He found such a Strat for the equivalent of $400 at the Sound City music shop in London on May 7, 1967, just a few days before Cream flew to New York to record its second album, *Disraeli Gears*. The guitar was serial no. 12073, a 1956 sunburst with an alder body and suitably worn maple fingerboard. He christened it "Brownie"

2009 Eric Clapton Signature Gray and Daphne Blue Stratocasters. *Fender Musical Instruments Corporation*

and used it during much of the early 1970s, especially on his solo debut, 1970's *Eric Clapton*, and Derek and the Dominos' 1970 album *Layla and Other Assorted Love Songs*. As he remembered, "Doing *The Johnny Cash Show* with Carl Perkins, touring with [Brownie] in a quartet that was quiet, funky, very, very strong—all of it hinged on the toughness of this guitar."

In 1970, Clapton acquired another Stratocaster that would become one of the most famous electric guitars of all time. "The problem was trying to find the maple necks [fretboard]," he said. "All the models that were current had the rosewood fingerboards. They [the maple-fretboard Strats] had kind of gone out of circulation, on this end of the scene [in England] anyway. It wasn't until I went through the States on tour that I started picking them up in pawnshops and guitar shops for a song. I'd buy four or five at a time."

At a guitar store in Nashville, Clapton purchased six late-1950s Strats and combined the best elements from his favorite three of the bunch; the other three were given to Pete Townshend, George Harrison, and Steve Winwood. This "parts guitar" he named

"Blackie," and after 1971, Brownie served as a backup instrument. Blackie was unique, blending elements from three '56 and '57 Strats, the modifications and repairs required to keep it serviceable over the years, and plenty of wear, sweat, and mojo from Clapton's own hands. The guitar was heavily used, from its first live appearance at the 1973 Rainbow Concert until its semi-retirement around 1985.

Clapton sold Brownie for $497,000 at a 1999 fundraising auction. Blackie was the star of another auction in 2004 that also saw the sale of Clapton's '64 ES-335 and fetched the highest price paid for a guitar at auction at the time, going to Guitar Center for $959,500.

—Dave Hunter and Michael Dregni

George Harrison

George Harrison plays his Strat, Rocky, onstage with Delaney and Bonnie in 1969. *Jan Persson/Redferns/Getty Images*

It's always a little heartwarming, somehow, to recall what gearheads the Beatles remained, even throughout careers graced with unfathomable levels of fame and recognition. They were, after all, musicians first and foremost, and the equipment used to make that music continued to be vitally important to them right up through the end of the band's run and beyond. When both George Harrison and John Lennon acquired Fender Stratocasters early in 1965, their childlike glee was virtually palpable. As revealed in Andy Babiuk's strenuously researched *Beatles Gear*, Harrison in particular had enjoyed trying a fellow musician's Stratocaster in Hamburg in 1960 and had been beaten out by a rival guitarist in an effort to purchase a used example in 1961. His subsequent use of Gretsch and Rickenbacker guitars through the early years of the band's success might have been a rebellion of sorts at his failure to acquire the original object of his desires: "I was so disappointed, it scarred me for life," the Beatle said in the TV documentary *The Story of the Fender Stratocaster*. When Don Randall sent a representative to New York to try to woo the Beatles over to

Harrison played this rosewood Telecaster in the Beatles' famous "rooftop" concert, their final live performance, as well as in the studio recording of "Let It Be." Legend has it that the rosewood Telecaster, constructed of the best body and best neck of two prototypes developed in 1968, was flown to London in its own seat and delivered to The Beatles by company head Don Randall himself. *Courtesy Julien's Auctions (juliensauctions.com)*

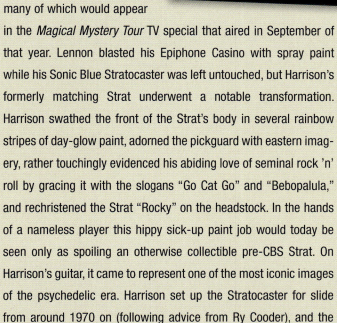

George Harrison's 1964 Stratocaster, Rocky. *Outline Press Ltd.*

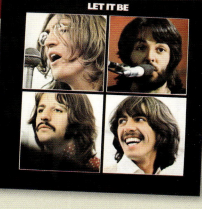

Fender mid-1964 during the band's U.S. tour, the effort apparently never made it past an underling in the Fab Four camp. Yet around February 1965, both Lennon and Harrison decided to tap that jones for what was then arguably the world's most popular solid-body electric, and they sent roadie Mal Evans out to purchase a pair of Stratocasters.

The guitars were matching Sonic Blue examples with pre-CBS features, and Harrison's at least would prove to be a used 1961 model. Both got immediate use from the Beatle guitarists during the recording of 1965's *Rubber Soul* album—and can even be heard together in the unison solo on "Nowhere Man" (as noted in *Beatles Gear*)—but Harrison's Stratocaster would make a more famous reappearance two years later as a key visual amid the band's psychedelic phase.

As London's legendary swing took a decidedly hallucinogenic swoop in spring 1967, the Beatles decided to paint several of their guitars to match the overriding mood, many of which would appear in the *Magical Mystery Tour* TV special that aired in September of that year. Lennon blasted his Epiphone Casino with spray paint while his Sonic Blue Stratocaster was left untouched, but Harrison's formerly matching Strat underwent a notable transformation. Harrison swathed the front of the Strat's body in several rainbow stripes of day-glow paint, adorned the pickguard with eastern imagery, rather touchingly evidenced his abiding love of seminal rock 'n' roll by gracing it with the slogans "Go Cat Go" and "Bebopalula," and rechristened the Strat "Rocky" on the headstock. In the hands of a nameless player this hippy sick-up paint job would today be seen only as spoiling an otherwise collectible pre-CBS Strat. On Harrison's guitar, it came to represent one of the most iconic images of the psychedelic era. Harrison set up the Stratocaster for slide from around 1970 on (following advice from Ry Cooder), and the guitar remains the property of the George Harrison estate.

Jeff Beck

Jeff Beck performs in 1973. *Robert Knight Archive/Redferns/Getty Images*

2004 Jeff Beck Signature Surf Green Stratocaster. *Fender Musical Instruments Corporation*

Among the several classic blues-rockers who evolved through the popular fat humbucker tones of the 1960s to more nuanced styles and sounds courtesy of the Fender Stratocaster, Jeff Beck is arguably one of the most masterful. Where others make admittedly good use of the instrument as a whole, Beck wields the Strat's versatile vibrato bar virtually as an instrument in itself and has taken the model as a whole to new heights of jazz-rock fusion in doing so.

The British guitarist made a big name for himself right from the start, after stepping into very big shoes in the Yardbirds as Eric Clapton's replacement, then splitting off to form the Jeff Beck Group with Ron Wood and Rod Stewart in 1967, all before he'd reached the age of twenty-five. Upon joining the Yardbirds, he at first inherited the red Fender Telecaster with rosewood fingerboard that Clapton had frequently played, which had been a "band guitar" of sorts, then set about acquiring his own, the now-famous Blonde Esquire with black replacement pickguard and sanded-down forearm contour. Come the 1970s, though, Beck became synonymous with, first, a humbucker-loaded Telecaster, then a '54 or '55 Gibson Les Paul that had been refinished in a dark oxblood color and had its original P-90s replaced with humbuckers. While the thick, creamy, sustaining Les Paul tones for a time seemed a Jeff Beck calling card, he was ever

striving for deeper expression from his work, and he finally found it in the emotive tremors of Leo Fender's original "Synchronized Tremolo Action."

Beck came out big time as a Strat fanatic on the 1976 album *Wired*, lacing the album with a newfound dexterity that would come to be his trademark and which was acknowledged by his appearance on the cover wielding an Olympic White example of his new love. For many fans, frenetic vibrato bursts of the album track "Goodbye Pork Pie Hat"—a tune written by Charles Mingus as a tribute to Lester Young—best define Beck's move to the Stratocaster. Through the course of the 1980s Beck further developed his style by dropping the pick in favor of using the fingers of his right hand to attack the strings. He recorded another of his classic Strat-fueled outings in *Jeff Beck's Guitar Shop* in 1989.

Rather than fawning over vintage models, Jeff Beck has long favored contemporary Fender Stratocasters, particularly those with the updated two-post vibrato and stainless-steel saddles. Fender's Jeff Beck Signature Stratocaster has gone through several incarnations and currently carries the noiseless ceramic pickups and roller nut that Beck favors.

In 1965, Jeff Beck bought a '54 Fender Esquire from John Walker (real name John Maus) of the Walker Brothers, and Beck used it to play some of the most groundbreaking music the rock and pop world had yet witnessed. The guitar, forever after referred to as "Jeff Beck's Esquire"—is known for its deep forearm and ribcage contours (sanded in by Maus himself), heavily scarred finish, and black pickguard. In 2006 Fender's Custom Shop put out this limited edition replica of Beck's famous Esquire. *Fender Musical Instruments Co.*

Ritchie Blackmore

Ritchie Blackmore and Deep Purple perform during their 1974 U.S. tour. *Fin Costello/ Redferns/Getty Images*

Often touted by devotees of the form as the original god of the über-metal solo, Ritchie Blackmore kept the Fender Stratocaster in the fold when most stadium rockers were turning to the fatter tones of Gibson Les Pauls, SGs, and Flying Vs to pound their Marshall stacks into submission. First with Deep Purple in the early 1970s and then with Rainbow after 1975, Blackmore established himself as the dark master of the Stratocaster, while also firming the foundations of a lead-heavy, medieval-influenced vein of hard rock and metal that has perpetuated to this day.

Like so many topflight artists, Blackmore modified his instruments considerably. He favored large-headstock, post-CBS Strats, mainly the early 1970s models with the "bullet" truss-rod adjustment points behind the nut, and is most noted for giving these a scalloped fingerboard to aid speed and finger vibrato. Blackmore

preferred a graduated scallop, which was fairly shallow up to the seventh fret and somewhat deeper thereafter. He also disconnected the middle pickup, which he never used; glued the necks in place, rather than relying on his Fenders' bolt-on attachments; and modified the vibrato tailpieces by removing some of the wood in front of the trem's inertia block in the back of the body. After they became available, Blackmore also added Seymour Duncan Quarter Pound Strat-style replacement pickups to the bridge and neck positions of his guitars.

During Rainbow's heyday, Blackmore also took to smashing plenty of Strats, usually as the grand finale to an explosive set, which would often culminate in a dummy amp stack bursting into flames after being assaulted with the unfortunate instrument. Rather than destroying one of his painstakingly modified guitars, though, he would usually inflict such punishment on a Strat copy that would be pieced back together for further abuse night after night.

Translating Blackmore's six-string hellfire and fury to a 20,000-strong arena crowd obviously required some gargantuan amplification, and all needs were ably met with a pair of 200-watt Marshall Major heads, each of which ran through two 4x12-inch speaker cabs. To induce these extremely robust tube amps into early distortion, and to warm up the tone of the otherwise bright Strats, Blackmore played through an Awai reel-to-reel tape recorder, which he set to "pause" and used purely as a preamp.

Ritchie Blackmore

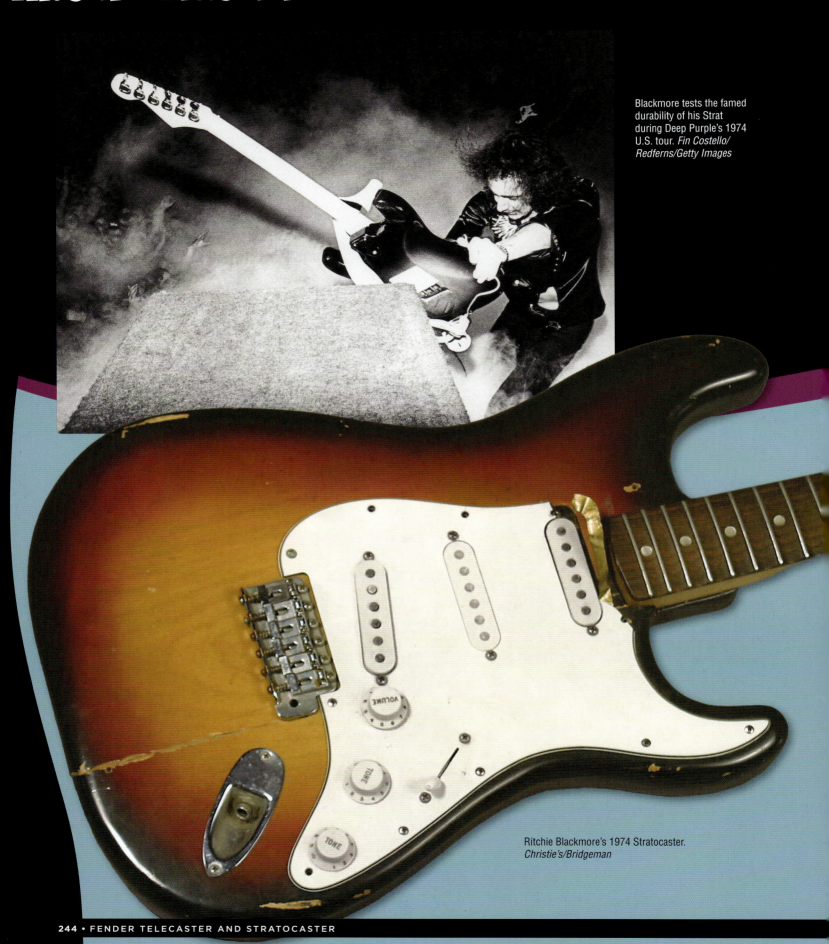

Blackmore tests the famed durability of his Strat during Deep Purple's 1974 U.S. tour. *Fin Costello/ Redferns/Getty Images*

Ritchie Blackmore's 1974 Stratocaster. *Christie's/Bridgeman*

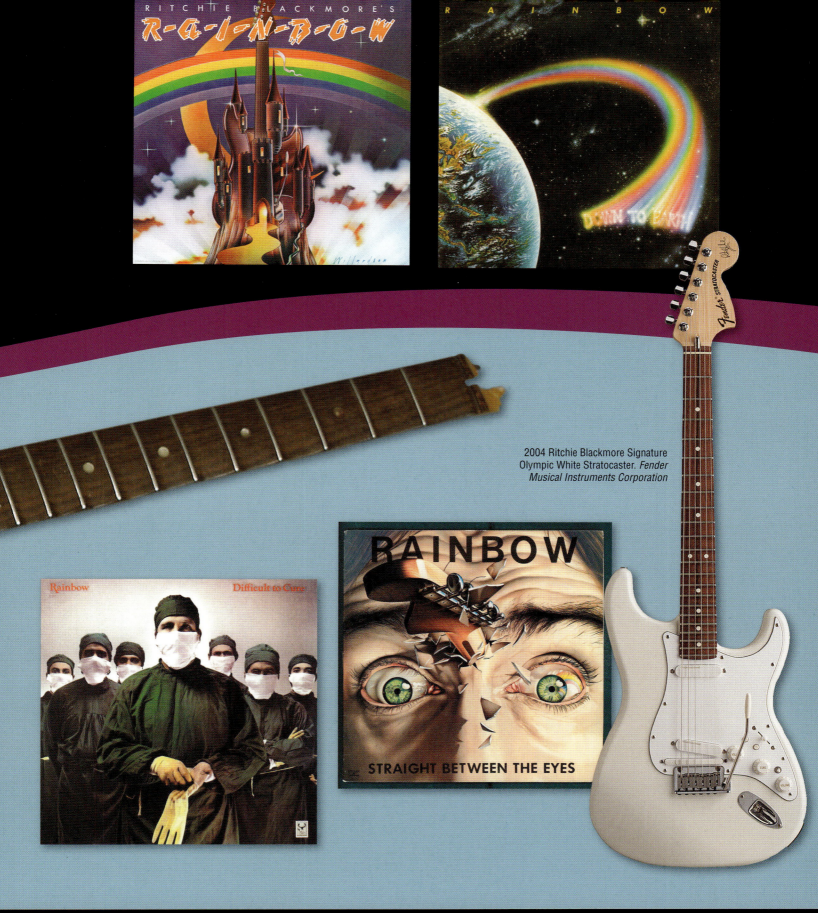

2004 Ritchie Blackmore Signature Olympic White Stratocaster. *Fender Musical Instruments Corporation*

1969 Candy Apple Red Stratocaster. *Fretted Americana, www.frettedamericana.com*

1969 Lake Placid Blue Stratocaster.
Chicago Music Exchange,
www.chicagomusicexchange.com

(continued from page 227)

Following the transitional mid-1960s changes, in late 1967 Fender replaced the Stratocaster's Kluson tuners with sets made for them by Schaller and stamped with the trademark reversed Fender "F" on the gear housing. In 1968 the coloring of the Fender headstock logo was essentially reversed to a more visible bold black lettering with gold outline and a much bolder model name. By this point, the "late-1960s post-CBS Stratocaster" had fully arrived. In 1967 the "maple-cap" neck was officially introduced (made with a glued-on maple fingerboard, rather than being a one-piece maple neck as used on guitars of the 1950s). This option gives plenty of late-1960s Strats more of the look of those made from late 1954 to mid-1959, although these lacked the dark wood "teardrop" behind the nut and the "skunk stripe" at the back, since the truss rod was installed from the front before the maple fingerboard was glued on, just as it had been for necks with rosewood fingerboards. Among the more detrimental changes of the late 1960s, however, was the move to polyester finishes around 1968. This "thick-skinned" finish, with its resilient, plasticky feel, was achieved with as many as ten to fifteen coats of polyester paint and is believed by many players to severely choke the tone of any guitar that carries it.

Many of the changes made from the mid- to late 1960s were purely cosmetic and should not have made a late-'65 Stratocaster "sound any worse" than, for example, an early-'64 Stratocaster. Given how greatly guitars produced even on the same day can vary, there are certainly Strats from throughout the 1960s that sound outstanding and plenty from the pre-CBS era that simply don't sound all that good. Regardless, the changes mark the most significant turning point in Stratocaster desirability for collectors, whatever wonderful music players might have made with post-'65 guitars. The laws of supply and demand have also made early CBS guitars more collectible than late CBS guitars, while the "law of Jimi Hendrix" has helped to make anything up to the end of the decade more prized than what came after.

Even so, it can't be denied that more significant issues of declining quality control, driven by increased production and an eye more on raw sales figures than the quality of the instruments, were beginning to take their toll on Fender quality by the late 1960s and certainly the early 1970s.

THE END OF AN ERA

In late 1971, several significant changes made to two critical components of the Stratocaster finally, and truly, signaled the end of the era of the guitar in its original form, broadly speaking. Many will point to the change to a thicker finish in 1968 as the first factory-induced detriment to the Stratocaster's tone (aside from the unquantifiable variations in wood resonance, variables in pickup construction, and so forth). When the neck attachment, truss rod, and bridge assembly were radically altered toward the end of 1971, it put the final nails into the coffin of the golden age of the Stratocaster.

In theory, the new Tilt Neck mounting system and bullet-head truss-rod adjustment point could have been seen as a good thing, but their fate as signals of a guitar that was already declining in so

1975 Rhinestone Stratocaster.
Chicago Music Exchange,
www.chicagomusicexchange.com

many other ways has fated them with a badge of dishonor, of sorts. The former part of this new neck construction involved a new three-screw neck mounting with built-in neck-angle adjustment plate that allowed the player or repairman to effect slight changes in the "tilt" of the neck without having to remove it to place a thin shim under the end, as the job was previously achieved. Accompanying this device was a newly designed truss rod with a bullet-shaped adjustment nut protruding at the headstock end of the neck, just behind the nut. The "bullet head" was far more accessible than the previous adjustment point, at the heel end (guitar end) of the neck, but was considered "ugly" by many players and, well, just different from "the classic Stratocaster."

The second major change was arguably more significant from a sonic standpoint, in that it altered the mass and material of the critical anchor points of the strings. In late 1971 Fender entirely reconfigured the original Synchronized Tremolo system, retaining what outwardly might have appeared to be a similar design but constructed of entirely different materials. The rolled-steel inertia block, so key to retaining satisfactory sustain in Leo Fender and Freddie Tavares's original design, was changed for a block of die-cast Mazak, an alloy of zinc, aluminum, magnesium, and copper. At the same time, the individual bridge saddles were changed from bent steel to die-cast Mazak. The lesser density of the Mazak, when compared to the steel of the previous components, brought a real change to the Stratocaster's tone, which many describe as giving it a "thinner," "lighter," or "brighter" voice. Once again, it's worth acknowledging that plenty of great music

has been made on Stratocasters constructed after these changes were introduced, but they delineate the real bottom that was finally hit in the Strat's gradual decline.

RETURN TO QUALITY

In 1985, William Schultz, then president of Fender Musical Instruments, along with Dan Smith and a team of other Fender managers and investors, rescued the Fender brand from near extinction under CBS. Under this new leadership, a newly revitalized Fender Musical Instruments Corporation went about building the brand back into one of the most successful musical instrument manufacturers in the world, and restored the renowned Fender quality of the '50s and early '60s along with it.

Several contemporary and modified Stratocasters proliferated and found their fans thanks to ever-increasing (or call it "returning") quality and a stronger and stronger brand. The guitars like the American Vintage Reissue Series, the Custom Shop Time Machine series—with their characterful, distressed Relic models—and even the Japanese and Mexican-made guitars produced in the image of models from the early to mid-1950s or early 1960s continue to form the main image in our collective notion of what "a Stratocaster" is or should be. If the Stratocaster is the world's most influential, and most copied, electric guitar, Fender is once again its most successful reinventor, and the future of Leo's grand design seems more ensured than ever before.

2012 Custom Shop 1956 Melon Candy Stratocaster. *Fender Musical Instruments Corporation*

David Gilmour

Dave Gilmour of Pink Floyd performs at the Miller Strat Pack concert on September 23, 2004, at Black Island Studios in London. *Jo Hale/Getty Images*

Some are born with great guitars, while others have great guitars thrust upon them. So it was, to some extent at least (and with Shakespeare's forgiveness), with David Gilmour, who made plenty of standout music with Pink Floyd on other instruments before acquiring a certain 1954 Strat toward the end of the 1970s. Historic in its own right, now doubly iconic for its use on several classic Pink Floyd recordings, Gilmour's 1954 Stratocaster carries the serial number 0001 on its neck plate.

This '54 Stratocaster, with a neck made in June of that year and a body dated in September, is certainly an early one (the Stratocaster was first released early in 1954 following several prototypes made in 1953), but it is not actually the first Strat made, as the serial number implies. Gilmour's Stratocaster wears a nonstandard finish that is sometimes referred to as Desert Sand or faded Olympic White, but is not quite like either of those two later Fender custom colors. It also has a gold-plated vibrato unit and jack plate and a gold-colored anodized aluminum pick-guard like those that would later appear on the Musicmaster, Duo-Sonic, and Jazzmaster. The common wisdom in vintage-Fender camps is that the eye-catching serial number was used to denote a special-order model, indicating this perhaps was the first Stratocaster with gold-plated hardware. In any case, Stratocasters made before Gilmour's

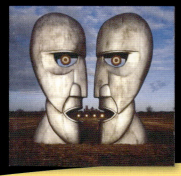

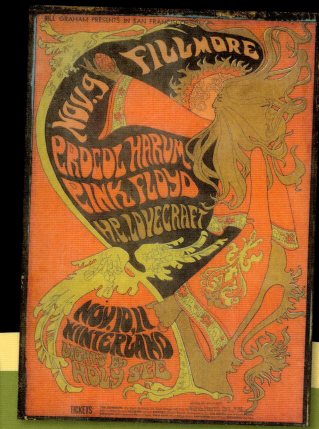

have been seen wearing higher numbers, so the 0001 most likely wasn't intended to denote the guitar's chronology—at least not among all Strats.

Gilmour's 0001 Strat followed a rather circuitous route into his loving hands. Owned at one time by pickup maker Seymour Duncan, the Strat was purchased by Pink Floyd guitar tech Phil Taylor in the mid-1970s for a reported $900. A couple of years later, Gilmour pried the instrument from Taylor by offering the tech the cash he was seeking toward the down payment on a house. The 1954 Strat was often used in the studio from around 1977 onward on several Pink Floyd recordings and on work Gilmour did for Paul McCartney and Brian Ferry. One of the easiest ways to see and hear it simultaneously, though, is to watch the video of the fiftieth anniversary concert for the Fender Stratocaster filmed at Wembley Arena, London, in 2004, when Gilmour picked up this legendary guitar for live renditions of "Coming Back to Life" and "Marooned."

2008 David Gilmour Stratocaster.
Fender Musical Instruments Corporation

Rory Gallagher

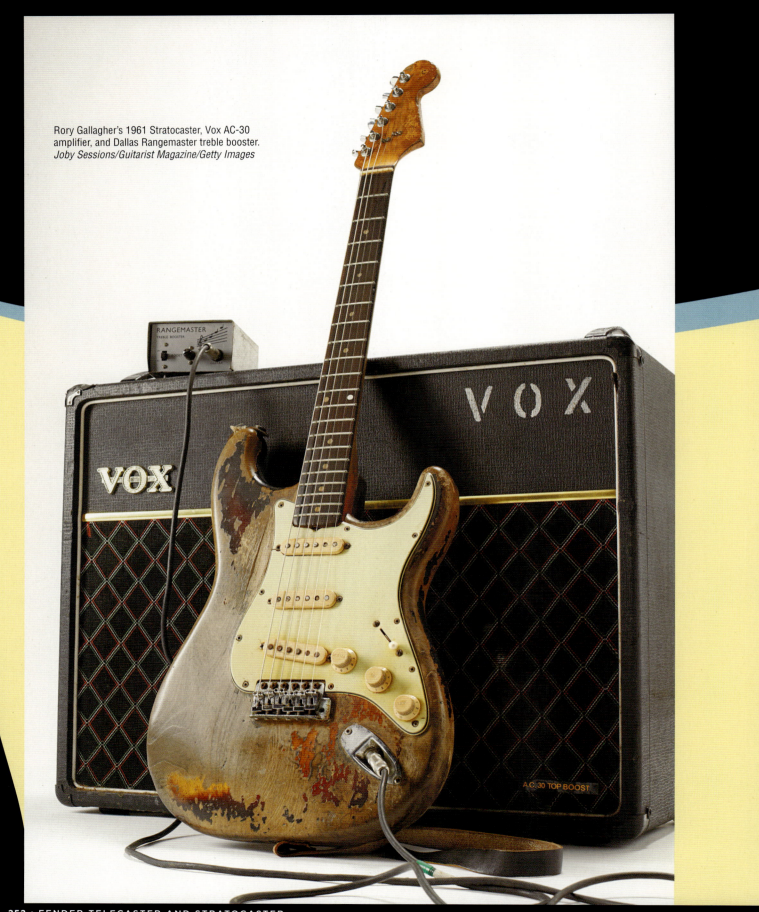

Rory Gallagher's 1961 Stratocaster, Vox AC-30 amplifier, and Dallas Rangemaster treble booster. *Joby Sessions/Guitarist Magazine/Getty Images*

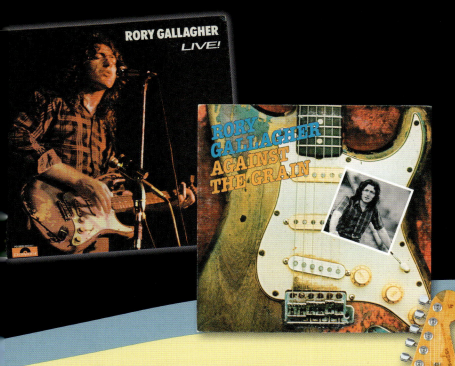

A mid all the battered Strats that have made their marks in the annals of the electric guitar, Rory Gallagher's leaves a bolder impression than most. This road-worn 1961 Stratocaster epitomizes the instrument of the hard-traveling, hard-playing, hard-living blues rocker and will eternally remain associated with the late Irish musician. When Gallagher bought this guitar in 1963, it was not only the first Stratocaster he had ever seen, but it was believed to have been the first Strat imported into Ireland. It was ordered for another local guitarist who thought he was buying a red Stratocaster and decided to pass it along to Gallagher when it turned out to be a Sunburst model instead. A fortuitous decision: Rory Gallagher and this passed-over Strat produced a mountain of fiery, emotive blues and helped to establish a Fender-based blues-rock tone that is idolized to this day.

In addition to its famous disappearing finish, Gallagher's Strat shows evidence of the wear and tear that will overcome any hard-gigged electric guitar. Its replaced tuners (mismatched, with five Sperzels and one Gotoh), single white-plastic fingerboard dot in place of one absent clay twelfth-fret marker, rewound pickups, and replaced potentiometers are all repairs of pure necessity, undertaken by an artist who made this his main instrument throughout his career.

Mike Eldred, the head of Fender's Custom Shop, who examined the original item in the course of creating Fender's Rory Gallagher Tribute Stratocaster, relates that there were many further modifications under the hood, too. "Inside it was pretty trashed. Replaced wood, bad wiring job, bits of rubber. It was a mess," Eldred told Patrick Kennedy for *Strat Collector* in 2004.

The most notable aspect of Gallagher's '61 Strat's decay, however, was not the result of abuse (Gallagher doted on the instrument and cared for it lovingly), but of its owner's body chemistry. According to brother Donal, who now owns the guitar, Rory had a rare blood type that gave his sweat extremely acidic properties. Gallagher sweated a lot in the course of any performance, and his Strat's sunburst finish paid the price. The amount of bare wood on this legendary '61 Stratocaster has helped propagate the belief that guitars with thinner (or no) finishes resonate more freely and have a better tone than those with thick, nonbreathable finishes. There might be something to this theory, but it's also a reasonable assumption that the magic that Rory Gallagher and his battered Strat made together had less to do with absent lacquer than it did with the artist's unchained heart, head, and hands.

2004 Rory Gallagher Tribute Stratocaster.
Fender Musical Instruments Corporation

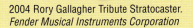

Robbie Robertson

Robbie Robertson of the Band plays alongside Bob Dylan at Madison Square Garden on January 29, 1974. *Gijsbert Hanekroot/Redferns/Getty Images*

Robbie Robertson's bronzed 1954 Stratocaster that he played at *The Last Waltz*. *Rick Gould*

Music fans who are unfamiliar with the intricacies of Robbie Robertson's career tend to know him primarily as the guitarist with the Band and Bob Dylan, and to picture him, if at all, with the odd monster of a Stratocaster that he wielded in much of the concert documentary *The Last Waltz*. Dig just a little deeper, though, and you quickly find that this understated artist boasts a career that stretches virtually from the roots of rock 'n' roll to span many of the high points in the history of popular music.

At age seventeen, Robertson joined formative rock 'n' roller Ronnie Hawkins and his band, the Hawks, in 1960 and toured the United States and Canada with the outfit until 1964. After a brief stint on their own, Robertson and the Hawks—which included Levon Helm,

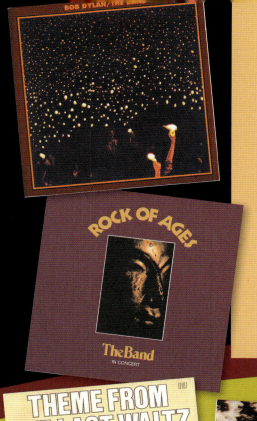

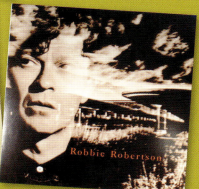

"I've had this souped-up old Stratocaster quite a while. It has number 0254 on the back. You can tell it's old 'cause the neck's a little thick. Before I used it in *The Last Waltz*, I had it bronzed, like baby shoes. That gave it a very thick, sturdy sound. A Stratocaster has three pickups: I had the one in the middle moved to the back with the other and tied them together. They have a different sound when they're tied together, and I don't like having a pickup in the middle, where you pick. I've got a Washburn whammy bar on that guitar."

—Robert Robertson, *Musician*, 1987

Garth Hudson, Rick Danko, and Richard Manuel—signed on as Bob Dylan's backup band in 1965, and upon signing to Capitol Records in 1967 as a band in their own right, changed their name to the Band. They released several successful albums of their own into the middle of the following decade, while returning time and again to their collaboration with Dylan.

Known as more of a Telecaster player through the early years of the Band, Robertson acquired a pre-CBS Stratocaster along the way, took to playing it more frequently, and decided to have it bronzed as a sort of monument in honor of the Band's final concert together, documented by Martin Scorsese in the film *The Last Waltz*. Robertson has often said this guitar was a 1958 Stratocaster, although the thicker neck profile, the round string guide on the headstock, and its 254 serial number might suggest an older guitar from 1954. While he used this freshly bronzed pre-CBS Stratocaster throughout much of *The Last Waltz*, the bronze shell, in addition to giving it "a very thick, sturdy sound," also added considerable weight. At times, Roberts lightened the load by switching to what appears to be a '57 Stratocaster in two-tone sunburst, although it's unclear whether this was his guitar or Bob Dylan's (certainly Dylan plays it on the finale, "I Shall Be Released"). Robertson later added a "double-locking" Washburn vibrato unit to the Stratocaster, taking it even further from its Leo-certified origins.

Bronze Strats aside, Robertson's wry, spare playing style has made him a true guitarist of note, and he has been admired by many prominent names in the music industry, in addition to legions of fans, for his rootsy tone and tasteful fills. Turning once again to the live documentary film, there are few better examples of his sound, or his musicality, than the performances on "The Night They Drove Old Dixie Down," "Ophelia," and "The Weight," the latter a Band classic, written by Robertson himself. Fender issued a Custom Shop Robbie Robertson Stratocaster available in the artist's preferred Moonburst finish as well as a lacquer-based bronze, and he has been seen playing one of two Fender Custom Shop Strats decorated by the Apache artist Darren Vigil Gray.

Wayne Kramer

2010 Wayne Kramer Signature Stratocaster. Fender Musical Instruments Corporation

The MC5 roared out of 1960s Detroit like a big-block V8 with open headers. Fueled by the twin guitars of Wayne Kramer and Fred "Sonic" Smith, their supercharged take on rock 'n' roll mixed garage, R&B, and psychedelia, with a boost of Sun Ra for good measure, and pushed the contemporary boundaries of volume and furor to the redline. The MC5 was also known for their political leanings and were one of the only bands of the era to talk the talk and walk the walk, holding the Grant Park stage in Chicago during the 1968 Democratic convention, for example, and escaping moments before the Chicago PD took over proceedings. (Rumor has it the Grateful Dead and Jefferson Airplane, though billed, were no-shows.)

Given their antiestablishment leanings, it might seem odd to some that Kramer's most iconic guitar was this "Stars and Stripes" Stratocaster, though as the guitarist explained upon Fender's release in 2011 of a heavily relic'd Signature Series model (complete with its "This tool kills hate" neckplate), "When I painted the guitar with this motif it was really to claim my patriotism in spite of what the country was doing at the time."

Wayne Kramer bends a note on his trademark Strat while performing with MC5 in Mount Clemens, Michigan, in 1969. From left, drummer Dennis "Machine Gun" Thompson, Kramer, Fred "Sonic" Smith, and Rob Tyner. *Leni Sinclair/Michael Ochs Archives/Getty Images*

Little is known of the original guitar, other than the fact that it's a CBS-era instrument and must have been fairly new when Kramer acquired it. Given its new vintage and the MC5's balls-out sonic assault, it doesn't seem a stretch to assume that Kramer—who also played Epiphones and Gibsons with the MC5—had the humbucker installed in the middle position. What Kramer has offered in regard to the Stars and Stripes Strat, however, is that it was the instrument he wielded on the evenings of October 30 and 31, 1968, when the MC5 recorded the incendiary performances at Detroit's Grande Ballroom that became the touchstone protopunk LP *Kick Out the Jams*.

The MC5 disbanded in 1972 and Kramer did two years in federal prison for selling cocaine to an undercover agent in 1975 (an incident immortalized in The Clash's "Jail Guitar Doors"). Upon release he formed the abortive Gang War with Johnny Thunders before going on to enjoy a solo career and work scoring television and films. Over the years, he and surviving MC5 bandmates reunited to perform with members of The Cult, Motörhead, Mudhoney, and other acts that they influenced. Kramer has also continued to spread his political beliefs through music, including his work with Jail Guitar Doors, a nonprofit that provides musical instruments to prisoners in the United States and Great Britain.

—Dennis Pernu

Lowell George

Lowell George of Little Feat at the Beacon Theatre in New York on April 7, 1978. *Richard E. Aaron/Redferns/ Getty Images*

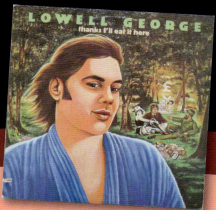

From his early days with Frank Zappa and the Mothers of Invention in the late 1960s, to the formation of his own band, Little Feat, to his short-lived solo career, Lowell George was well on course to becoming a significant hero of the Stratocaster before his untimely exit from the scene on June 29, 1979. Check out any of Little Feat's landmark 1970s recordings and, alongside that soulful voice, George's guitar tone stands out as one of the most distinctive of the era.

When George told *Guitar Player* interviewer Dan Kening in 1976 that he always preferred "to buy a stock guitar so if it gets stolen I can replace it easily," that really only told a fraction of the story of what went into creating that distinctive voice. Having had several guitars stolen on the road, George had taken to buying standard, off-the-shelf 1970s Stratocasters at the peak of his success, but the best known of these had several modifications that helped it achieve his signature tone. While the Strat's standard neck pickup served his mellower moments well, he put a slightly fatter Telecaster pickup to the bridge position for extra punch, which was given a serious goose by the addition of an Alembic Blaster preamp, housed in a replacement output-jack plate. Add to the brew a set of heavy-gauge flat-wound strings, put it in open-A tuning (like the more common open-G, but a whole step up), slip a Sears Craftsman $^{11}/_{16}$ socket wrench on your little finger for slide, and pump it all through a custom-made Dumble amplifier, and you're there. A long way from "off-the-shelf Strat" for sure.

Lowell George had at least two similarly equipped '70s Stratocasters, one with a natural finish and another in Blonde, as witnessed in photos and live concert footage from the era, but he likely owned several over the years. Not all had the Tele pickup or the Alembic preamp at all times, but they tended to evolve toward that ideal as he carted them out on the road and back into the studio again. The tone that this mighty concoction brought forth might arguably best be heard on Little Feat's live album from 1978, *Waiting for Columbus*, which eventually became their bestselling record. Dig the blistering slide tones on tracks such as "Fat Man in the Bathtub," "Dixie Chicken," and "Rocket in My Pocket" (its girth aided by some judicious delay)—and note, just as crucially, how important the use of restraint, and silence, is to his playing style, too—and you know it can be none other than Lowell George. All the more tragic, then, that he left us at the age of thirty-four after dying of heart failure just two weeks into his solo tour.

Randy Bachman

Randy Bachman and his Strat power Bachman-Turner Overdrive.
Michael Ochs Archives/Getty Images

There's a saying among hot rodders that anyone can build a hot rod, but it takes a real man to cut one up. This old adage refers, of course, to the act of taking torch and hacksaw to rare, vintage tin with the intention of modifying it to do things that Henry Ford never intended. When it comes to guitars, Randy Bachman is a first-class hot rodder.

Though he often has been seen taking care of business with a Gibson Les Paul and is known as one of the world's foremost collectors of Gretsch instruments, Bachman is also closely associated with the Fender Stratocaster, thanks to a guitar known as "The Legend." Bachman, founder of Canadian rock giants the Guess Who and Bachman-Turner Overdrive, obtained The Legend in the late 1960s. It had already been modified a bit by a previous owner, but Bachman was fearless when it came to laying the thing down on his workbench and applying chisel, saw, and sundry other tools, all in an effort to make the guitar do what he wanted it to do—things Leo never intended. As Bachman told photographer Rick Gould:

"Originally a black '59 Strat, the Legend was stripped to bare wood. The upper horn had my name in rub-on decals as well as a round metal Titano accordion

Randy Bachman's 1955 Stratocaster, serial number 7179, that he played with BTO. *Rick Gould*

logo. The guitar had been modded to be a 9-string and had extra tuners on it, which I took off, leaving three extra holes in the headstock. Also, the big curved part on the headstock had broken off when I threw the guitar into a speaker cabinet à la Pete Townshend. I also broke off the wang bar and had to redrill the tremolo block to accommodate a bigger screw-in arm that I had made by a blacksmith. It was a 'T' with an arm to grab over the pickups and a big one that went out back past the strap attachment. This allowed for extreme Hendrixian wang-bar tactics with feedback.

"In the back, I chiseled out a long channel, thinking I could create my own B-bender by cutting out the B saddle, stabilizing the trem block, and keeping just one spring on the cutout B saddle. Then I found out I couldn't hacksaw the trem block, so I just left it.

"When the nut broke to pieces, I didn't have a replacement, so I used my mother's metal knitting needle. It didn't have grooves and it was cool how the strings slid around for low bending. I sanded and steel-wooled the back of the neck like a violin neck with no finish, which made playing such an ease.

"I reversed the inny jack to be an outy, which I thought Fender always should have done anyway because it allows bigger jacks and L jacks to be easily used."

If it seems like all this gouging and soldering made The Legend a Stratocaster in name only, you ain't seen nothin' yet.

Reportedly, the guitar also featured a swapped-in rounder-profile Fender Jazzmaster neck and three on-off pots in place of the usual three-position selector, allowing Bachman to combine any two pickups, including the bridge and neck units.

Bachman: "My bridge pickup was a '50s Tele that was held to the pickguard with clear bathtub caulking, which prevented feedback and squeal. I had a Rickenbacker pickup at the neck for a while and then a '59 humbucker. The last mod was three off/on pickup switches that allowed for an amazing combination of pickups— neck and bridge, all three, bridge and middle, neck and middle, et cetera. Problem? Yes. I was too wild onstage and would hit them all. Of course the guitar would have no sound because all the pickups had been switched off."

"There's something about the Strat sound that just rings out," Bachman wrote in his book, *Vinyl Tap Stories*. "If you take that same guitar and run it through a small tweed Fender amp cranked right up, you get a really great bluesy sound."

As for The Legend, sadly it went the way of many other hard-touring rock 'n' roll axes: Bachman reports that it was stolen. "It would be the thrill of a lifetime to get the guitar back, but it was just a wreck, so unless someone knows what it is . . ." he said. "But what a sound and monster it was."

—Dennis Pernu

Randy Bachman

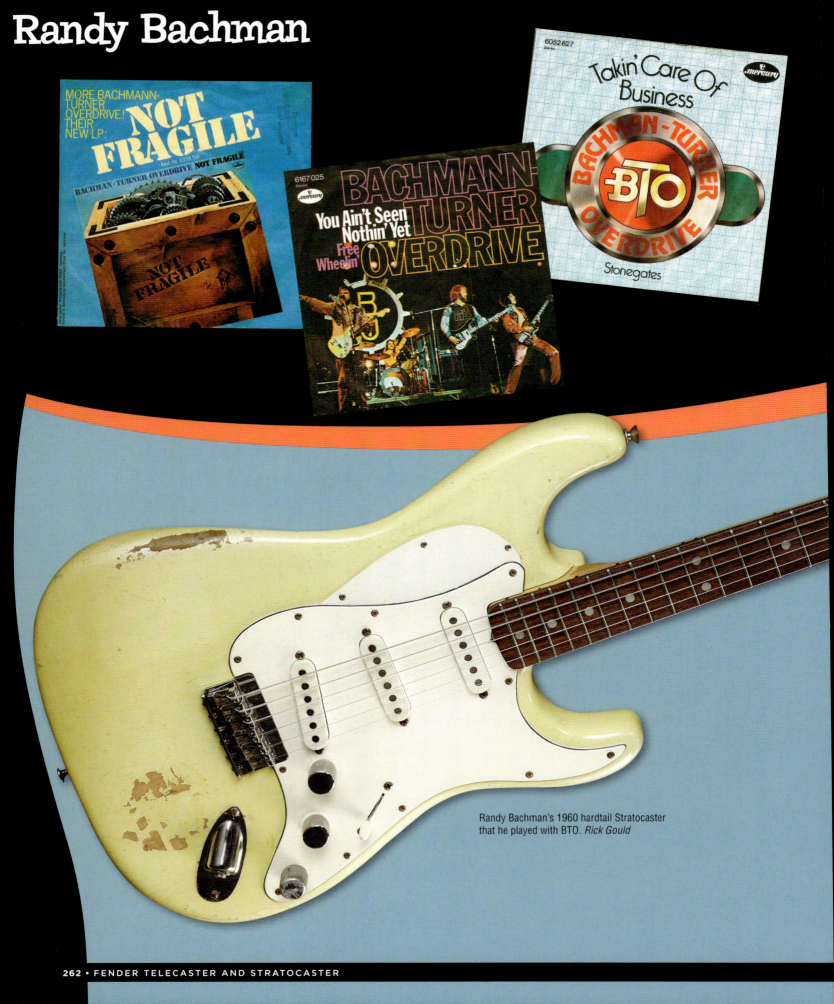

Randy Bachman's 1960 hardtail Stratocaster that he played with BTO. *Rick Gould*

"There are two iconic guitars that shaped the blues and rock 'n' roll—the Gibson Les Paul and the Fender Stratocaster. They each have their own distinctive look and sound, and because they are opposites in every way, every guitar player has to have both of them.

"The Strat was and still is the most recognizable image, sound, and pioneering guitar to ever make music. The first time I saw a Strat was with Buddy Holly & the Crickets on *The Ed Sullivan Show*. At the same time, I got a copy of *Out of the Shadows* from England and saw my first red Strat. The sound had me hooked.

"The Stratocaster is the most versatile and durable guitar ever made. The ability to interchange different Fender guitar necks, bodies, pickups, etc., made all Fenders in demand. No airline has ever destroyed one of my Fender guitars. To demonstrate their toughness, I have thrown a Strat off the roof of a house, climbed down, picked it up, and played it—and it was still in tune.

"They are the workhorse of most guitar players. In my early days, I had a '59 black Strat that I customized . . . This guitar was known as The Legend by many guitarists and fans as it was the guitar I played through the Guess Who years, into the Brave Belt years, which became the Bachman-Turner Overdrive years. Unfortunately, it was stolen, and my heart still aches when I think of that. There should be a death penalty for guitar thieves! If you've had one stolen, you'll agree.

"I have quite a collection of Strats now. My favorite is an Olympic White 1954, serial number 0717, that sounds so clear on the top end, it's like a pedal steel.

"It would not be out of line to change the "T" to a "D," and call this model of guitar a "Strad-icaster." The Fender Stratocaster is truly the Stradivarius of guitars."

—Randy Bachman, 2013

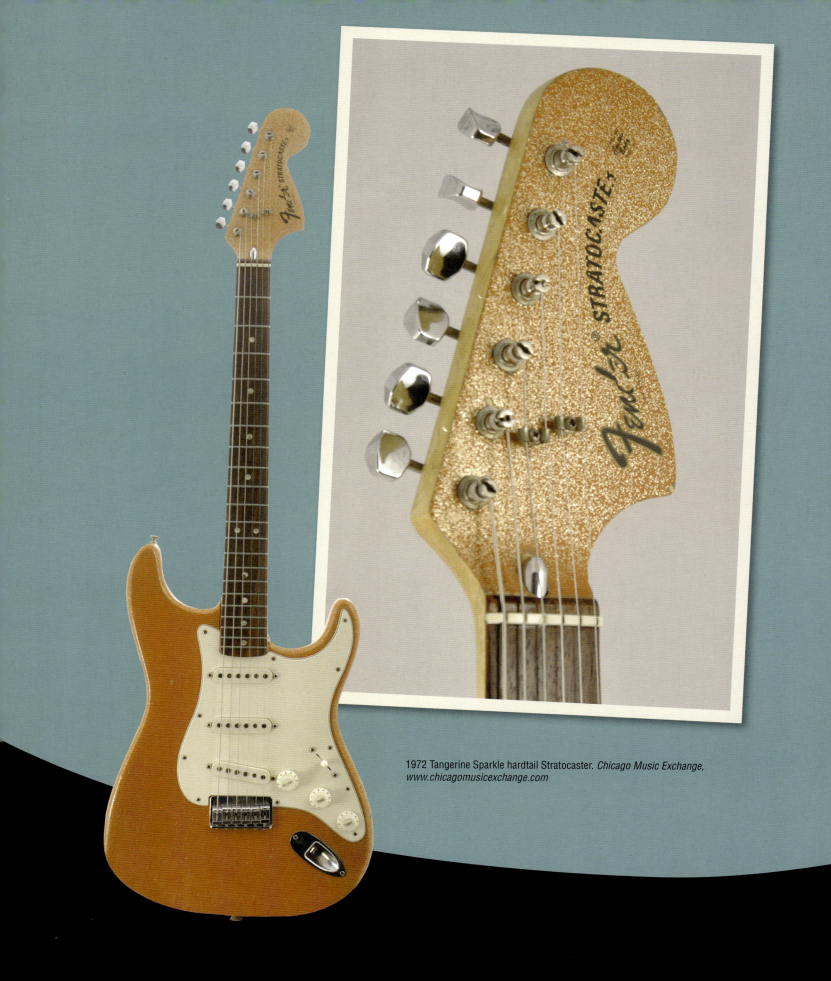

1972 Tangerine Sparkle hardtail Stratocaster. *Chicago Music Exchange, www.chicagomusicexchange.com*

Playing the guitar with the Faces, then separately with Rod Stewart, then the Rolling Stones—with several notable side projects and solo ventures laced throughout—pretty much gives you your choice of any guitar out there. And while archive shots of Wood in concert will often show the more unusual, arguably more dramatic metal-fronted Zemaitis models or his Lucite-bodied Dan Armstrong, a prized vintage Stratocaster has long been his go-to guitar, both on stage and in the studio.

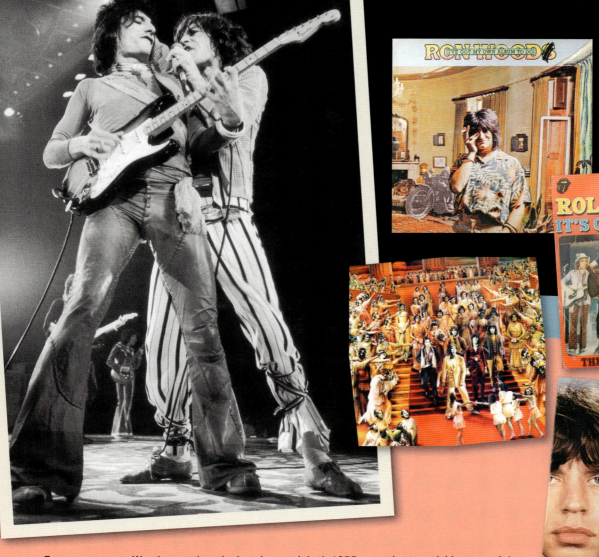

For many years Wood owned and played an original 1955 Stratocaster in two-tone sunburst, with a similar-looking 1956 Strat as backup. Entirely stock, the '55 is far and away the single guitar most seen in his Stones performances and remained a major ingredient in the recording of his 2010 solo album, *I Feel Like Playing*, which features collaborations with Billy Gibbons, Slash, Flea, and several other artists. As Wood told *Premier Guitar* magazine while promoting the album, "I think, like wine, the matured sound of a '50s Strat is more or less a stable part of my diet—like with Jeff Beck and Jimmy Page and Eric Clapton. They're just very comfortable. You get that reliable sound that comes from a '50s amp and a '50s guitar."

For many, Keith Richards's guitar tone might define that Rolling Stones sound, but watch any Wood-era Stones concert footage and you quickly appreciate how much he contributes to the band. Although he name checks Beck and Clapton in reference to the timelessness of the Stratocaster's appeal, his is quite a different approach to the instrument: He came up amid Britain's blues-rock scene of the late 1960s and early 1970s, sure, but for Wood the emphasis was always more on rock 'n' roll. Give him a Stratocaster and a tweed amp and he'll come out sounding more like a cranked-up Buddy Holly than a Buddy Guy, defining a groove that has long kept pace with the Stones, certainly, but was also right in step with his other great British rock 'n' rollers, the Faces and Rod Stewart. Nailing the groove, nailing the tone, and nailing the vibe—and doing it, more often than not, on a Stratocaster.

Robin Trower

Robin Trower bends a note on his Strat in 1975.
Colin Fuller/Redferns/Getty Images

Not unlike both Eric Clapton and Jeff Beck, British blues-rocker Robin Trower made the leap from playing a Les Paul with Procol Harum from 1967 to 1971 to being a Stratocaster fanatic in his solo work from 1971 on. What he did with that Strat, though, was quite different from either Beck or Clapton, and is perhaps more often associated with the playing and tone of Jimi Hendrix than with his British compatriots. For all the Hendrix associations, however—and Trower himself has frequently said that he isn't copying Hendrix, as such, but trying to carry on in his footsteps—it wasn't his admiration for the deceased legend that prompted his switch to the Stratocaster, but simply a "feel thing."

As Trower told Steve Rosen in *Guitar Player* magazine in 1974, he was struck by the Strat revelation upon arriving early for a sound check one day in 1971 while Procol Harum was on tour with Jethro Tull. He picked up Tull guitarist Martin Barre's Strat (a guitar that Barre had set up for slide), plugged it in, and yelled, "This is it!" Trower continues: "I then switched to Strat. Up to then, I had been playing Les Pauls. I always felt there was something missing on Les Pauls. They had a good fat sound, but they never had that 'musical' sound. When I played a Strat I realized it had that strident chord."

Trower first acquired a black Stratocaster that he would later deem "unplayable," which he demoted to backup status, making a white Strat from around 1973 or 1974—large headstock, bullet

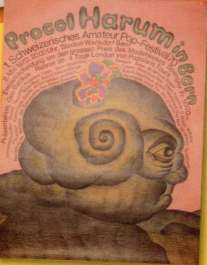

truss-rod adjustment, maple fingerboard—his main instrument through much of that decade. The artist dipped into the well-respected Squier JV series Stratocasters in the 1980s and has largely played contemporary Stratocasters since that time. Whichever Strat he straps on, though, he continues to prove that a true artist will sound like himself whatever gear he chooses to get the job done. That being said, a Fuzz Face, Uni-Vibe, and Vox or Tycobrahe wah-wah (or recent Fulltone equivalents) all run through a pair of 100-watt Marshall heads might also be part of the equation. The Fender Custom Shop has issued a Robin Trower Stratocaster made to the specs of his favorite 1970s model.

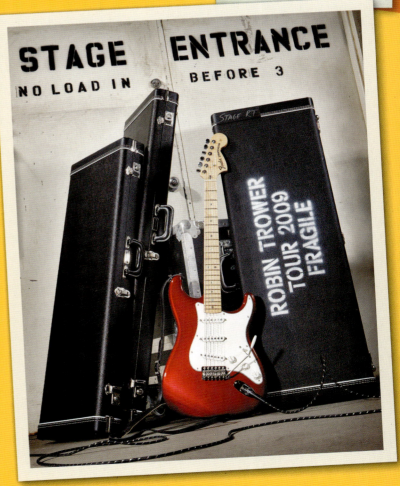

2009 Robin Trower Signature Midnight Wine Burst Stratocaster.
Fender Musical Instruments Corporation

Dave Murray

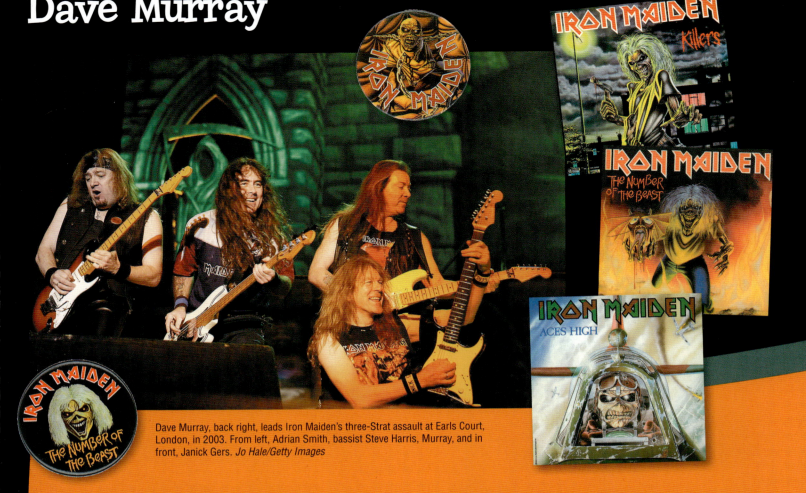

Dave Murray, back right, leads Iron Maiden's three-Strat assault at Earls Court, London, in 2003. From left, Adrian Smith, bassist Steve Harris, Murray, and in front, Janick Gers. *Jo Hale/Getty Images*

In the late 1970s, whilst acts like Zeppelin, Sabbath, and Deep Purple lounged poolside, content amid sacks of money, the New Wave of British Heavy Metal looked to blaze a fresh trail for metal. However, one guitarist in the movement's leading band did manage to bring a piece of rock history along for the ride.

In 1976, Iron Maiden's Dave Murray answered an ad in U.K. music mag *Melody Maker* purporting to offer the Stratocaster that once belonged to recently deceased Free guitarist Paul Kossoff. After double-checking the serial numbers, Murray laid down the equivalent of $1,400 for the axe—a princely sum for a working-class bloke. "[Kossoff] used that guitar on a lot of Free," Murray explained to *Gear Vault* in 2009. "I actually saw him many years ago using it during a Free performance of 'My Brother Jake' on an English television show called *Top of the Pops*. They were one of my favorite bands, and I had to have that guitar because it belonged to Kossoff."

The Stratocaster, comprising a 1957 body and a 1963 rosewood-board neck, is immediately recognizable for its unconventional H/S/H configuration. Murray reported that he added the DiMarzio 'buckers to obtain a thicker sound. The purchase and the modifications proved savvy: the Stratocaster appeared on Iron Maiden's first eight albums and was a constant sidekick to Murray on tour. "It was my main guitar," he said, "and I played everything with it: lead and rhythm, clean stuff, heavy stuff. It was real versatile."

One point of debate concerning this guitar appears to be whether it's the same white-with-mint-pickguard Stratocaster that appeared on the cover of Kossoff's *Back Street Crawler* solo LP released in 1973. Some maintain that Murray had the guitar painted; others claim that it was already black when it came to him. Given Murray's admiration of Kossoff and his understanding of the instrument's significance, as well as the substantial financial sacrifice he made to obtain it, it seems doubtful he would have had the guitar painted after obtaining it.

After endorsing ESP and Jackson in the late '80s and early '90s, Murray returned to Fender in 1995, and in 2009 his black Strat with loads of provenance was honored with a Signature Series model.

—Dennis Pernu

Bonnie Raitt

Bonnie Raitt is one of the blues' most respected slide players, and her instrument of choice is the Fender Stratocaster—specifically a rag-tag and road-weary 1965 Strat, a guitar from a turning point in Fender's history. Raitt acquired her stripped and heavily gigged example, which wasn't going to be anyone's prize, back before "vintage" Strats had much cache even in the best condition. The body and headstock had lost their paint and logos, respectively, as if awaiting a refinish, and the former had taken on a ruddy, natural brown stain. The pickups remained, though, and the guitar was otherwise functional and, it would seem, a tonally superior example of the breed, as Raitt has proven over the course of many years and nine Grammy Awards.

Other than its scruffy looks, this Stratocaster is exemplary of the "transition period" represented by early post-CBS Strats. It carries the large headstock that CBS execs purportedly introduced so the iconic electric guitar would be more recognizable on TV, pearloid dots rather than clay dots in the rosewood

fingerboard, and the three-ply white plastic pickguard characteristic of the era. Otherwise, the '65 Stratocaster differs little from its pre-CBS predecessors of at least a couple of years before.

Raitt's fluid style and sweet-yet-biting tone have helped make her playing instantly recognizable among myriad slide guitarists. She tunes her Strat in open G (D-G-D-G-B-D low to high) and uses a custom-cut glass wine bottle neck on her middle finger while attacking the strings with a clear plastic thumb pick and the bare (though fingernail-aided) fingers of her right hand. The seeming simplicity of many of her lead lines belies an innate melodic sensibility and an ability to hit straight at the hook of the tune, qualities that have helped her become one of few hardcore blues-slide players to cross over into mainstream success. Even on her major hits, songs like "Love Sneaking Up on You" and "Something to Talk About," that slinky, sweet slide oozes in and stamps Raitt's signature all over the tune just as assuredly as do her distinctive vocals.

Mark Knopfler

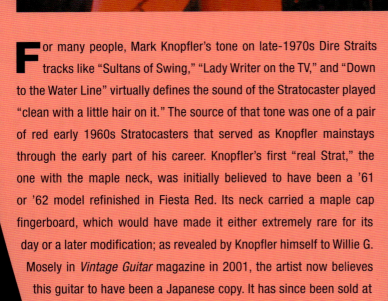

Mark Knopfler fingerpicks his Strat onstage with Dire Straits in 1980. *Mike Prior/Redferns/ Getty Images*

Mark Knopfler's 1954 Stratocaster, serial number 059. *Rick Gould*

For many people, Mark Knopfler's tone on late-1970s Dire Straits tracks like "Sultans of Swing," "Lady Writer on the TV," and "Down to the Water Line" virtually defines the sound of the Stratocaster played "clean with a little hair on it." The source of that tone was one of a pair of red early 1960s Stratocasters that served as Knopfler mainstays through the early part of his career. Knopfler's first "real Strat," the one with the maple neck, was initially believed to have been a '61 or '62 model refinished in Fiesta Red. Its neck carried a maple cap fingerboard, which would have made it either extremely rare for its day or a later modification; as revealed by Knopfler himself to Willie G. Mosely in *Vintage Guitar* magazine in 2001, the artist now believes this guitar to have been a Japanese copy. It has since been sold at auction for charity.

In 1977, Knopfler bought his second red Strat as a backup, this time a real '61 with a rosewood fingerboard, and it soon made

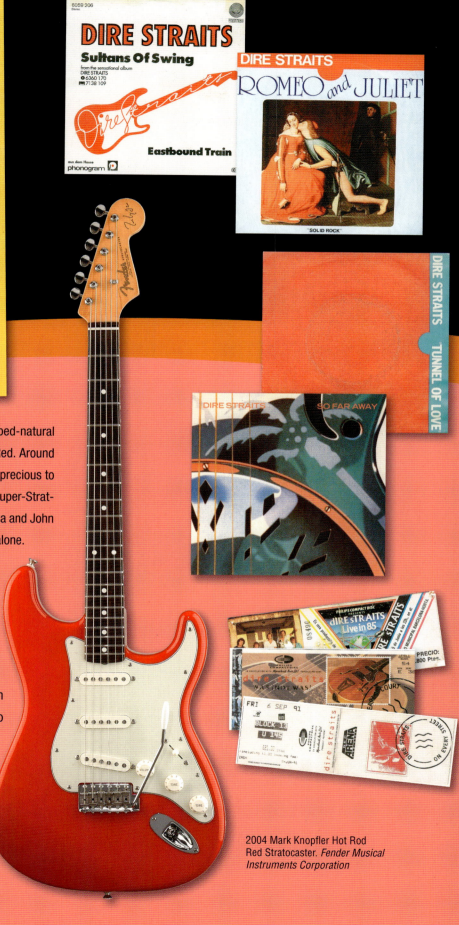

its way into the first string. Acquired used with a stripped-natural finish, Knopfler also had this one refinished in Fiesta Red. Around 1980, though, he declared his pre-CBS Stratocaster too precious to take on the road and moved to a series of Strat- and super-Strat-like guitars made initially by Schecter, then by Rudy Pensa and John Suhr of Pensa-Suhr in California, and later by Pensa alone. Regardless, he has always remained a "Strat guy" in most fans' estimations and has even returned to the pre-CBS fold in more recent years, sporting a genuine 1954 Stratocaster with the early serial number 059.

While Knopfler's musical adventures have segued through several avenues, it all seems to come back home to a common ground when you put a good Stratocaster in his hands. Pipe it through a brown-face early '60s combo with just a little compression in the front end, attack the strings fingerstyle with the right hand, and set that selector switch between the bridge and middle pickups for extra quack, and it's a tone that'll take you "South Bound Again" every time. Fender's Artist Series Mark Knopfler Stratocaster is based on the Fiesta Red '61 refin with rosewood fingerboard.

2004 Mark Knopfler Hot Rod Red Stratocaster. *Fender Musical Instruments Corporation*

Yngwie Malmsteen

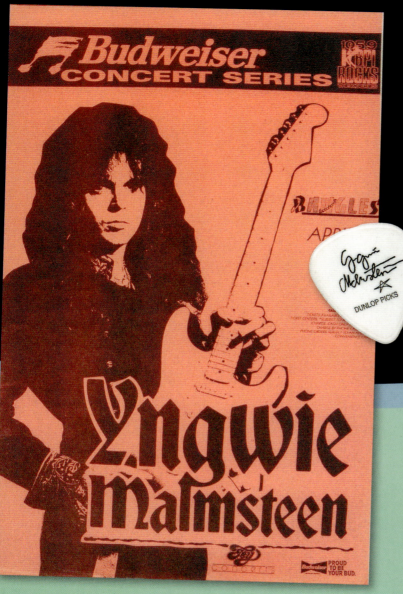

Yngwie Malmsteen Vintage White Stratocaster with scalloped fretboard. *Fender Musical Instruments Corporation*

Yngwie Malmsteen, hailed as the single-handed founder of a new classical-metal genre, brought a distinctive new voice to the shred-rock arena when he arrived on the scene in the early 1980s. Rather than indulging in the tapping and hammer-ons of Van Halen and others, Malmsteen displayed a fluid, legato-like alternate picking technique and an impressively vocal vibrato that enabled him to roll out neoclassical runs at breathtaking speeds. And while his early work with the bands Steeler and Alcatrazz, as well as his 1984 solo debut, *Rising Force*, helped him ascend the ranks of poodle-haired, Superstrat-toting virtuosi, Malmsteen did it all on a plain old (if uniquely modified) 1972 Fender Stratocaster, the first

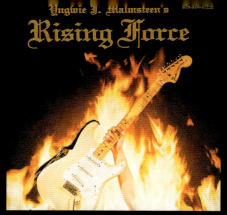

serious guitar he ever acquired as an aspiring teenage guitar hero in Stockholm, Sweden.

In 2005, Malmsteen told Hugh Ochoa of *StratCollector* that he first decided the course of his life in 1970, at the age of seven, while watching a documentary on the death of Jimi Hendrix. The show ran a clip of Hendrix burning his Stratocaster at Monterey, and although the young Malmsteen couldn't even see what kind of guitar was aflame, he knew he had to have it. A year later, on his eighth birthday, Yngwie's sister gave him Deep Purple's *Fireball* album and he discovered that Ritchie Blackmore played a Stratocaster, the same guitar Hendrix had played and burned. American-made guitars were rare and prohibitively expensive in Sweden in the 1970s, but Malmsteen eventually acquired a white 1972 Strat, and the instrument clicked for him right from the start.

Malmsteen created the famous "scalloped" divots in his Strat's fingerboard himself, after observing such construction on an old lute that had come in for work in a repair shop in which he apprenticed as a teenager. He first tried the technique on a few of his cheaper guitars, then took the file to his prized Strat. The Swede wasn't the first to perform on a scalloped fingerboard (his hero, Ritchie Blackmore, had been using the technique for some time), but his pyrotechnics on the instrument helped popularize the mod among the shred crowd. Although Malmsteen now has a large collection that includes many pre-CBS, 1950s and early-1960s Strats and several Gibsons, he has always expressed a preference for Stratocasters made between 1968 and 1972, largely because he feels the bigger headstock improves the resonance on those models. Unlike his colleagues in the genre during the early 1980s, Malmsteen eschewed Floyd Rose vibrato systems (again, for tonal reasons), and has always retained his stock Fender vibrato units. Other than the scalloped neck and jumbo frets, his '72 Strat, and the Fender signature models based upon it, are largely stock with minor modifications, including a DiMarzio HS-3 pickup in the bridge position (alongside standard Stratocaster pickups in the neck and middle positions) and a brass nut. None of these are the high-gain accoutrements one might expect from a shredder like Malmsteen, but ram these clean single-coils through upward of twenty Marshall JMP 50s, and the setup apparently gets the job done.

Yngwie Malmsteen

Richard Thompson

Much of Richard Thompson's unique style and tone might seem to come from his transmogrification of fingerstyle acoustic Scottish and English folk music to the electrified genre, but that shouldn't by any means imply that this British artist can't rock with the best of them. And while he has long enjoyed using alternative designs from smaller guitar makers, we will always consider him a "Strat player" first and foremost. Thompson was playing a mid-'60s Stratocaster when he cofounded folk-rockers Fairport Convention in 1967, but he acquired what would be his "number one" Strat in 1971 around the time of his departure from the band. The 1959 Stratocaster came into its own on 1982's *Shoot Out the Lights*, which *Rolling Stone* magazine declared one of the best rock albums of all time.

Thompson was born in the Notting Hill neighborhood of London in 1949, and he grew up listening to everything from

Richard Thompson picks his Strat in Leeds, England, on March 4, 2013. *Ben Statham/Redferns/Getty Images*

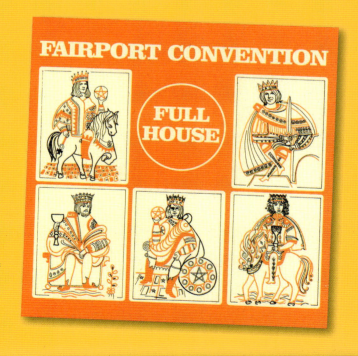

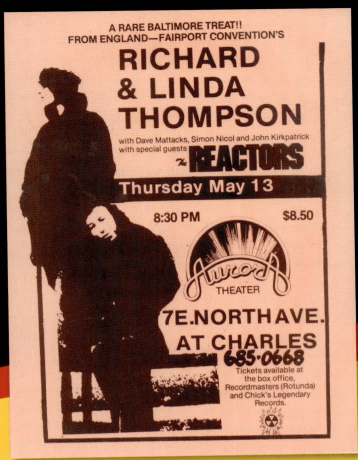

classic jazz and bebop to Scottish folk music. The diverse music of his childhood wove its way into the artist's playing style even today. Listen to Thompson's solo work on the title track from *Shoot Out the Lights*, or any of his standout electric playing, and you'll hear a wiry, angular style that is impossible to define. Although he was raised on rock 'n' roll and hit the stage himself when the London scene really was at its most exciting, both his tone and the riffs he applies it to have leaned more toward an edgily clean eclecticism than toward the heavy, humbucker-fueled blues-rock that was so many players' stock-in-trade in the late 1960s.

In Richard Thompson, we might even hear a player whose acoustic voice and playing style translates more accurately to his plugged-in approach, including his hybrid picking style (using a pick between thumb and index finger and the bare tips of the middle and ring fingers) and his frequent use of open tunings.

In the latter part of his career Thompson has frequently turned to electrics made by California builder Danny Ferrington, which often comprise clever twists on some of the basic Stratocaster specs. Time and again, though, he has returned to his '59, which was played so heavily in its first ten years of ownership that the original neck with rosewood fingerboard would no longer take a refret and was replaced by an all-maple neck from 1955. Thompson also plays a reissue-style Fender Stratocaster in Sonic Blue that his guitar tech, Bobby Eichorn, assembled from select pieces of different Fender guitars.

Quality means Confidence

Often copied but never equalled, Fender Fine Electric Instruments continue to lead the field in concept, design and precision manufacture. Musicians have long recognized the superiority of Fender Guitars and Amplifiers because high quality has always guaranteed complete dependability. No wonder Fender customers have such confidence . . . they won't settle for less than the genuine article. Neither should you. Choose Fender!

Quality...
a measure
of the
genuine

SOLD BY LEADING MUSIC DEALERS THROUGHOUT THE WORLD

Fender
SALES, INC.

SANTA ANA, CALIFORNIA

A 1960s Fender advertisement

Smoother playing, faster action

Why not visit your nearest dealer . . . see and hear for yourself.

Fender SALES, INC. · 308 EAST 5th ST. · SANTA ANA, CALIF.

STRATOCASTER TONE AND CONSTRUCTION

WHEN IT CAME TO DEVELOPING THE STRATOCASTER, Fender already had an excellent template on hand in the form of the Telecaster, a burgeoning success in the country market in particular and soon on the blues and rock 'n' roll scenes, too. Leo sought to do something quite different with the Stratocaster, of course, adding features and functionality that were gained mainly through the addition of new components, along with a few sexy new twists to the body and headstock styling. Even so, the fundamentals of the chassis—as we might call the body and neck woods—were largely in place, and functioning fine just as they were.

While any guitar's core tone might be shaped by the tonewoods from which it is constructed, it's also worth noting just how certain newly designed components that were added to that chassis to create the Stratocaster considerably shaped, and ultimately differentiated, the sound of the new instrument. If Leo had established his sound with the Telecaster, the Stratocaster certainly attained something that would also be recognizable as "the Fender sound," but was nevertheless quite different in its tonal fine points.

Classic elements of the Stratocaster design are as iconic today as they were in the early days, as shown by this pair of 2005 '70s Stratocasters. *Fender Musical Instruments Corporation*

The simple act of adding elements such as the spring-loaded, semi-floating vibrato unit and a trio of similar but slightly different single-coil pickups to the same ash-and-maple construction changed the voice of the Stratocaster in relation to the Telecaster. The alteration might seem subtle in the broad scheme of electric guitar tones, but to aficionados of either breed it is significant enough to render them two entirely different instruments. Otherwise, the ingredients in the Stratocaster still coalesce perfectly toward Leo Fender's original goal of creating a bright, clear, cutting guitar based on the sonic template of the lap steel guitar popular in Western Swing music at the time, with outstanding resistance to feedback and better sustain than the common hollow-body electrics of the day. Dissect the instrument, and it starts to look extremely simple: The foundation is found in a highly functional and playable bolt-on maple neck (classically with maple fingerboard, but a rosewood 'board alters the formula only slightly) and solid swamp ash body (later alder), all slightly amended by its clever vibrato bridge design with individually adjustable steel saddles. In addition to these, one intangible ingredient—its 25½-inch scale length—also makes an impact on the guitar's final voice. Drastically alter any one of the above, and a Stratocaster becomes an entirely different electric guitar.

ELEMENTS OF THE STRATOCASTER DESIGN

The key elements in the Stratocaster's basic design have been covered in the discussion of the guitar's development in History of the Stratocaster, and since its basic elements were developed using the Telecaster as a starting point, many of these elements were also covered in Telecaster Tone and Construction. However, it's also worth summing them up here, if only to point out the subtle variations and differences in the models. By "design," I mean the blueprint, as it were—specifications that are largely intangible, but nevertheless contribute to the guitar's sound and function.

The Solid "Slab" Body

This is an obvious ingredient, perhaps, since it forms the cornerstone of the Stratocaster's construction, but its contribution to the tonal formula can't be ignored. Aside from the sonic properties of the common tonewoods used in Stratocaster bodies, which will be discussed in their own right further along, the sheer method

Slab blanks and contoured bodies back up a 2010 Custom Shop 1959 Black Stratocaster. *Fender Musical Instruments Corporation*

Elements of the classic Stratocaster body displayed in a bare body and a 2010 Custom Shop 1967 Aged Olympic White Relic Stratocaster. *Fender Musical Instruments Corporation*

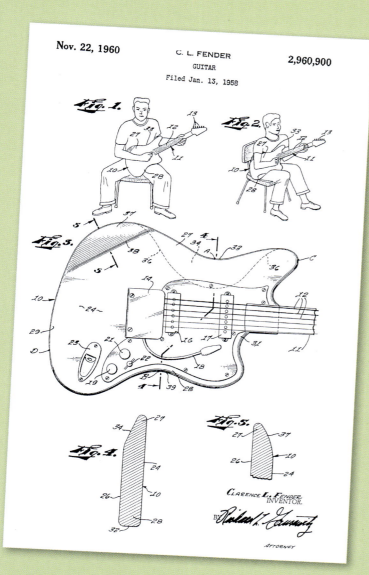

of construction of a guitar with a slab-styled body made from one or two pieces of the same wood, with minimal use of glue and lack of adornments, lends its own tonal characteristics to the instrument. It is difficult to quantify such factors, but suffice it to say that such a design allows a relatively unencumbered vibration of the wood itself, and since there is only one wood involved, it presents the pure characteristics of that wood without the complications of multiwood constructions or heavy adornments. The end result is heard in the Strat's clarity and tonal purity, which is emphasized by other elements of the design, but is certainly anchored here.

Also, while some players will talk of a Stratocaster as "lacking sustain," they are often actually hearing the single-coil pickups, which don't present the "fatness" and perceived sustain of, for example, a higher-gain humbucking pickup when played through the amplifier. Compare both types of guitars unplugged, however, and a good Stratocaster will usually hang in there sustain-wise with any popular set-neck, humbucker-loaded guitar you might put it up against.

The 25½-Inch Scale Length

Whether Leo Fender settled on the Telecaster's (and therefore, Stratocaster's) scale length by happy accident or by conscious design, it certainly worked toward achieving his goals for the instruments. In his lecture to the 1995 convention of the Guild of American Luthiers, guitar maker Ralph Novak stated that, of all factors that affect a guitar's tone, "scale length comes first, because the harmonic content of the final tone produced by the instrument begins with the string. Factors such as structure and materials can only act as 'filters' to tone; they can't add anything, they only modify input. Therefore, if the harmonic structure is not present in the string tone, it won't exist in the final tone." Scale length is, therefore, a cornerstone of design for any thoughtful maker and one of the first decisions to be settled when conceiving the voice of an instrument. The fact that Leo Fender settled on the 25½-inch scale seems perhaps to have been serendipitous, but the choice served to emphasize many of the other sonic characteristics that he was hoping to achieve with this guitar.

Put simply, the longer the distance between bridge saddle and nut slot, known as the "speaking length" of a guitar's strings (that is, its scale length), the more distance there is between the strings' harmonic points. Longer scale lengths have produced more of the sonic qualities often described as "shimmer" or "sparkle" or "chime." Leo copied the scale length of a Gretsch archtop guitar when designing the guitar that would become the Telecaster, but it turns out that the 25½-inch scale length accentuates the qualities he was looking for. Gibson uses a shorter 24¾-inch scale on many guitars, including the Les Paul family, the SG, the ES-175, and several others; in his shorter scale length, the tighter grouping of the harmonic points create a slightly warmer tone—in short, they don't ring as clearly—which itself is part of the whole Gibson electric tonal profile.

It so happens that Fender's narrow single-coil pickups, his choice of woods, the steel bridge construction, and the bolt-on maple neck all further accentuate harmonic clarity and high-end presence, so the total package really is working together toward Fender's desired tonal ends. But, as Novak put it, "if the harmonic structure is not present in the string tone, it won't exist in the final tone."

The slightly longer Fender scale length also increases the string tension. The strings feel firm under the fingertips, although the springs in the Stratocaster vibrato unit offer some "give" to the playing feel to partly counteract this. The 7¼-inch fingerboard radius on vintage Fender guitars (the curve at which the top of the fingerboard is milled) also contributes greatly to the guitar's playing feel and to some extent has always dictated how it was approached. Smaller than the radius used on any other popular model of guitar, this tight circle results in more curve to the surface of the fingerboard and, in one sense, a neck that can feel extremely natural and comfortable in the hand for basic open chords played in the lower positions in particular. The rounder the radius, though, the harder it can be to bend strings on the fingerboard or to do so without "choking out," a phenomenon whereby the curvature of the fingerboard mutes a bent string and causes it to die out prematurely. Obviously, plenty of players do bend strings successfully on the Stratocaster, and it has become the classic choice of several big-bending blues players in particular, such as Buddy Guy and Stevie Ray Vaughan.

The Bolt-Neck Construction

Even if the neck itself and mounting plate and wood screws that hold it in place are all "tangible" components, it is probably best to consider the so-called "bolt neck" in theory for its contribution to the Stratocaster's voice, regardless of the wood and hardware that comprise it. Leo Fender originally adopted the bolt-on neck for the Telecaster in the early 1950s, and a full discussion of its characteristics and contributions to tone are fully discussed on page 147.

(continued on page 296)

1959 Blonde Stratocaster with black-anodized pickguard. *Rumble Seat Music*

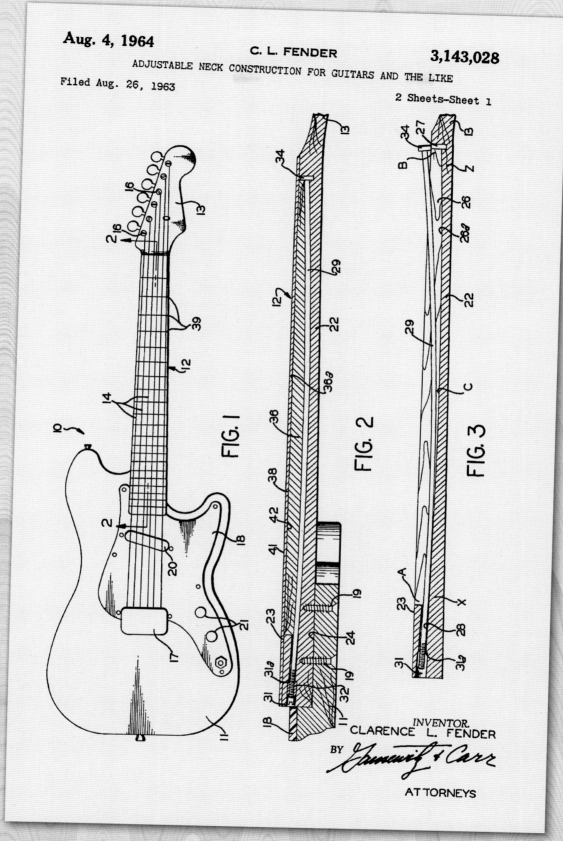

C. L. FENDER

ADJUSTABLE NECK CONSTRUCTION FOR GUITARS AND THE LIKE

3,143,028

Filed Aug. 26, 1963

2 Sheets—Sheet 1

FIG. 1

FIG. 2

FIG. 3

INVENTOR.
CLARENCE L. FENDER

BY *Gunewich & Carr*

ATTORNEYS

Leo Fender's 1963 patent drawing for the adjustable bolt-neck design
used on the Stratocaster as well as other Fender guitars.

Nils Lofgren

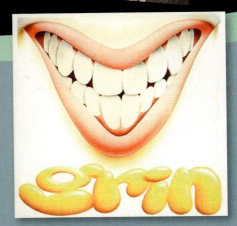

Nils Lofgren hits a high note at the Winterland Ballroom in San Francisco, California, in 1975. *Richard McCaffrey/Michael Ochs Archives/Getty Images*

Though he released four stellar albums in the early 1970s with his band Grin, Nils Lofgren got his foot in the door thanks to sessions with Neil Young, who famously drafted the teenaged guitar-slinger to play piano on Young's 1970 solo album, *After the Gold Rush,* despite Lofgren's lack of experience on the instrument. After Grin dissolved in 1974, Lofgren released a string of solo LPs before replacing Steven Van Zandt in Bruce Springsteen's E Street Band in 1984 for the massive *Born in the U.S.A.* tour.

It's through his appearances with Springsteen over three decades that Lofgren's become best known for a particular natural-finish 1961 Stratocaster. As the guitarist explained to *Fender News*, "My first guitar, in the mid-'60s, was a Tele; I got it because Jeff Beck played one. Soon after that, I saw Jimi Hendrix live . . . and the Strat soon became, to me—even more than the Tele—the instrument that I was most comfortable with, as far as having different sounds."

Lofgren has actually owned two 1961 models. The first was acquired from a friend in a trade for a 12-string acoustic. The more recognizable Strat, however, came into Lofgren's hands a bit later. "The other '61 I found in a pawn shop in Berkeley when I

Playing for the Boss: from left, Jake Clemons, Gary Tallent, Nils Lofgren, Bruce Springsteen, and Patti Scialfa perform at the Los Angeles Convention Center on February 8, 2013. *Kevin Mazur/WireImage/Getty Images*

was on the road in the late '60s," he told interviewer Peter Walker. "It was this ugly purple thing, but I bought it because it sounded great. I gave it to my brother, Michael, who is a master carpenter, to restore it. He stripped it and dyed it natural wood, and made a beautiful oak pickguard."

This "oakguard" Strat is also notable for its Alembic Blaster pre-amp unit, visible where the stock recessed output is usually located. When toggled on, the Blaster allows the player to increase volume without affecting tone. A rubber effects pedal knob in place of the traditional skirted Strat volume knob gives Lofgren the ability to use the Blaster to create swirling effects.

Finally, the guitar is outfitted with a Bill Lawrence double-blade pickup in the neck position. Also noteworthy is Lofgren's technique, which involves a downstroked thumbpick and harmonic-inducing upstrokes with his second and third fingers.

Lofgren is an enthusiastic Fender user through and through (on the road, he also uses a Jazzmaster, numerous other Stratocasters, and Fender amps). "I've found that with a Fender, you can lose your finesse and not totally lose it on the instrument, if you can understand that," he told *Premier Guitar* in 2009. "I like to lean into the guitar and use those five settings you can get out of a Strat. I like playing lots of different guitars, but I'll always reach for a Strat. It's the most beautiful electric guitar ever made."

—Dennis Pernu

Jimmie Vaughan

Jimmie Vaughan stands proud with one of his Signature Strats relic'd to mimic his original Olympic White 1963.

"He really was the reason why I started to play, watching him and seeing what could be done." So said Stevie Ray Vaughan of his big brother, Jimmie. What more really need be said?

Jimmie Lawrence Vaughan was born in March 1951 in Oak Cliff, Texas—T-Bone Walker's old stomping ground, on the edge of Dallas. Sidelined by a football injury when he was thirteen, a family friend gave Jimmie a guitar to occupy his time during his recuperation. From the moment his fingers touched the strings, he proved himself a natural talent. As his mother, Martha Vaughan, remembered, "It was like he played it all his life."

Jimmie launched his first band, the Swinging Pendulums, at fifteen and was soon playing Dallas clubs several nights a week. A year later, he joined one of Dallas's top local bands, the Chessmen, which opened shows for Jimi Hendrix. Hearing Muddy Waters and Freddie King play, Jimmie focused on the blues, founding the band Texas Storm in 1969.

In 1974, Jimmie formed the Fabulous Thunderbirds in Austin with singer and harpist Kim Wilson, drummer Mike Buck, and bassist Keith Ferguson. They released their debut album in 1979, *Girls Go Wild*, with a tough blues sound tempered by 1950s rock 'n' roll. With the 1986 *Tuff Enuff*,

Jimmie Vaughan Tex-Mex Olympic White Stratocaster. *Fender Musical Instruments*

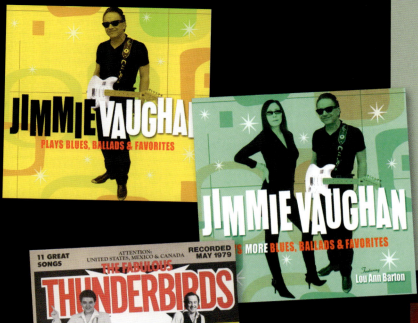

"Mine is the white one that I used on all the Fabulous Thunderbird records, and I also made *Strange Pleasure* with it. It's a '63. I customized it a little bit. I put a new neck on it and back then you couldn't get pick-ups so you had to scavenge them."

—Jimmie Vaughan, 2013

the title track single, and follow-up single "Wrap It Up," the Fab Thunderbirds found a widespread, national audience. The album became a Top 40 hit, peaking at number ten on the *Billboard* charts.

Shortly after, Jimmie left the 'Birds to play in a duo with his kid brother, which came to a halt following Stevie Ray's death in 1990. The duet album *Family Style* arrived shortly after. Ever since, Jimmie has remained a solo artist.

He's made music on many guitars, but his well-traveled, beat-up '62 Olympic White Strat has long been his trademark instrument. That Stratocaster has had much surgery, with a maple fretboard neck and plenty of other changes to keep it alive after all its years on the road.

The Jimmie Vaughan sound is a Strat through a Fender narrow-panel tweed Bassman. As Jimmie says, "You can get that sound through a Matchless and several different amps, but it's really basically all the same amp from my perspective—they all came from a Bassman. I mean there's always an exception, but for the most part, a Bassman it is."

—Michael Dregni

Vaughan plays his Strat behind his head with the Fabulous Thunderbirds in 1986. *Ebet Roberts/ Redferns/Getty Images*

Stevie Ray Vaughan

Stevie Ray Vaughan and Number One at the Oakland Coliseum Arena on December 3, 1989. *Clayton Call/Redferns/Getty Images*

Few players have done as much to establish the Fender Stratocaster as the American blues machine as Stevie Ray Vaughan. Devoted to the Strat, Vaughan owned and played several, but the name he gave his favorite of the bunch—"Number One"—really said it all.

Today, it's the guitar most associated with the late blues hero. Although Vaughan referred to the guitar as a '59 Strat, and it did have '59 pickups on it, the body and neck both carried date stamps from 1962, so it appears it originated from that year. However, by the end of the star's ownership of the instrument, it had really transmogrified into something of a Parts-o-caster.

Vaughan bought his '62 Strat at Hennig's Heart of Texas Music Store in Austin, Texas, in the mid-1970s, and it possessed a certain magic for him right up until his death in a helicopter crash on August 26, 1990. Store proprietor Ray Hennig, who knew Vaughan as a regular customer, told music writers Joe Nick Patoski and Bill Crawford, "He lived for that guitar. He told me it was the only guitar he ever had that said what he wanted it to say."

As much as Number One meant to him, Vaughan nevertheless set about modifying it to his specific requirements almost immediately. The most visible customizations included the reflective "Custom" and "SRV" stickers he added behind the vibrato bridge and on the replacement black pickguard, respectively, but several other alterations had more to do with the feel and playability of the instrument. He added a left-handed vibrato unit, installed a new set of gold-plated hardware, and replaced the original frets with jumbo frets. The neck would actually be refretted several times over the years—to the extent that, toward 1990, it just couldn't take another refret and was replaced with the original neck from another '62 Strat known as "Red."

2004 Stevie Ray Vaughan Stratocaster and 2004 Custom Shop SRV Replica prototype. *Fender Musical Instruments Corporation*

Stevie Ray Vaughan

Details aside, Number One is really best known for the huge tone Vaughan wrangled from it, which was aided, of course, by a set of pre-CBS pickups that seemed to have been wound slightly on the hot side and the artist's preference for heavy .013–.058 strings, but mostly by a muscular left hand and a ferocious right-hand attack.

If he wasn't playing Number One, odds are Vaughan was playing "Lenny," a Stratocaster he first saw in an Austin pawn shop in 1980. He was unable to afford its $350 price tag at the time, but the guitar was later given to him as a birthday present by his wife, Lenora, and six other friends who all chipped in $50 each. Named in tribute of Lenora, Lenny was an early 1960s Strat that carried its original rosewood fingerboard, pre-CBS pickups, and three-ply white scratchplate—which is not to say the guitar hadn't been modified in other ways. The body had been stripped and stained a rich brown, and a scrolled Victorian mandolin-style inlay had been added beneath the vibrato bridge, which itself was a contemporary replacement unit with die-cast saddles. Vaughan further modified the guitar to suit his needs.

First he added the customary reflective "SRV" stickers to the pickguard, and then later swapped the original neck for a modern-era all-maple unit given to him by Billy Gibbons of ZZ Top. Vaughan pressed Lenny into service most notably on the songs "Lenny" from *Texas Flood* and "Riviera Paradise" from *In Step*.

Number One is now in the hands of Stevie's brother, Jimmie Vaughan, while Lenny was sold to Guitar Center for $623,500 in Eric Clapton's 2004 Crossroads Guitar Auction.

THE RITES OF SPRING

FRIDAY MAY 4 AUDITORIUM SHORES

Stevie Ray
VAUGHAN
& DOUBLE TROUBLE

with
very special
guests

BUDDY
GUY

ERNIE
ISLEY

and

DOYLE BRAMHALL

Stevie Ray Vaughan's Lenny.
Robert Knight Archive/Redferns/
Getty Images

Eric Johnson

Eric Johnson performs in Hollywood, Florida, on March 14, 2012. *Larry Marano/Getty Images*

2004 Eric Johnson Signature Stratocaster. *Fender Musical Instruments Corporation*

Regarded in guitar circles as a tone freak's tone freak, Eric Johnson is famous for such niggling tweaks as using a rubber band to hold the bottom plate on his Fuzz Face fuzz box because he doesn't like its sound with the standard screws, and preferring the performance of his BK Butler Tube Driver when positioned on a wooden block that lifts it above the level of the rest of his effects pedals. Most players would be thrilled with any '57 Strat, but with ears like these, and a discriminating sonic sensibility to go with them, you can be sure Johnson isn't likely to settle on just any 1957 Fender Stratocaster. If Eric Johnson has chosen to ply his trade for years on one particular '57 Stratocaster, you can bet it's a breathtaking instrument. As such, this particular maple-neck sunburst Strat has become legendary among an elite crowd and is a fitting example of everything a great Strat should be.

As iconic a guitar as Johnson's Strat might be, it's no museum piece. Rather, it has been carefully modified to suit the needs of a hardworking and discerning professional. Johnson has the guitar refretted with jumbo wire as often as necessary to keep it feeling meaty and

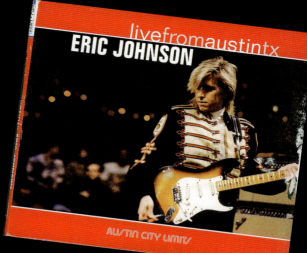

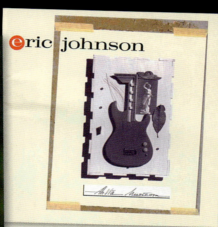

playable. As Johnson explained to Dan Erlewine in *How to Make Your Electric Guitar Play Great!*, rather than having the fingerboard planed down to a flatter radius than the vintage 7.25-inch radius that Fender originally used, he has his frets milled down slightly lower toward the middle of the neck so they remain higher toward the edges, making it easier to grip the strings for extreme bends. Johnson famously leaves the cover off the tremolo spring cavity on the back of the guitar because he feels it hampers the tone. He has had a nylon insert cut from an old Gibson bridge saddle installed in the high E string's steel saddle to soften its shrillness, a goal further pursued by rewiring the Strat's controls so the bridge pickup passes through a tone potentiometer rather than straight to the output the way a '57 was wired at the factory.

Achieving Johnson's famous "thousand-pound violin" tone involves far more than just the guitar, though, and several other elements of his rig deserve a portion of the credit. Johnson's guitar signal first runs through his choice of ingredients on a fairly basic but meticulously selected pedalboard, including the aforementioned Fuzz Face and Tube Driver, a Crybaby wah-wah, a TC Electronic Stereo Chorus Flanger, and an Echoplex tape-delay unit. From there, Johnson selects between a pair of blackface 1966 Fender Twin Reverb amps with JBL D120F speakers, a 1968 Marshall 50-watt Tremolo head and 4x12 cab, or a 1969 Marshall 100-watt Super Lead and 4x12 cab. A mighty arsenal, yet for all this, we've perhaps got to credit the player's hands for just a little of the mighty tone this rig generates.

BASIC TANGIBLE INGREDIENTS

(continued from page 284)

We might be tempted to use the old adage that the tone of any electric guitar is "more than the sum of its parts," and that is true in many ways for the seminal Stratocaster, but an examination of the individual contributions of several of these components does get us a long way toward understanding that sonic "sum." Back in the mid-1950s, when the Stratocaster first came together, Fender wasn't always aiming for the highest quality—in the pure and absolute sense—in any of these elements, but sought a marriage of good, robust performance with ease and efficiency of manufacture and repair. Fortunately, a certain unquantifiable magic seemed to reside in the results of this approach, and the pre-CBS Stratocaster gradually established itself as one of relatively few genuine top-tier classics of solidbody electric guitar tone.

Body Woods

The first Stratocasters were made with bodies of ash, the wood used for the Telecasters' bodies at the time. After 1956, that timber remained in use for some Strats, mainly those finished in custom-color Blonde, while alder became the standard wood for the Strat's body.

The tonal qualities of "swamp ash," which is harvested from the lower portions of ash trees grown in the wetlands of the southern United States, is discussed in detail on page 154.

In the late 1950s good ash became more difficult to get. Older, well-dried stocks were being used up, and newer timber was often proving denser and heavier. It made sense, therefore, to save the fewer good swamp ash blanks for blonde guitars, which made the most of exhibiting this tonewood's broad, attractive grain.

The majority of guitars made after the middle of the decade were made with alder wood, which has a finer, less dramatic grain that worked just fine under sunburst or opaque custom-color finishes. Alder was cheaper and easier to come by but still of a more than acceptable quality, and it exhibits a strong, clear, full-bodied and well-balanced sound, often with muscular lower-mids, firm lows, and sweet highs. In many ways it might be considered a more "open" sounding wood than swamp ash, one capable of producing a guitar with a more versatile and better-balanced tonal palette.

Guitarists sometimes have a tendency to latch onto the "first is best" rule regarding so many issues of vintage-guitar specifications,

1954 Stratocaster with an ash body. *Chicago Music Exchange, www.chicagomusicexchange.com*

but it seems to make the most sense to simply declare that there are two classic Stratocaster body woods. And while the glorious swamp ash might still carry an air of greater romance for many, you need only consider the fact that Jimi Hendrix, Stevie Ray Vaughan, Eric Clapton, and Ritchie Blackmore did most of their notable playing on alder-bodied Strats to see how futile such distinctions can sometimes be, in the "better or worse" sense, at least.

Neck Woods

The Stratocaster's radical, revolutionary body style made it instantly recognizable even from across a dimly lit concert hall, but the most distinctive characteristic of the guitar's construction is arguably its bolt-on maple neck. When he set out to design the Strat's predecessor, the Broadcaster/Telecaster, this entire configuration was high on Leo Fender's list of "easy to manufacture,

The classic maple neck with a rosewood fretboard on a 2008 Custom Shop 1960 Surf Green Stratocaster. *Fender Musical Instruments Corporation*

easy to repair," and we have already discussed the characteristics of the screwed-on joint itself, but the wood from which these necks were made is another significant ingredient in the formula.

As a hard, dense wood, maple contributes characteristics of brightness and clarity to the overall sound of the instrument when used in a guitar's neck. In addition to the goals regarding manufacture and repair, the Stratocaster neck therefore also aids Leo's sonic objectives. Even beyond their tonal characteristics, maple necks offer elements of response and performance that encompasses both the sound and "feel" of the guitar as an instrument. The immediacy of maple's response (merged with the "decoupled" effect of the bolt-on neck joint, as discussed earlier) helps to give the guitars a perceived "snap" and "quack," along with other characteristics that contribute to the classic twang tone.

The maple neck combined with an ash body also achieves clarity and articulation. While we might think of these as characteristics of the classic electric country guitar sound—the test-bed into which the Stratocaster was developed—they also give the guitar plenty of cutting power amid more distorted tones, and enhance its distinctive harmonic sparkle and "bloom" amid overdriven sounds. Listen to the way Stevie Ray Vaughan's Stratocaster manages to sound fat and juicy yet simultaneously crispy and articulate on tracks like "Scuttle Buttin'" or "Pride and Joy," the way Jimi Hendrix's playing exudes a marriage of gargantuan girth and delectable clarity on so many of his Strat-based cuts, or the multidimensional sonic complexity in so much of Eric Johnson's Stratocaster work, and you begin to understand what this guitar can do with some overdrive behind it.

Adding a rosewood fingerboard to an otherwise all-maple neck, as Stratocasters featured almost exclusively from mid-1959 until the mid-1960s, does add some warmth, roundness, and smoothness to the guitar's overall tone. Experienced makers estimate that these enhancements typically only contribute only 5 to 10 percent or so of the overall tone. As with any ingredient, though, the picture isn't entirely black and white. Rosewood from different parts of the world—whether it be Brazil, Madagascar, or India—also contributes to differences in tone. Brazilian rosewood, used by Fender up until the early 1960s, can be dense and ringing, but some makers, like Fender's Chris Fleming, consider the combination of Brazilian rosewood on maple to be "too bright." In recent years, Fender has sourced its rosewood from Madagascar.

As discussed in Part I, the switch from maple to rosewood likely occurred for reasons beyond tone. Though the Telecaster was an all-around rebel when it was introduced in the early 1950s, later in the decade it's likely that Fender wanted to bring a more traditional look (and the lack of the smudged-looking maple 'board that came with it) to the entire Fender line, and the Stratocaster was graced with this "upgrade" as well.

Neck and Headstock Hardware and Appointments

Since the Stratocaster has traditionally carried no fingerboard binding, no headstock overlay, and only simple dot inlays, there isn't much else to speak of as regards the guitar's austere neck appointments, although the nut, string retainer, and tuners still deserve a mention.

The bone nut used from the start of Stratocaster production is one of the guitar's few nods to guitar-making tradition. Bone is known for its resonance and sustain-enhancing properties, and as an organic material, its irregularities can lead to slight changes in performance from one nut to the other.

For ease of manufacture, Fender necks are created without the back-angled headstocks that many others use to create adequate string pressure in the nut slots. Necks are carved so that the headstock sits on a slightly lower plane than the fingerboard, so the break angle from the nut down to the first few tuner posts is entirely adequate, but the B and high-E strings in particular (the only unwound strings when the guitar was introduced) have to make a much longer journey to their tuner posts. To correct for this, Fender used a string retainer, which pulled down on the B and E strings slightly to produce adequate pressure in the nut slots and help prevent a droning sound being produced from the dead lengths of these strings between nut and tuner posts. This retainer started out as the same round, slotted disc in use on the Telecaster and changed to a thinner, bent-steel "butterfly" retainer midway through 1956, with a small spacer added beneath it in 1959 to reduce the downward pull on the B and

high-E strings, thereby improving return-to-pitch stability when the vibrato was used. Many later guitars from the early 1970s onward carried two "butterfly" retainer clips to achieve the same results on the G and D string pair.

The asymmetrical, six-in-line headstock design is another visual characteristic of the Stratocaster and of all classic Fender guitars. As discussed in Part I, the headstock design has performance benefits in addition to creating a distinctive style. Fender's headstock design enables a straight line for each string from nut slot to tuner post and therefore resists the tuning instabilities that can occur when strings stick or hitch in nut slots from which they must break at angles out toward their respective tuners on wider headstocks, such as those used by Gibson, Gretsch, Epiphone, Rickenbacker, and many others. Such "hitching" is usually compounded further when a vibrato bar is used, which requires a smooth and direct path for the strings' short slide through the nut slots in order to retain adequate return-to-pitch stability. Although the straight string path was already in line on the Telecaster, its functionality proved even more significant on the Stratocaster.

The Kluson tuners loaded onto pre-CBS Telecasters are another part of their classic vibe, and many players and makers will tell you that they have a slightly different "sound" than the heavier replacements by Schaller or Grover, which some players added to their guitars. The design of these tuners' back cover changed slightly over the years, namely in how the brand name was stamped into these gear covers, from a single-line "Kluson Deluxe" to no line (no brand stamp), back to single line, and finally double line—with "Kluson" and "Deluxe" stamped on

opposing edges of the cover—by the mid-1960s. In 1967 the Kluson tuners were dropped in favor of Schaller tuners that were made in West Germany to Fender's own design, and stamped with the new, thicker "F" of the Fender logo.

Truss Rod

The Stratocaster's original truss rod was installed through a channel routed in the back of the maple neck, which was afterward filled with a strip of darker walnut, creating a look that has come to be known as the "skunk stripe." From around mid-1959, with the introduction of the rosewood fingerboard, the truss rod was installed through a route made in the face of the neck, which was concealed by the fingerboard when the neck was completed. In both cases, access to the adjustment nut was found at the body end of the neck, requiring that the player either loosen the neck screws to raise the neck heel from its pocket, or dig into the pickguard (usually damaging it slightly) to make changes in neck relief. This would seem one factor that went against Leo's criteria that the Stratocaster (and all of his creations) be easy to service, and Fender did eventually, post-CBS, move the adjustment bolt to the headstock end of the neck in the latter part of 1971. Rather ironically, perhaps, the "bullet head" truss-rod design is loathed by many fans of the vintage (that is, "original") pre-CBS Stratocaster design, and guitars

that carry it are often considered, by some at least, to be from the nadir of Fender's Stratocaster production, although usually for several reasons other than (or in addition to) this truss-rod bullet.

Vibrato Bridge Assembly

Fender called its revolutionary bridge unit the "Synchronized Tremolo," but let's call it what it actually is: a vibrato. Where tremolo fluctuates the volume of a signal, vibrato fluctuates its pitch, which is exactly what this unit did—and still does with great effect. Whatever you call it, though, the bridge hardware developed by Leo, Freddie Tavares, and others on the Fender team was an ingenious piece of engineering for its day, and continues to be among the favorite vibrato units the world over even today. The vibrato's most obvious effect upon the sound of the Stratocaster is heard when it is in use, inducing anything from a gentle shimmer to a deep dive bomb. Leave your hand entirely off the "whammy" bar, though, or even remove the bar altogether, and this clever piece of hardware still makes its mark upon the Strat's tone.

The Stratocaster's lauded Synchronized Tremolo imposes several specific sonic elements upon the guitar's tone, and indeed renders it a very different sounding instrument—in its fine points, at least—than it would be with the strings anchored by any of a number of "hardtail" bridge configurations (just check out the sound of the lesser-seen, so-called "hardtail" Stratocaster to hear the difference for yourself). While the Telecaster's distinctive bridge affects that guitar's tone partly in the way that it interacts with the pickup suspended within it, the Stratocaster's vibrato bridge impacts its tone in multifarious ways primarily according to how its constituent components interact more directly with the guitar's string vibrations and body resonance.

2008 Robin Trower Signature Stratocaster with a modern version of the 1960s F-logo tuners. *Fender Musical Instruments Corporation*

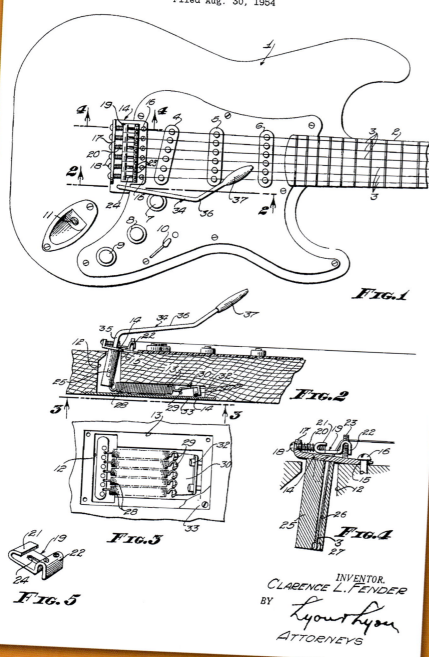

April 10, 1956

C. L. FENDER

2,741,146

TREMOLO DEVICE FOR STRINGED INSTRUMENTS

Filed Aug. 30, 1954

FIG.1

FIG.2

FIG.3

FIG.4

FIG.5

INVENTOR.
CLARENCE L. FENDER
BY
Lyon+Lyon
ATTORNEYS

Leo Fender's 1954 patent drawing for the tremolo bridge design used on the Stratocaster.

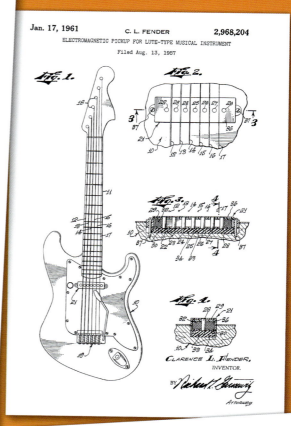

Jan. 17, 1961

C. L. FENDER

2,968,204

ELECTROMAGNETIC PICKUP FOR LUTE-TYPE MUSICAL INSTRUMENT

Filed Aug. 13, 1957

FIG.1.

FIG.2.

FIG.3.

FIG.4.

CLARENCE L. FENDER,
INVENTOR.
BY
ATTORNEY

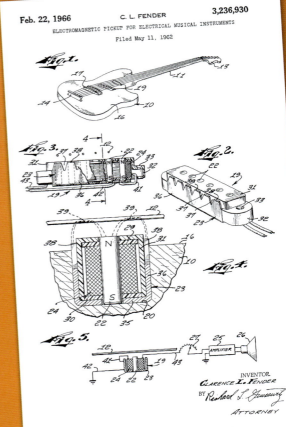

Feb. 22, 1966

C. L. FENDER

3,236,930

ELECTROMAGNETIC PICKUP FOR ELECTRICAL MUSICAL INSTRUMENTS

Filed May 11, 1962

FIG.1.

FIG.3.

FIG.2.

FIG.4.

FIG.5.

AMPLIFIER

INVENTOR.
CLARENCE L. FENDER
BY
ATTORNEY

Leo Fender's 1957 and 1962 patent drawings for single-coil pickup designs.

The vibrato bridge's individually adjustable, stamped-steel saddles contribute brightness and clarity to the Strat's tone, as does the steel bridge plate beneath them, to some extent. The truly ingenious element of the design, however, is hidden under all of this, in the form of the solid steel "inertia block" (or "sustain block"). Bolted to the underside of the bridge plate, and drilled with holes through which the strings pass (and into which those strings' ball-ends are anchored), the inertia block was Leo and company's brilliant means of replacing the resonant mass lost by the necessarily flexible coupling of vibrato to guitar body. As such, it provides a great means of retaining adequate—indeed, impressive—sustain in a guitar that has its strings anchored in a moving part. Stratocaster aficionados swear by the original, heavy, cold-rolled steel inertia blocks used on the guitars made between 1954 and 1971, as well as the many high-quality reproductions of such that are out there on the market. The less-dense, die-cast Mazak block introduced later in 1971, and others made with softer, sonically inferior alloys, are said to thin out the tone and inhibit the guitar's sustain. All in all, though, the bridge and its original sustain block are impressive for their contributions of warmth, sustain, and low-end solidity that might otherwise be absent. These elements are crucial components of the Stratocaster's overall tonal picture, which can be characterized as a ringing chime and jangle with a slightly silky sizzle in the highs, an air of gentle compression and a somewhat scooped midrange, coupled to a firm bass response.

In addition to the sonic elements contributed by the bridge and inertia block, the springs that help it perform its stated vibrato function add considerably to the playing feel of this guitar. Bend a Strat's G-string hard, for example, and you will note how the bridge plate tips forward slightly. Pick an open high-E string and bend the G-string (without picking it) and note how the pitch of that E dips with the upward bend. That's a clear indication that there's some give in the Strat's vibrato, and your fingers are aware of this elasticity when they play a vibrato-equipped Stratocaster. This "give" can make a Stratocaster feel easier to play than a Telecaster, for example, which has the same scale length. Many players will also tell you that the sympathetic "reverberation" of the vibrato's springs, set in motion by the vibrations transferred

when you pick a note or a chord, also contribute to the sonic brew of the Stratocaster. You can certainly hear this when you play a Stratocaster unplugged, although it might be more difficult to detect once you're amped up.

Pickups

We might infer something about Leo Fender's integrity as a designer from the fact that he didn't merely rejig the mounting arrangement of the existing Telecaster bridge pickup, add a cover, stick it on the new guitar, and call it a Stratocaster pickup. Certainly the newly designed pickups used on the Strat were similar to those that the Tele carried at the time—even once you stripped the Tele pickup from its bridge and base plate—but they were different in enough ways to make them an entirely new unit in the Fender camp. A traditional Telecaster bridge pickup is made from fiber top and bottom plates that form a "bobbin" of sorts that is wider than that of the similarly constructed Stratocaster pickup (which is the same in all three positions). The wider Tele pickup bobbin is capable of holding a greater number of turns of 42 AWG wire than that of the Stratocaster pickup, an average, in the early years, of around 9,200 or more turns of wire in the Tele pickup to the Strat pickup's average of around 8,350 turns. The thinner profile of this pickup, and the fewer turns of wire it holds, both contribute to a notable difference in tone. It might be subtle, and most players would still certainly describe both as characteristic of "the Fender sound," but it's a difference worth noting.

Most readers will be familiar with what we call "the single-coil tone" in the general sense, but even among that breed of pickup there's a great variety of sounds according to shape and design. Working from what we just explored in the Stratocaster design, the thinner the pickup (to some extent, at least), and in particular, the narrower and more tightly focused its "magnetic window," the brighter and tighter its sound. Simultaneously, less coil wire wound around a similar bobbin, in relative terms, also enhances clarity and focus. Meanwhile, the fact that Fender continued to use alnico rod magnet sections as pole pieces also enhanced brightness, note definition, and a certain tautness in the tone (compared, on the other hand, to a Gibson P-90 pickup, which gains a certain thickness and edginess from having steel pole pieces in contact with bar magnets below the coil and a much wider coil besides).

The sonic elements of Leo's design goals with the Stratocaster and with his Fender electric guitars in general have been discussed several times in this book: namely, he wanted the clarity, brightness, and definition needed to help guitarists cut through the erstwhile mud on the average bandstand or recording of the day. Having established the tonal significance of scale length, body and neck wood selection, and construction methods, and the sonic impact of the Synchronized Tremolo bridge, it's clear that the design of the Stratocaster pickups also furthered Leo's ends. Hang these narrow, relatively low-output pickups in their "floating" mountings in the Strat's plastic pickguard (where they don't contact any resonating body wood directly), and you have a bright, clear, somewhat glassy, twangy, and jangly guitar, and one that is particularly well suited to the demands of the music scene at the time of its arrival.

What comes across as twangy and jangly from the Stratocaster's bridge pickup, however, translates as warm and juicy from the neck pickup. Move the exact same pickup approximately 4½ inches forward from the bridge toward the neck, and it is now "hearing" the strings at a wider vibrational arc and transmitting that as a fatter and often louder-sounding signal. While many

Tele players claim they can never quite achieve the same meat and muscle from a Strat's bridge pickup as they get from a Tele's bridge pickup, most will concede that they'd kill for a Strat's neck pickup tone in their Telecaster. As we have already seen, though, there are so many factors contributing to that final tone that you really can't "fake it" through a pickup swap.

In addition to the effort put into the pickups' design, Leo Fender, Freddie Tavares, and the team put considerable thought into their placement. To some extent, the inclusion of three pickups might first have been largely a USP (unique selling proposition) for the sales team—as quoted in *The Fender Stratocaster* by A. R. Duchossoir, Tavares said, "Leo said it's quite a thing to have two pickups now, so let's have three!"—but the trio would considerably enhance the guitar's versatility (even to an extent, as below, that wasn't yet fully realized). More consciously utilitarian, though, was the decision to slant the bridge pickup in relation to the others, a trick that was already performing well on the Telecaster. Tavares to Duchossoir once more: "The rear pickup is slanted for a very important reason. That was because when you pluck the instrument way back near the bridge, everything is more brilliant, but you lose the depth. So the reason for the slant was to get a little more vitality, or 'virility,' into the bass strings and still maintain all the brilliance that we wanted."

Stratocaster pickups were wound with Formvar-coated 42 AWG wire throughout most of the 1950s, until Fender switched to plain enamel-coated wire in the early 1960s. Strat aficionados will swear by their preferences for one type or the other, and authorities on the fine points will often declare that there is a difference in sound between the two. The thicker Formvar insulation made for fatter coils that were also, at times, wound slightly more loosely, whereas the enamel-coated wire could be packed in more tightly. Whatever the wire, though, great music has undoubtedly been made on guitars carrying

The Stratocaster's classic controls and switch layout remains on the updated 2012 Aztec Gold American Deluxe Stratocaster FSR. *Fender Musical Instruments Corporation*

Classic features of the first Stratocasters live on today on a 2009 Custom Shop 1958 Candy Apple Red Stratocaster. *Fender Musical Instruments Corporation*

pickups wound with both types, so this can get into rather nit-picky territory. In a more cosmetic alteration, if one that often remains unseen, Fender changed from black fiber pickup-bottom plates to dark gray bottom plates around the end of 1964, then used lighter gray plates from 1968 onward.

CONTROLS AND SWITCHING

The original Stratocaster switching layout, and the one honored by traditional "reissue" style Strats today, offered a master volume control, individual tone controls for the neck and middle pick-ups, and a three-way switch that enabled selection of each pickup alone, but not in combination. Most players today, if faced with an incomplete complement of tone controls, would prefer to have one on the bridge pickup at least, to tame the potentially over-bright tone from that pickup, and many rewire their Strats in that way. But "bright" was the rule of the day, and routing the bridge pickup straight through with a no tone pot provided a means of ensuring maximum treble from that position.

As for the use of a three-way switch on a guitar that would prove to offer so many more potential pickup selections in combination, well, as Leo told Tom Wheeler in *Guitar Player* magazine in 1978, "There weren't too many convenient styles of switches back then. It wasn't a matter of what we would like so much as . . . of what we could get." Regardless of the implied limitations of the switch, players soon discovered that they could find the usefully funky "in between" pickup sounds of the bridge and middle or middle and neck together by simply balancing the switch carefully between its intended positions. Noticing this trend, component manufacturers soon offered an aftermarket five-way switch, and Fender finally began installing one at the factory in 1977.

Put them all together—and put them together in just the right way—and these constituent parts coalesce into the sublime whole that we have come to know as the Fender Stratocaster, one of the most, if not the most, influential electric guitars ever produced.

Robert Cray

Robert Cray and his Strat. *Joby Sessions/Guitarist Magazine/Getty Images*

While his style is often pigeonholed as straight-up blues, Robert Cray's music is really an amalgam of classic genres that he has blended into something all his own—part soul, part R&B, and yes, part blues. Whatever you call it, though, most would agree that his tone is seminal Stratocaster at its best. "Every time somebody asks me about where my music comes from, I give them five or six different directions—a little rock, soul, jazz, blues, a little gospel feel. Then there are some other things that maybe fall in there every once in a while, like a little Caribbean flavor or something," the guitarist says on his website, robertcray.com.

Robert Cray was born into a musical family in Columbus, Georgia, in 1953. His family moved often to follow his father's military career. Cray started playing the guitar in his early teens, joined his first band while still in junior high school in Newport News, Virginia, and moved to the Northwest at the age of twenty-one, where he soon formed the Robert Cray Band in Eugene, Oregon. Several years of paying dues all along the West Coast led to a deal with Mercury Records in 1982, but Cray's star truly ascended in 1986 with the release of his third

album, *Strong Persuader*, which earned him a Grammy Award. Since then, Cray has gone on to earn another four Grammy Awards, fifteen nominations, and sold more than twelve million records.

From the start, Cray was drawn to the Stratocaster, and for many listeners, his playing has come to define the clean-yet-rich nature of the guitar's natural voice. His spare, tasteful playing style enables that guitar to be heard in a pure setting, too—classy enough to make do with a few powerful, well-landed notes where less mature players might assault you with a blizzard of riffage, Robert Cray's playing is a virtual lesson in elegant restraint that manages to be utterly moving every time. His intimate technique is enhanced by his use of the bare flesh of his

right-hand thumb rather than a pick and running it all through both a Matchless Clubman and a Fender Vibro-King set relatively clean, with just an edge of breakup when he picks hard. Rather than using the Strat's vibrato (he removes the bar from his own guitars or chooses hardtail variations), Cray induces an emotive shake in his tone, using a classic left-hand finger vibrato, although he is also fond of bringing in the Vibro-King's tremolo to assist in some classic retro tones. Fender released the Custom Shop Robert Cray Signature Stratocaster in 2003, a hardtail model with vintage-wind pickups and Cray's favorite Inca Silver finish, which is flanked by the more affordable standard-run Robert Cray Stratocaster.

2004 Robert Cray Signature Violet Stratocaster.
Fender Musical Instruments Corporation

The Edge

The Edge and Bono onstage during the Lovetown tour in Australia in 1989. *Bob King/ Redferns/Getty Images*

In the alternative punk and new wave scenes of the late 1970s and early 1980s, the Stratocaster was often seen as a square traditionalist, the conventional weaponry of classic rockers and bluesers. As such, for a time there at least, it just wasn't much in favor with what you might call the "hip crowd"—players who were taking up the big names' alternatives like the Jazzmaster and Jaguar, the Les Paul Special and Junior, and other "second-tier" electrics. In using a 1970s Stratocaster to log many of his most notable tones, however, U2's the Edge (a.k.a. Dave Evans) helped drag this seminal Fender toward indie's cutting edge, making it once again acceptable to a younger, up-and-coming generation.

While the Edge is reported to own more than two hundred guitars and commonly takes more than forty on tour at any time, Stratocasters take up a bigger chunk of his collection than any other model. As is the way with so many struggling musicians, though, the Strats that peppered early U2 recordings weren't the prized pre-CBS models. In the early days, he plied his trade on several workaday 1970s Stratocasters with large headstocks, three-bolt necks, and bullet-head truss rod adjustment nuts and forged an instantly recognizable signature sound in the process. Some of the earliest U2 photos from around 1977 and 1978 show the guitarist wielding a mid-'70s Stratocaster with sunburst finish, and a black '73 Strat was often his main squeeze through the 1980s, when the '76 Gibson Explorer was resting. The Stratocaster's bright, glassy cutting power can certainly be heard amid the whirl of the Electro-Harmonix Deluxe Memory Man delay pedal and Vox AC30 of the early recordings.

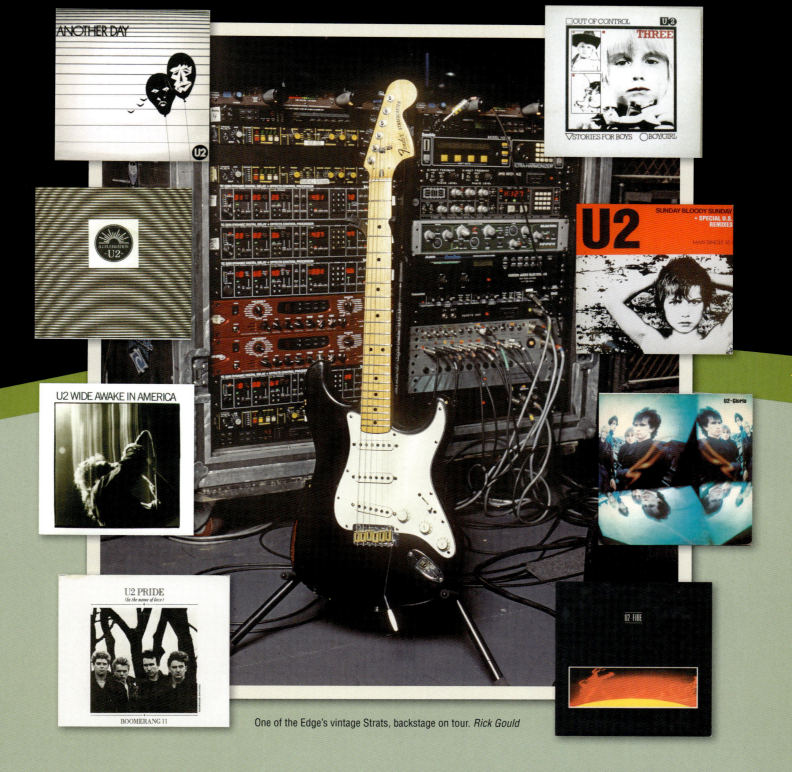

One of the Edge's vintage Strats, backstage on tour. *Rick Gould*

Where the Stratocaster had previously been known primarily as a lead instrument, the Edge took its percussive rhythmic capabilities to new heights. Neither a "lead" nor a "rhythm" player, per se, he established a rhythmic momentum on the instrument that allowed U2's early songs, in particular, to display plenty of air and space, while eliminating any real need for solos or chord parts in the traditional sense. Listen, for example, to his churning, bouncing performance on "Where the Streets Have No Name" from 1987's *The Joshua Tree*, and hear how well Leo Fender's goal for a "bright, cutting" tone works in a context he could in no way have envisioned when designing the guitar in 1953 and 1954. In its own way, and for its time, it was as fitting a tribute to the traditional that the alternative could make.

John Mayer

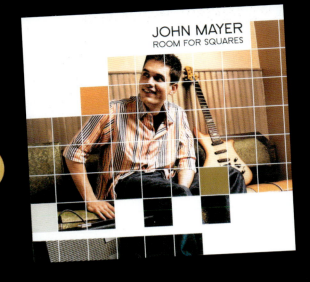

John Mayer swears by his Signature Stratocaster backstage at the Hard Rock Calling festival in London on June 28, 2008. *Joby Sessions/Guitarist Magazine/Getty Images*

One of the leading lights of a new breed of popular guitar hero, emerging just when it seemed that maybe guitar heroes had forever fallen from popular music, John Mayer has proven he can hang with the likes of Eric Clapton, Buddy Guy, and Robert Cray on stage at the Crossroads Festival and still make adolescent fans swoon with his next chart-topping hit. Peel away the tabloid stories and Mayer, at his core, is really just a guitar player, and one that has long favored Fender's seminal Stratocaster.

Mayer's star ascended so swiftly that Fender recognized him while he was still just in his mid-twenties. In 2005 the company

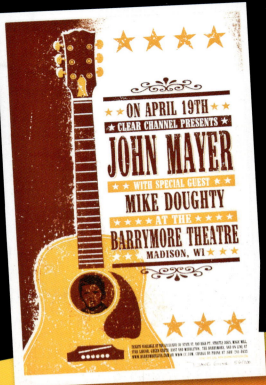

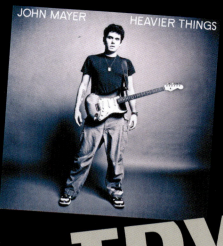

TRY!

JOHN MAYER TRIO
WITH STEVE JORDAN
AND PINO PALLADINO
LIVE IN CONCERT

issued a John Mayer Stratocaster in three-tone sunburst, black, and Olympic White, as well as a heavy-relic black rendition from the Custom Shop, but Mayer launched his own career on the back of an earlier Artist Series guitar, a Stevie Ray Vaughan Stratocaster that he purchased with money saved from his job at a gas station. He boasts an extensive guitar collection today, but still takes his signature models and contemporary Strats out on the road alongside other newer gems such as a Custom Shop rosewood Stratocaster.

John Mayer was born in Bridgeport, Connecticut, in 1977 and was raised in nearby Fairfield. His early musical skills were given a bump at Boston's Berklee College of Music, although he left that estimable institution after just two semesters, moved to Atlanta, and set about igniting his musical career. After a notable performance at Austin's SXSW music festival in March 2000, Mayer signed first to Aware Records and then to Columbia, which rereleased his previously

Internet-only debut album *Room for Squares* to major commercial and critical success. The album track "Your Body Is a Wonderland" earned Mayer a Grammy Award in 2003, his first of seven Grammies earned from nineteen nominations.

When fully amped with Strat in hand, John Mayer has a playing style that exhibits classic blues tendencies, laced with a versatility that signals his contemporary pop sensibilities. At other times, though, he can be far more adventurous than this mélange might imply, evidenced by his collaborations with Herbie Hancock, Kanye West, and Dead & Company. For some tabloid-minded fans, John Mayer might be a household name more for his romances, but music clearly fuels his fire, and he certainly helped to bring the Stratocaster back into the Top Forty nearly sixty years after it first hit the scene.

2006 John Mayer Signature Cypress Mica Stratocaster. *Fender Musical Instruments Corporation*

Sonny Landreth

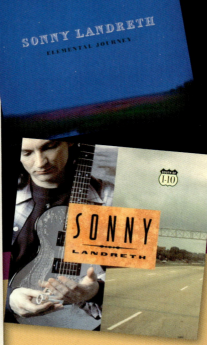

Sonny Landreth slides on his Strat. *Jack Spencer*

Sonny Landreth is famed for his slide guitar mastery, a virtuosic style of slide that he usually plays on Stratocasters. He developed a style of playing bottleneck with his pinky finger, but also fretting the guitar behind the slide at the same time, creating more developed chords, variegated sounds, and complex voicings. Landreth is also known for his right-hand technique, combining slapping, tapping, and picking with all of his fingers.

Born in Canton, Mississippi, in 1951, he settled in Breaux Bridge in southern Louisiana. Throughout his career, he's drawn on the musical traditions of the region in crafting his own, unique sound.

"When I first started listening to Delta blues, I didn't even know what a slide was," Landreth told *Vintage Guitar* magazine in 2012. "I had learned a right-hand finger-style approach from Chet Atkins, so when I listened to the Delta players and discovered a lot of them like to slide, putting the two of those together set me on my path. Looking back on it I realize that my jazz heroes who played trumpet and my blues heroes with a guitar were all seeking to emulate a human voice and to have that character in their playing. I think that really helped me a lot: Slide lends itself to that, but even more so [than fretted playing]."

Landreth has always been faithful to the Stratocaster. His main guitar is a 1966 sunburst Strat that's appeared on most of his albums since his 1981 debut with *Blues Attack*. He also uses several modern Strats, including a '57 Reissue Strat with Lindy Fralin Vintage Hot pickups, his own Signature Strat with Michael Frank-Braun noiseless single coils, and his main touring Strat with a DiMarzio DP181 Fast Track 1 bridge pickup and DiMarzio Virtual Vintage neck pickup. "I like the idea of changing the pickups," he explains. "I wanted to create different colors and have different voices."

—Michael Dregni

2009 Custom Shop 1956
Desert Sand Stratocaster.
*Fender Musical
Instruments Corporation*

INDEX

1964 Stratocaster and Band-Master amp with original shipping cartons. *Rumble Seat Music*

DAVE HUNTER is a writer and musician who has worked extensively in the United Kingdom and the United States. He is the author of *The Gibson Les Paul, Star Guitars, The Guitar Amp Handbook, Guitar Effects Pedals, The British Amp Invasion, The Guitar Pickup Handbook,* and several other titles. Hunter is also a regular contributor to *Guitar Player, Vintage Guitar,* and *Premier Guitar* magazines in the United States, and *Guitar Magazine* in the United Kingdom. He is a contributing essayist to the United States Library of Congress National Recording Preservation Board's Permanent Archive. He lives in Portsmouth, New Hampshire, with his wife and their two children.

TONY BACON is a leading author on guitar history. He has written, edited, or contributed to many highly regarded books on the subject, and co-founded music-book publisher Backbeat UK. He is based in London.